Britain

Britain

Red Guide

Edited by
Reginald J. W. Hammond

Ward Lock · London

Maps reproduced by kind permission of Map Productions Ltd.
Based upon the Ordnance Survey map with the sanction of the
Controller of H.M. Stationery Office

Drawings by Christopher White

Filmset by Keyspools Ltd, Golborne, Lancs
Printed in Spain

Contents

Maps

Introduction

The best of Britain! A fantastic commission within the compass of a single small volume. But this book sets out to show just that, mainly in gazetteer form, and to pinpoint the major items of interest, architecturally or historically, within Britain. The country is divided into convenient regions and a glance at the contents pages will quickly show these divisions. The holiday resorts and main centres are succinctly described and nearby items of particular interest included. Buildings, ancient monuments, historic houses and beautiful gardens, essentially those to which there is public access, have all been noticed. Where possible admission times have been included.

The places coming in for particular mention in the "Of Special Interest" sections are entirely of the Editor's own choosing. The omission from these lists of any particular item does not infer its lack of note or interest for there are, indeed, many more items deserving of mention than our space permits. Even so, by a careful use of these lists and the relevant gazetteer entries, the Editor is confident that the visitor will be able to extract the most rewarding return from his visit, whatever his taste.

Ancient Monuments

A great many of the ancient monuments of Britain, from prehistoric dolmen to abbey, castle or house, come under the protection of the Ministry of Public Building and Works. This Government department zealously guards and preserves our ancient heritage, and for the most part, there is public access to the properties, admission times being standard, as set out below. Throughout the book they are identified by the use of the letters AM.

Standard hours of admission are:

	Weekdays	Sundays
Mar–Apr	9.30–5.30	2–5.30
May–Sept	9.30–7	2–7
Oct	9.30–5.30	2–5.30
Nov–Feb	9.30–4	2–4

Many monuments are also open from 9.30 on Sundays in summer.

The National Trust

The letters NT indicate land or buildings administered by the National Trust for Places of Historic Interest or Natural Beauty. This organization for more than 70 years has existed to preserve, against the spread of industrialization, much of the beauty of Britain. Today the Trust owns for the permanent enjoyment of the public about 350,000 acres of England, Wales and Northern Ireland and some 200 houses of outstanding architectural or historical importance. Subject to local requirements the public usually have full access to all the Trust's open spaces, and to many of the buildings, though in the latter case a small fee may be charged. A similar organization, the National Trust for Scotland, owns or has covenants over much land and property in Scotland.

Great Houses

The mansions and manor houses of Britain are an integral part of our great heritage. They illustrate many periods of architecture though more especially that of Tudor and Elizabethan times. Many of the smaller properties are in private occupation and only the exterior views may be seen. The larger houses, however, economically difficult to maintain, have been opened to the public and attract ever-increasing numbers to view their treasures, art collections, paintings, tapestries and furniture. Where possible opening times of these houses has been given, though it should be noted, these are liable to change from time to time.

Gardens

Most of the famous gardens to which there is frequent public access have been noted in our lists. In addition, however, there are very many more private gardens, of special charm and beauty, that are made available to the public on perhaps one or only a few days of each year, generally at a time when the particular garden is at its floral best. Many of these gardens are opened in connection with the National Gardens Scheme under the auspices of the Queen's Institute of District Nursing. Full particulars may be obtained from the Organising Secretary, National Gardens Scheme, 57 Lower Belgrave Street, London, S.W.1. Other gardens are shown under the Gardeners' Sunday Scheme, a list being obtainable from the General Organizer, White Witches, Claygate Road, Dorking, Surrey, or for Scottish gardens, the General Organizer, 26 Castle Terrace, Edinburgh, 1.

Church Lane, Ledbury

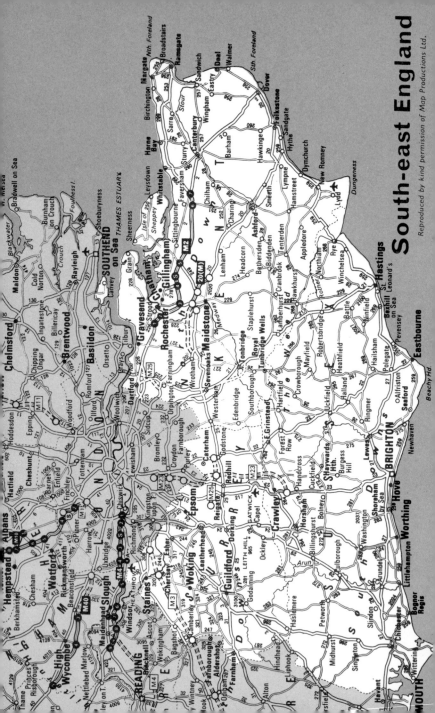

South-east England

Reproduced by kind permission of Map Productions Ltd.

South-east England

Kent - Surrey - Sussex

Kent

Probably the most historic of English counties. The Roman occupation of Britain commenced in Kent, the first Saxon invaders under Hengist landed at Ebbsfleet in 449, the Jutes established themselves here, and St. Augustine and his monks arrived in 597 to found his Christian cathedral. Four of its early ports were included in the famous Confederacy of the Cinque ports. The rolling Downs stretch across the county from north-west to south-east and south of them is the Weald, a fertile region of orchards, market gardens and hopfields well-deserving the name 'garden of England'. Chatham, Gillingham and Rochester at the mouth of the River Medway form an important industrial area. But it is on account of its wonderful sandy coastline that the county lays claim to fame. Along the coast are a string of popular holiday resorts from Whitstable, Herne Bay and Margate round to Folkestone, Hythe and Rye. Canterbury, 18 miles back from the shore, is the ecclesiastical capital of England and the magnificent cathedral draws thousands of pilgrims. The county town is Maidstone, a busy agricultural centre. Throughout the county there are many famous mansions and gardens open to the public.

Surrey

The county of Surrey adjoins Greater London south of the Thames. Beyond the suburbia which stretches way out from the capital are the beautiful chalk downs running from Caterham westward to Farnham, providing endless walking country and magnificent viewpoints. With no coastline and therefore without a holiday resort in the generally accepted term, the county nevertheless attracts many visitors with its hilly and wooded scenery, its antiquities, country mansions and open spaces being second to none.

13

Sussex

A popular county offering immense variety of scenery. The undulating land is guarded in the south by the magnificent ridge of the chalky South Downs which enter the county in the west and meet the sea at Beachy Head. Mostly they are clothed with springy turf which is a joy to walk on. Among the Downs nestle many beautiful villages. North of the Downs is the fertile Weald with many centres of charm and beauty. And on the south a grand coastline with a string of resorts including some of the most famous in Britain. Brighton is the largest of our seaside resorts and the fame of its many attractions is world-wide. Worthing, Eastbourne and Hastings, to some lesser degree perhaps, can provide most of the needs of the discerning holidaymaker. Littlehampton and Bognor Regis among others have their special appeal.

Beachy Head and the Lighthouse

Of Special Interest

Acrise Place (5m NW of Folkestone). Home of Papillon family since 1666. Elizabethan house with Georgian front. Costume collection. Gardens. June–Sept, Thurs, Suns, 2.30–6.
Arundel Castle (Arundel). Historic castle of Duke of Norfolk in fine grounds with park and lake. (See notices.)
Bedgebury Pinetum (Bedgebury Park, 12m SE of Tunbridge Wells). Large area of trees in research plots. Daily.
Bodiam Castle (3m S of Hawkhurst). Moated, curtain-walled castle, one of best preserved examples of medieval military architecture. (NT). Apr–Sept, daily from 10. Weekdays only in winter.
Boughton Monchelsea Place (Linton, 4½m S of Maidstone). Battlemented Elizabethan manor house in large deer park. Easter–Oct, Sats, Suns, Bk Hols. Also Weds in Aug. 2.15–6.
Box Hill (2½m S of Leatherhead). Fine expanse of down and woodland and grand picnic spot. The Mickleham Downs adjoin (NT).
Chanctonbury Ring (2m W of Steyning). Ancient camp site surrounded by ring of trees with magnificent views over Sussex Weald.
Chartwell (1½m S of Westerham). Churchill Memorial Museum, the former home of Sir Winston Churchill. Mar–Nov, Weds, Thurs, 2–6. Sats, Suns, Bk Hols 11–6.
Chiddingstone Castle (near Edenbridge). 18c house in large park. Oriental collections of art. Easter–Oct, Daily except Mons, 2–5.30. Sats, Suns, Bk Hols 11.30–5.30.
Cissbury Ring (1½m E of Findon). Largest of the South Downs earthworks constructed about 300 B.C. Site of intensive flint-mining industry of early Neolithic times (NT).
Clandon Park (3m E of Guildford). 18c house in Palladian style with fine plaster-work, furniture, pictures (NT). Apr–Sept, Mons, Weds, Sats, Suns, 2–6. Bk Hols 11–6.
Claremont Woods (S of Esher). Large woodland with lake and specimen trees originally laid out by William Kent. (NT). Daily.
Danny (Hurstpierpoint). Elizabethan mansion built 1593. May–Sept, Weds, Thurs, 2–5.
Glynde Place (4m SE of Lewes). 16c house, pictures, needlework and pottery. Easter, then May–Sept, Thurs, Sats, Suns, Bk Hols 2.15–5.30.
Goodwood House (4½m NE of Chichester). 18c flint-work house, ancestral home of Duke of Richmond and Gordon. Pictures, sculpture, china. Extensive park. May–Sept, certain days 2–6 except during Goodwood Race Week. Park always open.
Great Dixter (Northiam). 15c house with Great Hall in Lutyens designed garden. Easter–Sept, daily except Mons, 2–5.
Hatchlands (East Clandon). House with Adam interior, large park. (NT). Apr–Sept, Weds, Sats, 2–6.
Hever Castle (Edenbridge). Moated 13c castle. Formal gardens and lake. Easter–Sept, Weds, Suns, Bk Hols, also Sats in Aug, Sept, 2–7.
Ightham Mote (Ivy Hatch, 2½m S of Ightham). Moated 14c manor house. Mar–Nov, Fris afternoon only from 2.

Arundel Castle

Knole (Sevenoaks). Home of the Sackvilles and one of the largest private houses in England. Jacobean interior. Large park (NT). Weds, Thurs, Fris, Sats, Bk Hols, 10–12, 2–5. Closed Jan, Feb.

Loseley House (3m SW of Guildford). Elizabethan mansion built 1562. Furniture, paintings. Jun–Sept, Fris, Sats, 2–5.

Nyman's Gardens (5m S of Crawley). Lovely gardens of rare trees, shrubs and flowers. (NT). Apr–Oct, Tues, Weds, Thurs, Sats, Suns and Bk Hols, 2–7.

Parham (2m W of Storrington). Elizabethan house built 1577. Great Hall, Long Gallery, furniture, needlework and paintings. Gardens and pleasure grounds. Easter–Oct, Weds, Thurs, Suns, and Bk Hols, 2–5.30.

Penshurst Place (5m SW of Tonbridge). Gothic style mansion with beautiful formal gardens. Easter–Jun Weds, Thurs, Sats, Suns, Bk Hols. Jun–Sept, also Tues, 2–6.15.

Petworth House (5½m E of Midhurst). Rebuilt 1696 by 5th Duke of Somerset. 13c chapel, park. (NT). Apr–Oct, Weds, Thurs, Sats and Bk Hols, 2–6.

Polesden Lacey (Bookham). Greville collection of pictures, tapestries, furniture. Large gardens. (NT). Mar–mid Dec, Sats, Suns, Bk Hols, 11–6. Weds, 2–6. Gardens all year.

Richborough Castle (1½m N of Sandwich). Remains of late 3c Roman fort built on original site of landing of Romans in A.D. 43. (AM standard hours).

Sheffield Park Gardens (Sheffield Park). Gardens, lake, park, woodland. (NT). Apr–Oct, daily 11–7.

Upnor Castle (1½m NE of Strood). Blockhouse for the defence of Medway estuary. (AM standard hours).

Winkworth Arboretum (2½m SE of Godalming). Hillside of rare shrubs, lake. Views over North Downs. Daily.

Wisley Gardens (2m NE of Ripley). Extensive gardens of Royal Horticultural Society. Weekdays only, 10–7.30.

Resorts and Centres of Interest

Abinger (Surrey). Residential village set amongst woodland. The restored church is partly Norman. By churchyard gate are the old stocks. On Dorking road is old Crossways Farm associated with George Meredith. Near Abinger Hammer, a former centre of the iron industry, are Abinger Roughs (NT) a wooded ridge giving good views.

Alfriston (Sussex). Picturesque old-world village 4m NE of Seaford on west bank of Cuckmere river. The fine old cruciform church is late 14c and one of the finest specimens of flint-work in England. The thatched Old Clergy House (NT. open) dates from 1350. The 15c Star Inn has curious old wood carvings. At Lullington, across the river, the church is one of smallest in England. 1m E is Windover Hill (600 ft.) on the face of which is cut the Wilmington Giant, or Long Man. At Wilmington are remains of 12c priory (Apr–Oct 10–5, Suns 2–5). 1m S of Litlington is Charleston Manor where the gardens are open.

Arundel (Sussex). Medieval town on River Arun with magnificent castle owned by England's premier Duke (open weekdays). In the park is Swanbourne Lake, a beautiful feature. The parish church dates from 1380. Sharing the same roof is the Roman Catholic Fitzalan Chapel, the burial place of the Fitzalans and Howards. The Roman Catholic Church of Our Lady and St. Philip Neri, opened 1873, is built in 13c Gothic style.

Battle (Sussex). Market town 7m NW of Hastings on site of Battle of Hastings. The present remains of the Abbey (now incorporated in a school) with 14c Gatehouse, stand on site of original abbey founded by William the Conqueror. 3m SE is Beauport Park where the fine garden is open daily.

Bexhill (Sussex). Quiet resort and residential town. Shingle beach and sand at low tide. Rowing and sailing. The De la Warr Pavilion is striking modern concert hall and entertainment centre. Egerton Park has seawater swimming bath, tennis courts and pavilion for indoor sports, and a museum. 2m W is Gooden Beach with its golf course.

Birchington (Kent). Bracing seaside resort and part of large borough of Margate. Good sandy beach. Golf at Westgate. Yacht Club at Minnis Bay. Quex Park with chapel of Quex family. The Powell-Cotton Museum contains zoological and ethnographical collection. St. Nicholas-at-Wade is quiet village 3m SW.

Bognor Regis (Sussex). Pleasant south coast resort with extensive sands and all the usual amenities of a popular holiday centre. Sea-fishing from pier. Hotham Park is large natural park with woodland, shrubs, and children's zoo. To west is Aldwick, then Pagham with popular sandy beach. To east is Felpham where the sandy shore is much patronised by day tourists.

17

Bramber (Sussex). Village 4m N of Shoreham of main street of mixture of modern houses and delightful old timber-framed cottages. The ruined castle (NT) is open daily. The church is small Norman building. Potter Museum (weekdays). St. Mary's House is 15c timbered building with quaint flagged courtyard (daily except Mons).

Brighton and Hove (Sussex). Extensive and popular south coast resort (administratively separate boroughs) with 5-mile long seafront. Pebble beach, piers, promenades, gardens, bathing pools. Theatres, cinemas, aquarium and all sports. The Royal Pavilion (open daily) was built at the bidding of the Prince Regent, afterwards George IV. Several museums and fine public parks. Racecourse. To E is Rottingdean with bathing pool. 5m NW is Devil's Dyke and 6m NE Ditchling Beacon (views).

Broadstairs (Kent). Bracing resort renowned for its safe sandy beach especially ideal for children. The pretty Viking Bay is bounded on one side by steep chalk cliffs, and on the other by the picturesque pier. Rowing, sailing. Annual regatta, weekly sailing races. Charles Dickens lived for some time at Bleak House where he wrote much of 'David Copperfield' and other works. St. Peter's Parish Church dates in part from 11c. North Foreland with its lighthouse and golf course is 1½m N.

Burwash (Sussex). Small town of picturesque houses and tree-lined main street. The church has Norman tower with shingled spire. Bateman's (NT) once residence of Rudyard Kipling, is charming Elizabethan house.

Canterbury (Kent). The chief cathedral city of Britain and flourishing country market town on River Stour. Various entertainments and sports facilities. Annual Cricket Week in early August. Golf at Scotland Hills, 1½m. The 15c Church of St. Dunstan-without-the-Westgate preserves in a vault the head of Sir Thomas More (1535). The 15c Falstaff Inn has good oak panelling and ironwork. The massive West Gate is 14c but incorporates Roman brickwork and is now museum. Holy Cross Church is 14c. Flanking the river are the Weavers' Houses, half-timbered Ghent-like buildings, where Hugenot and Walloon weavers set up their looms in 1685. St. Thomas's Hospital is almshouse founded in 1180. The Royal Museum shows Roman and Saxon remains. In Butchery Lane is Roman Pavement. The earliest cathedral was erected in the 6c but the present buildings date from 11–15c. The great Central Tower is 235 ft high. Of particular interest are: Christ Church Gate (1517), 14c nave, 12c choir; Trinity Chapel, specially built to receive the Shrine of Thomas Becket, tombs of the Black Prince (1376) and Henry IV (1413), and the Corona. To N of cathedral are the monastic buildings. The remains of the Abbey of St. Augustine (AM), coeval with the Cathedral, both having been founded in 597, are now incorporated in the Central College of the Anglican Communion. St. Martin's Church is one of the oldest churches in use in England. Of the Norman castle only a shell of the keep remains. In Dane John Gardens is artificial mound, thought to be Romano-British burial mound. Close by is capstan from Nelson's 'Foudroyant' and a

Grand Parade, Eastbourne

monument to Christopher Marlowe. Of interest too, is Stephenson's locomotive 'Invicta' which ran on first railway built in southern England.

Chichester (Sussex). Pleasantly situated cathedral city about equidistant from the western boundary of the county, the South Downs on the north, and the Channel towards the south. The wall by which the Romans surrounded it is for the most part still standing. The cathedral is unique in Britain in that its Campanile, or Bell Tower, stands detached from the main building. At junctions of the four main streets is octagonal market cross erected in 1500 and a beautiful example of its type. St. Mary's Hospital is almshouse of note. At head of Chichester Harbour, 3m, is Bosham, a charming and peaceful village in favour with artists and yachting people. 3m N is Goodwood House and Park.

Chilham (Kent). A pretty village in orchard land with several timbered houses. Chilham Castle is notable 17c mansion by Inigo Jones. Norman castle keep in park. Ground only, May–Oct, Thurs and Suns 2–6.

Deal and Walmer (Kent). Sister towns, now incorporated, together forming a pleasant resort and popular fishing centre. Shingle beach, bathing, boating, sports and entertainments. Several golf courses in vicinity. Pier. Deep sea angling. Deal Castle, Walmer Castle and Sandown Castle were all erected in 16c as part of Henry VIII's coastal defence scheme. (AM standard hours.) Walmer castle is official residence of the Lord Wardens of the Cinque Ports. Sandown Castle is now little more than a few arched foundation walls. 5m offshore are the Goodwin Sands. 6m S is St. Margaret's Bay.

19

Dorking (Surrey). Ancient market town in setting of wooded hills and vales. The nearby Box Hill is famous beauty spot.

Dover (Kent). Prosperous port, busy commercial centre, and cross-Channel ferry terminal at south-east corner of England. Pebble beach backed by lofty, chalk cliffs except in centre of bay where River Dour reaches sea. The sea-front is divided between the docks and the residential seaside quarter. The Port is one of largest artificial harbours in the world and the nearest port to the Continent. Fishing facilities are available from Prince of Wales Pier, the Southern Breakwater and the Admiralty Pier, St. Mary's Church is notable for its fine western tower. Dover College stands on site, and includes portions of, an old Benedictine priory. The 12c Refectory is one of the largest secular Norman buildings in England. Maison Dieu Hall (open) has fine collections of paintings and arms and armour. Connaught Park has gardens and sports facilities. Dover Castle (AM Standard hours) is Norman and later. The massive keep was built about 1180. St. Mary's-in-Castro Church occupies site of the original Roman fort. The Roman Pharos, or lighthouse, stands nearby. In Northfall Meadow is granite memorial marking spot where M. Bleriot landed after his historic cross-channel flight in 1909. The Western Heights, above the town, give magnificent views. There are here the remains of the Knights Templar's Church of 12c date. 1m W along coast is Shakespeare Cliff, a sharply-pointed peak in the chalk cliffs. 3m NW is South Foreland with its lighthouse (open) where Marconi carried out some of his experiments.

Dungeness (Kent). A steep-sided promontory formed of shingle with close views of Channel shipping and good facilities for angling with deep water close inshore. Lighthouses and nuclear power station of interest.

Dymchurch (Kent). Village with 5m stretch of clean firm sand. Quaint mixture of modern bungalows pitched among old half-timbered cottages. 3m S is New Romney, a Cinque Port, but now a mile back from the sea.

Eastbourne (Sussex). Large and popular coastal resort at eastern foot of South Downs. Three miles of promenades. Sloping shingle beach with flat sand at low tide. Pier with pavilions and theatre. Several golf courses, all sports and entertainments. Daily band music at Bandstand off Grand Parade. The Great Redoubt (model village, aquarium) is circular fort built 1806. Devonshire Park is popular entertainment centre with Congress Theatre, Winter Garden and famous croquet lawns and tennis courts where the South of England Lawn Tennis Championships are held annually in September. There is a lifeboat, and lifeboat Museum. Towner Art Gallery displays collections of British artists. The parish church dates from 12c. Hampden Park is fine wooded tract to N of town with sports facilities. 2m SW is Beachy Head (516 ft) with extensive seascapes and its lighthouse offshore. Westward of Beachy Head is Birling Gap a remarkable dip between lofty cliffs, beyond which are the famous Seven Sisters chalk cliffs.

Epsom (Surrey). Famed for its racecourse on the nearby Downs which is

The Leas, Folkestone

the scene of the world-famous Derby and Oaks horse races each year in June.

Eynsford (Kent). Pleasing old-world village with timbered cottages and 15c bridge over River Darent. There are remains of 12c castle with high curtain wall and stone hall (AM standard hours). 2m SE is Brands Hatch. The Lullingstone Roman Villa (AM standard hours) shows splendid mosaics and unique remains of Christian chapel. Lullingstone Castle is 18c house with 16c gateway (1st Weds in May–Sept 2–6).

Folkestone (Kent). Populous south coast resort with extensive pebble beach, and busy cross-Channel port. From the Leas, a lofty promenade, there is uninterrupted view towards the French coast. The Leas Cliff Hall is fine concert pavilion with restaurant. Full entertainment and sports activities, golf at Hythe. The Lower Sandgate Road (toll for vehicles) connects with Sandgate a restful place at the foot of Shorncliffe heights. Of Sandgate Castle, coeval with those at Deal and Walmer, little remains. To E is the Warren, a wildly beautiful stretch of fallen cliff. 2m N is Caesar's Camp, a conical knoll (400 ft) with ancient earthworks.

Frensham (Surrey). Attractive village on River Wey. Frensham Common is popular expanse with Great Pond and Little Pond, lakes, sailing, fishing, swimming.

Friday Street (Surrey). Well-known beauty spot 2m N of Leith Hill. Enchanting village of red brick cottages and little lake. Leith Hill (NT 965 ft) is highest point in SE England. From the tower at the summit is magnificent panorama.

Godalming (Surrey). Attractive little town on banks of River Wey with narrow streets and old half-timbered houses. The Regency Town Hall is now a museum. The parish church has a crooked spire. Charterhouse School was founded in London in 1655. 3m SE is Winkworth Arboretum and nearby Hascombe Court with its attractive gardens.

Guildford (Surrey). Ancient county town on River Wey. The steep High Street is picturesque with the 18c Guildhall and its projecting clock a prominent feature. Of the Norman castle little more than the massive keep survives. The new cathedral on Stag Hill is fine modern building designed by Sir Edward Maufe, R.A. Abbot's Hospital is early 17c almshouse. Lewis Carroll is buried in the cemetery. He died in a house called 'The Chestnuts' on Castle Hill in 1898. 2m SW is Loseley House. 4m W is the Hog's Back, a lofty chalk ridge (500 ft) with extensive views. To S is Holmwood Common. To NE, 3½m, is Sutton Place with its pleasant gardens (open).

Hailsham (Sussex). Pleasant town 7m N of Eastbourne and chief market centre for the county. The early 15c church has embattled and pinnacled chequer-work tower from which curfew is still rung. Michelham Priory, 2½m W, consists of parts of 13c Augustinian priory, a Tudor wing and 14c gatehouse, and one of largest moats in England (open Apr–Oct). 2½m S is Polegate with its fine red-brick windmill (1817).

Hastings and St. Leonards (Sussex). Popular coastal resort offering a wide selection of modern attractions. The beach of shingle and sand affords good bathing, there are swimming pools and baths, a pier, and magnificent Pavilion at White Rock. Full sports facilities, numerous public parks and gardens, and a full programme of indoor entertainment. The present ruins of Hastings Castle are fragments of the mighty structure erected by William the Conqueror (daily in summer; on application in winter). St. Clement's Caves (daily) are extensive excavations in the cliff rock. There is a Lifeboat House. The Fishermens' Quarter is quaint area of narrow streets and a beach dotted with 'tackle-boxes' or 'net-shops'. East Hill (lift) is wide expanse of heath and greensward with fine Channel views. Ecclesborne Glen is picturesque gorge with winding path, crags and tiny rivulet. 2m further E are Fairlight Glen and Fairlight Down (599 ft). 3m N is Beauport Park. 6m N is Brede Place.

Herne Bay (Kent). Bracing Thanet resort with total sea frontage of nearly 7 miles. Broad level promenades and extensive beach of shingle. Golf, boating, sea fishing. Pier with concert pavilion. Memorial Park is large recreation ground with sports facilities. Herne church has massive flint and stone tower and some old brasses of interest. 3m E are the sister towers of Reculver (AM).

Hindhead (Surrey). Picturesque resort nearly 900 ft above sea level and one of southern England's finest viewpoints. Gibbet Hill (NT) overlooks the Devil's Punchbowl (NT) a deep combe with heather and bracken.

Hythe (Kent). Pleasant resort 5m W of Folkestone. Shingle beach with stretch of sand at low tide. Boating on Royal Military Canal. Scene Valley Golf Course. Borough museum. The parish church shows Norman to Early English work with magnificent chancel. The crypt contains fantastic collection of human skulls and bones thought to be of victims of the 'Black Death' of 1348. On the coast are Martello towers, relics of the Napoleonic scares. To SW is Romney Marsh. 1m N is Saltwood where at the castle (July-Aug Weds 2.30–6) the four assassins of Thomas a Becket are said to have rested on the eve of the murder. 2m NW is Westenhangar with its racecourse. 2½m W is Lympne were is old Norman castle (open in summer) and Lympne Airport.

Leatherhead (Surrey). Attractive town on River Mole, with 18c bridge, Tudor houses and a 16c inn with overhanging gables. 12c–15c church. To W is Bookham Common (NT). Open spaces in the vicinity include Leatherhead Downs, Fetcham Downs, Ranmore Common, Effingham Hill, Headley Heath, Oxshott Heath, the famous Box Hill and Mickleham valley.

Lewes (Sussex). Ancient county town on hill above banks of River Ouse, 8m NE of Brighton. Castle with 14c Barbican (open daily). Barbican House, High Street, is museum. The church of St. John-sub-Castro was built 1839 on site of original Saxon church. In Southover church lie remains of William the Conqueror's daughter Gundrada. Anne of Cleves House (weekdays) has display of old furniture, tapestries and bygones. Glynde Place is 4m SE.

Littlehampton (Sussex). Popular resort at mouth of river Arun with large open green between the town and the sands. Pier, amusement park, harbour, golf, museum. Rustington is pleasant coastal suburb (sand at low tide). Angmering, 4m NE is old-world village. Its seaside portion, 1m away, has a variety of sports and pastimes including tennis, golf, boating, fishing, bathing and riding. 4m N is Arundel with its famous castle.

Littlestone-on-Sea (Kent). The seaward extension of Romney with pebbly beach and sand at low tide. Golf. There are sand dunes at Greatstone 1m S. A mile further is Lydd-on-Sea.

Maidstone (Kent). County town and modern business centre on River Medway but retaining a number of old buildings. All Saints Church is Perpendicular structure erected by Archbishop Courtenay and has good stalls and sedilia. The Archbishops Palace is Elizabethan. The 16c Chillington Manor is art gallery and museum. Excursions can be made to Allington (3m) for Allington Castle, and Aylesford (4m) for Kit's Coty House, the chamber of a prehistoric long barrow (AM).

Margate (Kent). 'Merry Margate' but nevertheless a charmingly laid out holiday resort with miles of green lawns and gardens fringed with golden sands, and excellent public parks. Unrivalled facilities for bathing, sport and entertainment. There is a fine 5-mile coast walk along cliffs to Kingsgate, the North Foreland and Broadstairs. There is Harbour pier and a Jetty with lifeboat house. Immediately eastward is Cliftonville, within the borough, with cliff-fringed sandy beaches and greensward. 1m S is Salmestone Grange (open Sats 12–5 Jun–Sept).

Midhurst (Sussex). Old market town overlooking River Rother, a feeder of the Arun, and good centre for excursions on wooded downland. Beneath steps of Town Hall are the old stocks and pillory. To north is Cowdray Park (polo) and the ruins of the 16c mansion of the Viscounts Montague.

Newhaven (Sussex). Busy cross-Channel terminal for the Dieppe service and small fishing port with fine harbour and yachting at mouth of River Ouse. From the Breakwater and East Pier are good angling prospects. Lifeboat station (open). Shingle beach.

Newlands Corner (Surrey). Famous beauty spot (600 ft) on North Downs between Merrow and Shere. There are far-reaching views.

Pevensey (Sussex). Twin village with Westham, 4m NE of Eastbourne, of quaint cottages and fragrant gardens. The Norman castle stands within extensive remains of Roman fortress of late 3c date (AM Standard hours). The Mint House (open weekdays' is interesting old building said to date from 1342. Town Hall with museum. The church is Early English structure of green sandstone. Pevensey Bay, 1m S, is developing seaside resort. 4m N is Herstmonceux Castle occupied by Royal Greenwich Observatory (grounds only open).

Petworth (Sussex). Picturesque little town of narrow streets and old houses. Petworth House (NT), with its important collection of paintings, is situated in vast grounds. 6m W is Midhurst with nearby Cowdray Park.

Ramsgate (Kent). Popular holiday resort built on and between two lofty chalk cliffs. Excellent bathing at Main Sands and many other spots along nearly three miles of sandy foreshore. Busy harbour, the two piers of which provide fine promenades. Yacht club, annual yachting week. Full programme of entertainment and sports events in season. Greyhound stadium at Dumpton Park. At 1m W is Pegwell Bay with vast expanse of sand at low tide (shrimping). At Ebbsfleet is Viking ship 'Hugin' commemorating the 1500th anniversary of the landing at this spot of Hengist and his warbands. 2m inland is Minster much visited for its famous church and abbey.

Reigate (Surrey). Old market town at foot of North Downs. The church shows some Norman features. There are several Queen Anne buildings and scanty remains of old castle in park where are some caves. On nearby heath is Reigate windmill in which occasional Sunday services are held.

Rochester (Kent). Busy commercial centre on River Medway. Of main historical interest are remains of the Norman castle with its massive keep and the Cathedral, in plan very similar to that at Canterbury. At the Elizabethan Restoration House Charles II stayed a night on his return to England in 1660. Close to the river is Temple Manor, a 13c hall, with vaulted undercroft, of house of Knights Templars (AM standard hours). 4m E is Cobham Hall, a 16c mansion showing work by Jones, Adam and Wyatt.

Margate Seafront and Sands

Romney Marsh (Kent). A great tract of alluvium and shingle extending from Hythe to the Sussex border, separated from the sea by the Dymchurch Wall, a 20 ft high embankment, an area of meadows, fences and dykes.

Runnymede (Surrey). Historic Thames-side meadows (NT) where King John affixed his seal to Magna Carta in 1215. Museum. Magna Carta Island is private. The wooded slope of Cooper's Hill nearby commands widespread views and has Runnymede Memorial on summit.

Rye (Sussex). Ancient and romantic town with characteristics more Flemish than English, attracting artists, writers and photographers to its picturesque ensemble of houses, inns, gateway, and hilly streets. The sea has receded 2m from this 'ancient town' attached to the original Cinque Ports. The Landgate (*c.* 1360) is only survivor of the three portals which guarded the town. The church dates from 1120. The pendulum of the tower-clock swings inside the church. Picturesque buildings include the 18c Town Hall, the Old Stone House, and the Ypres Tower (once a prison and now museum). Lamb House was once occupied by Henry James (N.T. Weds in summer 2–6). 3m SE is Camber (golf) with fine sands and dunes.

St. Margaret's Bay (Kent). Charming resort in Rural District of Dover 6m S of Deal. The bracing and picturesque bay is ideal for a quiet holiday. Bathing and boating. On Leathercote Point is memorial to the Dover Patrol (1914–18). St. Margaret's-at-Cliffe, the mother village, is 2½m inland. There is a fine Norman parish church.

Sandwich (Kent). An ancient port, chief of the Cinque Ports of Kent. Now the sea is 1½m distant where the sandhills and foreshore give some of the best bathing in this part of the country. Golf. Quaint gables and overhanging storeys give a Flemish aspect of the town. At N end of High

Street is ancient Barbican and toll-house. St. Clement's Church has arcaded Norman tower. St. Peter's church dates from 12c. 1½m N is Richborough Castle (AM).

Seaford (Sussex). Quiet, sheltered resort 2m E of Newhaven. Shingle beach with good bathing, boating and sea-fishing. Two golf courses, tennis, bowls. At eastern end of promenade is Martello tower, the last of the 74 placed at short intervals along the coast between Seaford and Folkestone. The parish church shows Norman work. To E are downland walks with Seaford Head, the site of a prehistoric camp. In 2m is Cuckmere Haven at the mouth of the Cuckmere river. 2m W is pretty Bishopstone with church showing Saxon, Norman and Early English work. 2m NE is Hindover, a favourite picnic spot with good views over Seaford Bay while 5m N is Firle Beacon (718 ft).

Selsey (Sussex). Delightful resort on Selsey Peninsula. To west of Selsey Bill is sandy shore, while to east is steeper shingly beach with deep water close inshore.

Sevenoaks (Kent). Well situated dormitory town in wooded scenery. The church is Perpendicular in style and has some interesting monuments. The old grammar school was founded in 1432. 1½m SE is Knole (open) one of the largest mansions in England. Further SE (5½m) is Ightham Note. Combe Bank, with its Adam work is 2½m W.

Shoreham (Sussex). Seafaring town midway between Brighton and Worthing appealing to lovers of old churches and quaint and picturesque corners. Buckingham Park is fine natural open space with sports facilities. Two-mile long beach with swimming, rowing, yachting and fishing. The old bridge (toll) is picturesque timber structure. Nearby is Shoreham airport.

Steyning (Sussex). Quiet but considerable village 5m N of Shoreham. Long main street, several old inns, ancient grammar school and picturesque half-timbered houses. 2m W is Chanctonbury Ring (783 ft) with glorious panorama over the Weald.

Sunbury-on-Thames (Surrey). Popular riverside resort with boating and angling. Racecourse at Kempton Park. The church dates in part from 12c. Sunbury lock is prominent feature of this reach of the Thames.

Tunbridge Wells (Kent). A former spar but now busy centre near county border with Sussex in wooded country. The Pantiles, or parade, is architectural feature with picturesque houses and shops, and chalybeate well. There is a museum and art gallery. To SW are the High Rocks, queer shapes of sandstone rock. 8m SE is Lamberhurst, with the beautiful gardens of both Owl House and Scotney Castle open on certain days. Old Scar Manor (NT) is 6m NE. Penshurst Place is 6m NW.

Walton-on-Thames (Surrey). Residential town and resort on River Thames with bathing, boating and fishing. Annual regatta in June.

Westerham (Kent). Small town with some pleasant houses and inns and Quebec House (NT open) once home of General Wolfe. 2m S is Chartwell, the former home of Sir Winston Churchill, now Churchill Memorial Museum (NT).

Westgate-on-Sea (Kent). Popular resort within borough of Margate. St. Mildred's Bay and West Bay are sandy shores joined by substantial sea walls and promenades. Entertainment in Westgate Pavilion. Numerous schools in the town.

Whitstable (Kent). With Seasalter and Tankerton a Thames estuary resort popular with sailing folk. Bathing from shingle beach. Sea angling, golf and other sports. The town's oyster industry has a record of 2,000 years behind it.

Winchelsea (Sussex). A once busy and important maritime town, an 'ancient town' with Rye, included in the confederation of the Cinque Ports. It retains a few vestiges of its antiquity including three gateways of the former walled town. The parish church has remarkable stained glass and some good monuments. The Old Court House (museum) is modern restoration of a Tudor rebuilding. Winchelsea Beach (1m) has shingle beach. 1m NE is Camber Castle.

Woking (Surrey). Residential town in north-west part of county. St. Peter's church dates from Norman times. There is a mosque erected in 1889. Good centre for excursions to many places of interest—Ripley, Pyrford, Chobham and Bisley among others.

Worthing (Sussex). Famous holiday resort with good bathing (shingle and sand), boating and fishing, a long sea frontage, splendid countryside and Downland rambles and good golf, tennis and bowls. Pier with pavilions, parks and gardens, library and museum, theatre. 2m NE is Sompting where the church has late-Saxon tower of type known as 'Rhenish holm'. At High Salvington a windmill is prominent feature. Highdown Hill (NT) is outlying spur of the South Downs (prehistoric earthworks). $2\frac{1}{2}$m E is Lancing with good sandy beach and various recreational amenities. Cissbury Ring (NT) is 3m N.

Worthing

Southern England

Southern England

Dorset - Hampshire - Isle of Wight - Wiltshire

Dorset

This southern county between Hampshire and Devon covers an area of
974 square miles with a population of 338,000. It has a coastline along the
English Channel of some 78 miles. Much of the county inland is chalk
downland with characteristic bare rounded hills and few trees and is
intensely farmed. In breaks in the chalk however, there are extensive areas
of wooded and scenic beauty. The county town is Dorchester, but Poole
is the largest town. Along the Channel coast is a string of resorts with
Canford, Swanage, Weymouth and Lyme Regis attracting most attention.
Beauty spots include Lulworth, Charmouth, Abbotsbury, Kimmeridge
and Studland. The county is rich in notable churches and beautiful
houses, and is literally dotted with sites of antiquarian or historical interest,
outstanding among which is the prehistoric fortress of Maiden Castle,
2 miles south of Dorchester.

Hampshire and the Isle of Wight

This southern county which, with the Isle of Wight, extends to an area of
some 1,660 square miles is bordered on the north by Berkshire, south by
the English Channel, eastward by Surrey and Sussex, and to the west by
Dorset and Wiltshire. Principal rivers are the Avon, Test, Beaulieu,
Blackwater, Hamble and Loddon, and these with numerous streams all
provide good fishing. The county is predominantly agricultural. Hampshire's county town is Winchester, a beautiful cathedral city onetime capital
of the ancient kingdom of Wessex and of England. The naval dockyard
at Portsmouth is one of the greatest in the world and Southampton has
for centuries been a centre of world trade and an important world passenger
traffic port. Along the coast are many popular holiday resorts, and inland
great wooded tracts of which the New Forest is best known.

The Isle of Wight, separated from the mainland by the Solent channel,
is deservedly one of the most popular holiday places in the south of England.
A range of chalk downs is ringed by a coastline of many small resorts
offering sandy beaches and innumerable holiday amenities.

Wiltshire

A county of rich and varied landscape, of extensive chalk downland and fertile valleys, of dignified towns, and strings of small but attractive villages. The broad Salisbury Plain occupies a great part of the southern half of the county, with the rolling Marlborough Downs to the north-east. In the north-west the landscape is mainly Cotswold in character. Salisbury, with its magnificent cathedral, is the county town but most administrative functions are carried out at Trowbridge. Prosperous towns include Bradford-on-Avon, Chippenham, Devizes, Marlborough and Swindon. Among prehistoric sites, of which there are many, Avebury and Stonehenge stand supreme. White horses, cut in the chalk downs, are to be seen at Westbury Hill, Cherhill, Marlborough, Milk Hill, Hackpen Hill, Broad Town and Pewsey. Wilton House, home of the Earl of Pembroke, is of great historical and architectural interest, and the National Trust gardens of Stourhead, Stourton, are outstanding.

Of Special Interest

Athelhampton (Puddletown 5m NE Dorchester). Among the finest of English medieval houses. Great Hall with timbered roof, fine staircase, 15c Great Chamber, thatched stables. In grounds are lovely water and walled gardens and 15c dovecote. Apr–Sept, Weds, Thurs, 2–6. Also Bk Hols, Suns and Mons, and Suns in Jun and Jul.

Avington Park (5m NE of Winchester). Handsome 17c mansion with fine ballroom and state rooms where Charles II and Nell Gwynne once lived. (May–Sept, Sats and Suns, 2.30–5.30).

Beaulieu Abbey (6m SE of Lyndhurst). Remains of Cistercian monastery founded by King John in 1204. Its Great Gatehouse, now called Palace House, forms part of residence of Lord Montagu. The former monks' refectory serves as the parish church. Motor Museum.

Breamore House (3m N of Fordingbridge). Magnificent Elizabethan manor house dating from 1583, with fine works of art. (Apr–Sept. afternoons except Mons and Fris).

Carisbrooke Castle (Isle of Wight). Medieval castle, added to later, on site of late Roman fort. Charles I imprisoned here 1647–8. Isle of Wight County Museum. (AM standard hours).

Cerne Abbas (8m N of Dorchester). 15c gatehouse and 14c guest house of once powerful monastery. Open daily. St. Augustine's Well in village. On hillside is Cerne Giant, a stupendous figure cut in the chalk.

Compton Acres (Canford Cliffs, Poole). Magnificent gardens overlooking Poole harbour and Purbeck hills. Apr–Oct, daily, 10.30–6.30.

Corsham Court (4m W of Chippenham). Fine Elizabethan structure with Georgian state rooms and furnishings by Adam and Cobb. Collection of old masters. Grounds by Capability Brown and Georgian bath house. Wed, Thurs, Apr–Oct. All Suns through year and daily (except Mons and Fris) mid July–mid Sept, 11–6.

The Courts (Holt, 2m E of Bradford-on-Avon) (NT). Garden with hedged vistas

Cloisters, Beaulieu Abbey

and fine trees. Apr–Oct, Tues, Weds, Thurs, 2–5. 17c house with porcelain, Weds only.

Creech Grange (3½m S of Wareham). Restored William and Mary house displaying fine furnishings and good collection of paintings. Wooded garden. Jul–Aug, Weds, Thurs, Suns, 2.30–5.

Exbury Gardens (4m SE of Beaulieu). Beautiful woodland gardens with many azalea, rhododendron and other flowering shrubs. (Afternoons except Sats in spring months).

Forde Abbey (Thorncombe, 4m SE of Chard). Former 12c Cistercian monastery, later converted and enlarged. Famous set of Mortlake tapestries from Raphael cartoons. Beautiful grounds. May–Sept. Weds 2–6. Also some Suns.

Great Chalfield Manor (Melksham) (NT). 15c moated house with notable Great Hall. Mid Apr–mid Oct. Weds 12–1, 2–5. The church nearby is 13c.

Hale Park (4m NE of Fordingbridge). Georgian country mansion designed and built in 1715 by Thomas Archer, architect, for himself. Tapestries, portraits. (Afternoons, Jul to Sept, Weds, Thurs, Suns and late Summer Bk Hol).

Hurst Castle (2½m SE Milford). Coastal defence erected 1544 by Henry VIII and later additions. (AM standard hours).

Jane Austen's House (Chawton, 1m SW of Alton). The novelist's old home in the village street is preserved as a museum and contains personal and family relics. (Daily 11–4.30 except Mons and Tues, Nov–Mar).

Kingston Lacy (2½m NW of Wimborne). 17c home of the Bankes family. Paintings. Grounds, Easter, then May–Sept. Sats, Suns, Bk Hols, 2–6.

Lacock Abbey (Lacock, 3m S of Chippenham) (NT). Augustinian abbey remains of cloister, sacristy, chapter house, kitchen etc. Tudor Mansion with octagonal tower and twisted chimney stacks. Cloisters Apr–Oct daily except Fris 2–6. Other months Mons, Weds, 2–4. House Apr–Sept, Weds, Thurs, Sats and Bk Hols Mons 2–6.

Langford Castle (3m S of Salisbury) House on unusual triangular plan (1591) with later alterations. Fine pictures and furniture. Gardens. Apr–Sept Weds 2–5.30.

Littlecote (3m W of Hungerford). Tudor manor, notable Great Hall, armoury, Long Gallery and chapel. Furnishings. Grounds. Apr–mid Oct. Tues and Weds 10–1, 2–5 and Mons, Sats and Sun afternoons.

SOUTHERN ENGLAND

Longleat (4m SW of Warminster). The magnificent Renaissance home of the Marquess of Bath. State Rooms, pictures, furniture. Extensive parkland wherein the famous lions roam. Daily 10–6 (summer), 10–4 (winter).

Maiden Castle (2m SW of Dorchester). Finest of Dorset earthworks dating from 1c B.C. Huge oval triple ramparts surround extensive plateau. (AM regularly).

Minterne (2m N of Cerne Abbas). 30-acre shrub garden, bamboo walks, rhododendrons, azaleas, Japanese cherry walks, etc. Apr–Jun, Suns and Bk Hols 2–6.

Mottisfont Abbey (NT) (5m NW of Romsey). 18c mansion incorporating parts of a former 12c priory. The drawing-room displays Rex Whistler paintings. (House and grounds, Apr–Sept, Weds and Thurs afternoons).

Netley Abbey (Netley). Remains of Cistercian abbey of 1239. (AM standard hours).

Old Sarum (2m N of Salisbury). Vast earthworks of late 11c Norman town. Originally Iron Age hill fort and then Saxon settlement. Museum. (AM standard hours and Sun mornings).

Osborne House (Isle of Wight). Private residence of Queen Victoria 1845–6 and where she died 1901. State Apartments, Swiss Cottage museum and grounds. Easter–Sept, Mons, Weds, Fris, 11–5. Also Tues and Thurs from Whitsun.

Porchester Castle (3m E of Fareham). Roman shore fort of late 3c, walls and bastions still standing. Medieval castle with late Norman keep and Norman church of Augustinian priory. (AM standard hours).

St. Giles's House (Wimborne St. Giles). House built 1650 by 1st Earl of Shaftesbury and containing rare collection of furniture, pictures, tapestries and porcelain. Unique 18c shell grotto in grounds. Easter then mid-May–mid-Oct, Weds and Suns 2–6. Also daily except Mons in Aug.

Sandford Orcas Manor (3m NW of Sherborne). Small Tudor House with collections of furnishings, china, glass. Notable gardens. Daily, except Mondays in winter months.

Smedmore (1m SE of Kimmeridge). 18c manor house. Paintings and rare collection of antique dolls. Gardens. Jun-Sept. Weds 2.30–6.

Stonehenge (2m W of Amesbury). Famous remains of prehistoric (18c–15c B.C.) religious or governing centre, once consisting of outer circle of massive sarsen stones capped by lintels, a second circle of upright 'Blue Stones', a horseshoe of sarsen trilithons, an inner horseshoe of 'Blue stones', and a central Altar Stone. (AM standard hours and Sun mornings in summer).

Stourhead (Stourton, 3m NW of Mere) (NT). 19c mansion built for member of Hoare banking family. Collections of works of art including Chippendale furniture. Pleasure grounds, lakes, woodland (daily 11–7). House Easter–Sept except Mons and Tues. Winter also except Thurs. Closed Dec–Feb.

Titchfield Abbey (3m W of Fareham). Remnants of house of Premonstratensian Canons of 13c converted to mansion. Chapter house and other monastic buildings. (AM standard hours).

The Vyne (Sherborne St. John). 16c house with later additions, chapel of 1150, Long Gallery, gardens. (NT Apr–Sept. Weds and Bk Hol. Mons 11–6, Suns 1–6).

Wilton House (Wilton, 2m W of Salisbury). Magnificent seat of Earl of Pembroke, 16c–19c house by Inigo Jones, Holbein and James Wyatt. State rooms, with famous 'Double Cube' room, paintings, furniture, sculpture. Parkland, lawns, gardens. Apr–Sept, Tues–Sats, 11–6. Suns in Aug–Sept 2–6.

Yarmouth Castle (Isle of Wight). Last to be built of Henry VIII's coastal defence castles. (AM standard hours).

Resorts and Centres of Interest

Abbotsbury (Dorset). A pretty village near the West Fleet, 9 miles west of Weymouth, with two great attractions, a Swannery and Sub-Tropical Gardens. Other objects of interest are St. Nicholas Church (early 16c but showing parts of an older building), remnants of its old Abbey of St. Peter, and St. Catherine Chapel on a nearby hill.

Amesbury (Wilts). Former small village on River Avon attracting many visitors on account of numerous prehistoric remains in the neighbourhood. Antrobus House is museum and social centre. 2m NE is Woodhenge, a prehistoric circle, and 2m W the famous Stonehenge (AM).

Avebury (Wilts). (6m W of Marlborough). Village centre for number of ancient monuments on the Marlborough Downs. The great Avebury Stone Circle dating from about 1900 B.C. is represented now by huge circular earthworks. A museum (NT) contains articles found during excavations. Other antiquities nearby include Silbury Hill, West Kennett Long Barrow, Windmill Hill earthworks and Woodhenge, Durrington. Avebury Manor is Elizabethan with good garden.

Bournemouth (Hants). In its short history the town has developed into one of the country's most popular holiday resorts with a resident population of some 150,000. Six miles of golden sands are sheltered by sandstone cliffs. Where the cliffs have eroded picturesque chines have been formed. Pine trees line many of the streets. There are parks and gardens, while its Pavilion, Pier and Winter Garden with famous symphony orchestra are well-known. Eastward, but within the borough, are the popular resorts of **Boscombe, Southborne** and **Pokesdown**.

Bradford-on-Avon (Wilts). Lovely old town of stone buildings with ancient bridge with rare bridge chapel. 10c Saxon St. Lawrence's Church and Norman parish church. Many fine 17c and 18c houses—The Hall, Westbury House, John Halls Almshouses. At Barton ($\frac{3}{4}$m) is 14c tithe barn (AM).

Brading (Isle of Wight). Small town mid-way between Ryde and Sandown, convenient for downland walks. The principal street straggles uphill to the church of Transitional-Norman architecture of interest on account of its Oglander chapel. The Old Town Hall has beneath it the old stocks and whipping-post. Wax museum. Bull Ring. At Yarbridge is Roman Villa.

Bramshaw (Hants). Pretty village with church showing traces of Norman and EE work. The attractive churchyard contains old yews and many ancient tombstones. Much common land in vicinity is now NT property. To S beyond Brook is Canterton Glen where is the Rufus Stone recording the violent death of William Rufus in 1100.

Bridport (Dorset). Chief centre for production of fishing rods, lines, twines and cordage. Wide main street, red brick buildings and wooded background. **West Bay**, the holiday portion, lies on the coast 2m south. Here there is bathing, boating, bowls, tennis and golf.

Brockenhurst (Hants). Residential village of old and picturesque cottages on southern outskirts of the New Forest.

Bursledon (Hants). Charming boating centre on Hamble river. Monuments in late 13c church recall times when battleships were built here. Strawberry cultivation is local pursuit. Hamble is noted yachting centre. To W is Netley Abbey.

Cadnam (Hants). Village at important road junction on New Forest boundary, 6m W of Southampton. Pretty cottages and famous Sir John Barleycorn Inn claim many visitors in summer months.

Calbourne (Isle of Wight). Village 4m SW of Carisbrooke. Winkle Street is attractive row of old-world stone and thatch cottages. There is a water-mill (open). Nearby are Westover and Swainstone, fine mansions in extensive parks.

Carisbrooke (Isle of Wight). Village 1m W of Newport, and good centre for downland walks. The famous Norman castle, on a wooded hill, was place of imprisonment of Charles I. The Well House with 161-foot well is of interest. The priory church has noble tower and interesting memorials.

Christchurch (Hants). Important town on outskirts of the New Forest with venerable Priory, ruined castle (AM) and long open river front. Small boat sailing in harbour. Along the coast are developing resorts of **Highcliffe**, **Barton** and **Milford-on-Sea**. Hengistbury Head commands magnificent seascapes.

34

Corsham (Wilts). Town of pleasant 17c–18c houses, 12c–15c church, and Elizabethan and Georgian Corsham Court. Local quarries for Bath stone.

Cowes (Isle of Wight). Famous yachting centre at mouth of River Medina and facing the Solent. Cowes Castle is headquarters of Royal Yacht Squadron, premier yacht club of Britain. Car ferry service to Southampton. 1m SE of East Cowes is Osborne House, stately marine residence of Queen Victoria and where in 1901 she died.

Devizes (Wilts). Old market town in heart of county with some attractive Georgian architecture. Two churches (St. John's—St. Mary's) retain Norman work. The museum has many prehistoric relics. 19c castle on site of Norman stronghold.

Dorchester (Dorset). Historic market centre and county town built on high ground west of the spur of land between the river Frome and its tributary, the Winterborne. 15c St. Peter's Church, in High Street, is of ancient origin. Adjoining is County Museum. Other buildings of interest include Judge Jeffrey's Lodgings, the old Grammar School, and old Crown Court of Tolpuddle Martyr fame. Numerous ancient forts and earthworks in the district include Maumbury Ring, Poundbury, and Maiden Castle, finest of them all.

Emsworth (Hants). Bright little place well-known to local sailing men (regatta). On border between Hampshire and Sussex, the little River Ems marking the boundary. There are some oyster fisheries. To E a road connects with Thorney Island. To N is peaceful village of Westbourne and Racton where church has monuments to Gunter family.

Fareham (Hants). Town on rising ground above the Wallington River, busy port with coastal trade. The church shows Norman and possible Saxon work. 3m W is Titchfield Abbey. To E is Portchester Castle.

Fordingbridge (Hants). Quiet little town on River Avon with quaint seven-arched bridge. The graceful church of stone and flint has an embattled tower. 3m N is Breamore where is almost complete Saxon church, and Breamore House, a fine Elizabethan manor house (open).

Freshwater Bay (Isle of Wight). Bracing resort in tiny bay near southwestern corner of the Island. Rock and pebble beach with some sand at low tide, but there is plenty of sand and good bathing at Compton Bay a short distance eastward. Golf on Afton Down and sea-fishing. Features of nearby cliffs include Freshwater Cave, the Arched Rock and Stag Rock. The village of Freshwater lies 1m inland. The parish church contains memorials of the Tennyson family. Needles Down (400 ft) gives fine seascapes. Alum Bay has coloured cliffs, with twelve distinct shades of colour in the sandstone best seen after rain.

Godshill (Isle of Wight). Village of thatched cottages, tea gardens and 15c church, one of the prettiest and most visited places in the Island. Model village in old rectory grounds.

Gosport (Hants). Busy seaport and naval centre on west bank of Portsmouth Harbour (ferry). Constant panorama of passing ships of all kinds. Open air salt water baths.

Hamble (Hants). Noted yachting centre at mouth of Hamble River at junction with extensive Southampton Water. To NW is Netley Abbey.

Hayling Island (Hants). Situated east of Portsmouth and divided from mainland by strait connecting the two harbours of Langstone and Chichester. Wooden trestle bridges cross the strait. It is a low, flat tract about 4m long and 4m wide. On southern shore is long sandy expanse sloping gently from a steeper margin of shingle. Ideal for children.

Ibsley (Hants). Ancient village 1m N of Ellingham cross-roads. Its little church has a Queen Anne service of plates and contains a curious monument to Sir John Constable and his wife (1627). 4m S is Fordingbridge.

Isle of Wight. As a holiday resort the Island is thoroughly up-to-date, the seaside towns and inland centres offering many facilities for sport and entertainment. The Island is a paradise for children and there are few danger spots for paddling or bathing from gently shelving sands. There are numerous golf courses and many resorts hold regattas. Cowes is world famous as a yachting centre.

Lee-on-Solent (Hants). Small resort with low gravelly cliff overlooking the Solent. Boating and yachting. The coast walk westward to Titchfield Haven gives magnificent prospect across the Solent and up Southampton Water. Golf on Chark Common.

Lulworth Cove (Dorset). Beauty spot on the south coast, this perfect cove lies between Swanage and Weymouth beneath high limestone cliffs where Purbeck Hills reach the coast. There is little room on the sand and pebble beach during the height of the season. A mile from the cove is Durdle Door, a great naturally-formed rock arch and many caves biting deep into the cliff face. At East Lulworth is the burnt-out shell of Lulworth Castle.

Lyme Regis (Dorset). Pleasant sheltered coastal resort with fine sea views. The Cobb, an 870 foot curved stone pier, forms an extensive harbour. Good bathing from shingle beach, and tennis, golf and entertainment available. Westward lies the Landslip, a vast extent of fallen cliff.

Malmesbury (Wilts). Picturesque town on Marlborough Downs whose principal feature is the ruin of the monastic Abbey church. A splendid ornate Market Cross dates from time of Henry VII. 14c clock tower to parish church. Among old houses is St. John's Hospital, almshouse of 13c. 6m NW is **Tetbury** with pillared market hall and 18c church with box pews.

Marlborough (Wilts). Small but attractive town on River Kennet. Very broad main street of red-brick houses and inns is scene of late summer Mop Fair. Marlborough College is well-known school. To SE is Savernake Forest with its many fine avenues of beech. To W is Fyfield Down Nature Reserve and prehistoric Ridgeway across the downs.

Central Bournemouth

Milford-on-Sea (Hants). Pleasant watering place, fresh and bracing, 4m from Lymington. The turf-bordered shore gives excellent bathing. The village of Milford is slightly inland. To E the shingly shore curves round to the spit on which is Hurst Castle with its white lighthouse. There are good views across to the Isle of Wight.

Milton Abbas (Dorset). Village of thatched cottages amid lovely scenery. Wooded chalk hills form a semi-circle around the picturesque valley and lake enfolding the old Abbey church and the mansion. The present Abbey was begun in 1322 but not completed until 1539. 3m NW is Bulbarrow Hill (902 ft) with fine views over Blackmore Vale.

New Forest (Hants). A hundred thousand acres in extent, with open heath, lawns, greens, slades and dells interspersed with woods and plantations, trickling streams, quiet villages, ancient churches and quaint cottages its chief features. Deer and ponies roam freely. **Brockenhurst**, **Ringwood** and **Lyndhurst** are excellent centres for many walks and drives.

Newport (Isle of Wight). Commercial capital of the Island on River Medina 5m S of Cowes. The Old Grammar School is stone structure used as lodging place of Charles I. Old buildings include God's Providence House (1701) the Chantry House (1612) and the Castle Inn (1684). In Avondale Road is Roman Villa, showing mosaic floors and baths. 1m W is Carisbrooke with its castle.

Petersfield (Hants). Pleasant little town amid attractive surroundings 10m W of Midhurst. In Market Place is statue of William III on horseback. The church has a Norman chancel arch and some EE windows. 3m S is Butser Hill (889 ft).

Wilton House

Poole (Dorset). Seaport and holiday town with vast landlocked harbour excellent for sailing. Good sands and bathing at Branksome, Canford Cliffs and Sandbanks, all within the borough. Brownsea Island (NT) of fir groves, miniature glens and hills lies within the harbour.

Portchester (Hants). Village on Portsmouth Harbour notable for its castle (AM), a Norman structure built in a corner of a Roman fortress of 3 or 4c date. Early 12c church with lichened west front has Roman relics.

Portland (Dorset). Connected with the mainland by the notorious Chesil Bank, Portland is a mass of limestone rock with some ten small villages and hamlets. Overlooking the harbour on the north is Portland Castle (AM) built by Henry VIII. Museum at Avice's Cottage, Wakeham. At Portland Bill, the extreme tip of the peninsula, are a small beach, lighthouse, and the curious Pulpit Rock.

Portsmouth and Southsea (Hants). Important naval port in the Royal Dockyard of which is preserved Nelson's flagship 'Victory'. Dickens House (Museum) is Georgian house in Landport where the novelist was born in 1812. **Southsea** is the holiday portion with many attractions and a constant parade of ships passing to and from the harbourage.

Ringwood (Hants). Ancient market town prettily situated on east bank of River Avon 9m N of Christchurch. Angling for salmon and coarse fish in Avon. 2m N is Ellingham with 12c Priory church noted for its traceried chancel screen and unique tympanum.

Romsey (Hants). Pleasant market town on river Test notable for its

Norman Abbey Church. Close by is building known as King John's Hunting Lodge (museum).

Ryde (Isle of Wight). Popular resort with extensive sands on Solent shore facing Spithead. The long pier is steamer ferry point from Portsmouth and railhead of short Island railway. Long esplanade and flower gardens. Entertainments and many sports facilities, but mainly yachting (Royal Victoria Yacht Club). 2m E is Seaview a pretty seaside village with good bathing and prawn and lobster fishing. To W is Binstead and beyond the slight remains of Quarr Abbey founded in 1132. The new abbey was erected in 1908–14 for Benedictine monks exiled from Salesmes, France. Nearby is Wootton Creek, a favourite yachting resort.

Salisbury (Wilts). Classic cathedral city on River Avon near southern edge of the great chalk downland of Salisbury Plain. Ancient houses, good hotels and shops. The magnificent Early English cathedral remains the only medieval cathedral in Western Europe which, except for the 404 ft spire, is one man's design (James Wyatt). The Cloisters are 13c, Chapter House Early Decorated style. The Cathedral Close is beautiful with mellow residences among which is Mompesson House (NT) with fine wood and plaster work and carved staircase. Museum of local interest. The Guildhall dates from 1795 and has good collection of pictures.

Sandown (Isle of Wight). Pleasant seaside resort with extensive sands and ideal as a family holiday choice. Golf and various sports and entertainment. Pier and esplanade. Blue Lagoon is roof garden with swimming pool.

Shaftesbury (Dorset). Ancient hill-top market town overlooking Blackmore Vale. Chief interest lies in the Abbey ruins, remains of a Benedictine nunnery founded in A.D. 888 by Alfred the Great. Museum on site. The much-pictured Gold Hill rises behind the Town Hall. There are wide views over Cranborne Chase from Zigzag Hill 2m SE.

Shanklin (Isle of Wight). Ideal holiday resort with extensive sands. Undercliff esplanade and pier. Various sports and entertainment. To west is Shanklin Chine a fissure in the cliff with cascade and canopy of foliage and path and steps from top to bottom. The old village with thatched cottages makes a quaint picture. Luccombe Common is good picnic spot. There are glorious rambles through the Landslip and over the Downs.

Sherborne (Dorset). Ancient warm-tinted stone town famous for its Abbey Church and its school. Other interesting buildings include Almshouses founded in 1437, remnants of its old castle built 1107–1135, the curious Conduit in Cheap Street, and many old houses.

Southampton (Hants). Great seaport and transatlantic terminal. Much damaged during the war, the City still retains many ancient structures including parts of its medieval wall and the north or Bargate (museum), 14c Wool House (maritime museum), 15c God's House Tower (museum of archaeology) and 16c Tudor House (museum of antiquities). The Pilgrim Father's Memorial commemorates the departure in 1620 of the *Mayflower* and the *Speedwell*. Modern buildings include the Civic Centre and the University.

Studland (Dorset). One of the prettiest villages in England set in woodland, with sea and downs combining to make a picture of rare charm. Bathing from sand and dunes. Golf links within easy reach. The common along the shore is good picnic spot, as also is Shell Bay nearer Sandbanks. To S is Ballard Down separating the bay from Swanage.

Swanage (Dorset). Popular seaside resort with sandy shore, good boating and bathing, tennis and golf. Fine seascape extends from Peveril Point to Ballard Down and over the Purbeck Hills to **Corfe** with its Norman castle (AM), old stone houses and inns. **Studland**, 4 miles north, is unspoilt village with sandy beach.

Titchfield (Hants). Quiet village of quaint old cottages, wide market place with a few shops. The church, part Saxon, has low western tower with shingled spire. Titchfield Abbey or Place House (AM) lies ½m N.

Totland Bay (Isle of Wight). Restful resort and residential quarter at western tip of the Island. Bathing from pebble beach with sand at low tide. Boating and various sports. Colwell Bay (1m) has excellent sands.

Ventnor (Isle of Wight). Popular resort on south-east coast below St. Boniface Down (787 feet). Sand and fine shingle beach, pier, Winter Gardens Pavilion. Golf on Week Downs. 1m E is Bonchurch. Its tree-shaded pond is bird sanctuary. The modern church is built in Norman style but the diminative old church is true Norman and only 48 ft long by 12 ft wide.

Wareham (Dorset). Attractive town of broad streets, fine churches and picturesque old inns and good centre for excursions in the Isle of Purbeck. In restored St. Martin's Church is effigy of T. E. Lawrence. At Bovington, 8m NW, is Cloud's Hill (NT) his former home, and Tank museum of Royal Armoured Corp.

Warsash (Hants). Little place on eastern bank of Hamble River celebrated for crab and lobster teas. Yachting. Ferry to Hamble.

Weymouth (Dorset). Modern seaside resort in glorious bay 5m across. Extensive sands with good bathing and boating. All sports and lively entertainment. Cut in the Downs behind the town is the White Horse, an equestrian figure of George III on horseback. At Preston 2m NE is Jordan Hill Roman Temple.

Wimborne (Dorset). Small but interesting market town serving a large agricultural district in East Dorset and rich in historical associations. The present Minster was built soon after the Conquest and although many additions and alterations have been made, each successive architect has tried to preserve features of the older building. The chained library and a 14c orrery, or astronomical clock, are features of the interior.

Winchester (Hants). Former *Venta Belgarum* of the Romans, and Saxon capital of the Kingdom of Wessex, now a busy focus of prosperous agricultural country. Of the castle built by William I only the Great Hall remains.

In it hangs the Round Table at which King Arthur is said to have sat with his knights. Winchester Cathedral, begun by Bishop Walkelyn in 1079 and completed at the Reformation shows gradations from pure Norman to Late Perpendicular. The Library contains the famous Winchester Bible, the earliest surviving English manuscript of the twelfth century. Wolvesey Castle was rebuilt in 1138 and contains fine Norman work. Other buildings of note include Winchester College founded by William of Wykeham in 1382, and the massive West Gate (museum). Along the river stands the 12c Hospital of St. Cross, an almshouse from which is distributed the historic Wayfarers' Dole.

Wroxall (Isle of Wight). Village in hollow of the high Downs 2m N of Ventnor. On high ground is Appuldurcombe (AM Standard hours) seat for centuries of the Worsley family. 2m NW is Godshill, a pretty village of thatch and stone.

Yarmouth (Isle of Wight). Terminus of car ferry service from Lymington at mouth of River Yar. The castle dates from time of Henry VIII (AM standard hours). Yachting centre with annual regattas.

Weymouth

London

The area defined by the Registrar-General for census purposes as Greater London covers 720 square miles and has a population of slightly under eight millions. The principal and larger part lies to the north of the River Thames. Fortunately for the visitor the major sights are confined to a relatively small central area consisting of the so-called West End and of the ancient City.

Royal London

Banqueting House (Whitehall, S.W.1). One of few remaining parts of old Whitehall Palace, and outstanding example of work of Inigo Jones. Cromwell held his parliaments here. The painted ceiling by Rubens is notable. Weekdays 10–5, Suns in summer.

Buckingham Palace (The Mall, S.W.1). The London residence of the British Sovereign. Rebuilt by Nash in 1825 and refaced in 1913 in Portland Stone from designs by Sir Aston Webb. The Royal Mews are open Weds 2–5 and additionally Thurs in summer, 2–4. The Queen's Gallery is in reconstructed private chapel as art gallery, daily except Mons 11–5, Suns 2–5.

Clarence House (Stable Yard, St. James's, S.W.1). London residence of Queen Elizabeth, the Queen Mother, built 1825 for William IV, the Duke of Clarence.

Hampton Court Palace (Hampton Court). Stately palace built by Cardinal Wolsey and given to Henry VIII. There are about 1,000 rooms, most of which are occupied by royal pensioners. State Apartments with pictures, furniture, tapestries; Great Vine, Maze, Great Hall, Great Kitchen and Cellars, Orangery, open throughout the year from 9.30. Tudor Tennis Court and Banqueting House, Apr–Sept only. Gardens daily.

Houses of Parliament (Parliament Square, S.W.1). The building, completed in 1857, is in rich Gothic style and occupies an area of 8 acres. The designs of Sir Charles Barry were accepted after the destruction by fire of St. Stephens Chapel, the former meeting place of the House of Commons for over three hundred years. The Clock Tower is 316 ft high. Big Ben, the hour bell, weighs $13\frac{1}{2}$ tons. The great Victoria Tower is 323 ft high and 75 ft square. In the House of Lords Chamber is the Sovereign's throne and facing it the Woolsack, on which the Lord Chancellor sits.

Houses of Parliament

The House of Commons chamber was designed after bomb damage by Sir Giles Gilbert Scott. The Palace of Westminster is open on Sats, Easter Mon and Tues, Spring and Summer Bk Hols and Tues, all Mons, Tues and Thurs in Aug, and Thurs in Sept (when House is not sitting), 10–4.30. For debates in House of Lords from 2.40, Tues and Weds and from 3.10 on Thurs—in House of Commons from 4.15 (Fri 11.30).

Jewel Tower (Westminster, S.W.1). Restored fragment of the Old Palace of Westminster dating from 14c. Moat. Open throughout the year 10–4.30 or 6.30.

Kensington Palace (Kensington Gardens, W.8). William III house reconstructed by Wren and Kent. Birthplace of both Queen Victoria and Queen Mary. Now 'Grace and Favour Residences' and occupied in part by the London Museum.

Lambeth Palace (Lambeth Palace Road, S.E.1). For over 700 years the London residence of the Archbishops of Canterbury. Gatehouse built in 1490, Lollards Tower in 1436. Ancient chapel restored after war damage. Great Hall open daily, except Suns 10–5.

Marlborough House (Pall Mall, S.W.1). Built by Wren in 1709 for the Duke of Marlborough and later a Royal residence. Now a Commonwealth centre. Easter-Oct, conducted tours at 12.30, 1.30 and 3.30. Weekends and Bk Hols, 2–6. The Queen's chapel is always open.

Palace of Westminster. See Houses of Parliament.

St. James's Palace (St. James's Street, S.W.1). 'Our Court of St. James's' to which foreign ambassadors and ministers are still accredited. No longer the sovereign's official residence though part (York House) often used by members of Royal Family. Services in Chapel Royal on Sunday mornings in winter open to public.

Tower of London (Tower Hill, E.C.3). The fortress, including the Moat, now drained, occupies an irregular pentagon of 18 acres, the circuit of the outer walls being nearly two-thirds of a mile. The central Keep or White Tower dates from 1078. Overlooking river is St. Thomas's Tower, with Traitors Gate beneath it. The chapel of St. John is one of the most perfect specimens of Norman architecture extant. Armouries, Crown Jewels, Gun Wharf. The picturesque State Dress uniforms of the Yoeman Warders has remained unchanged since the reign of Henry VII. Weekdays from 10; Suns (May–Oct only) from 2.

Westminster Hall (Parliament Square, S.W.1). From 1224 until 1882 the Law Courts were held here. The scene of the trial of Charles I and of the proclamation of Cromwell as Lord Protector. Hall begun by William Rufus in 1097 and rebuilt by Richard II in 1397. Notable oak roof. Weekdays 10–4. When House sitting closes 1 hour before House meets.

Pageantry

Military. Troops usually stationed in London are the Household Cavalry at Knightsbridge Barracks; the King's Troop, Royal Horse Artillery at Regent's Park Barracks; and battalions of the Guards at Wellington Barracks (St. James's Park) and Chelsea Barracks. In summer the Guards full dress is scarlet tunic and blue trousers, and the various regiments may be distinguished from the plumes in the bearskin caps and by tunic button spacing. The Grenadier Guards wear a white plume; the Coldstream Guards, red; the Irish Guards, blue; the Welsh Guards, white with strip of green; the Scots Guards, none. The Foot Guards furnish the Queen's Guard (Palace sentries). Mounted escorts are provided by the Household Cavalry of Life Guards (red tunics and white plumes) and the Royal Horse Guards (blue tunics and red plumes).

Changing of the Guard
    Buckingham Palace. Daily at 11.30.

    Horse Guards. Weekdays at 11, Suns 10.

Trooping the Colour (Horse Guards Parade, S.W.1) Annual ceremony on Sovereign's birthday in June.

Ceremony of the Keys (Tower of London). Ancient ceremony that has taken place nightly (9.40–10) for over 700 years. Written application necessary to Constable's Office.

Major Sights

Bank of England (Threadneedle Street, E.C.2). Fortress-like building between Threadneedle Street, Princes Street, Lothbury and Bartholomew Lane. A military guard is mounted nightly. Entrance Hall only open to public.
Chelsea Royal Hospital (Royal Hospital Road, S.W.3). Wren-designed buildings occupied by the Chelsea Pensioners. Great Hall with interesting portraits, museum, grounds. Weekdays 10–12, 2–6, Suns 2–6. Chapel service, Suns 10.50.
County Hall (Westminster Bridge, S.E.1). English Renaissance style building, headquarters of the Greater London Council.
Dickens House (48 Doughty Street, W.C.1). Dickens lived here from 1837–39 writing final parts of 'Pickwick Papers', 'Nicholas Nickleby' and 'Oliver Twist'. Museum of relics. Weekdays 10–12.30, 2–5.
Discovery (Victoria Embankment, W.C.2). Jointly with nearby HMS *Crysanthemum*, headquarters of the London Division of the R.N.V.R. The ship was used by Captain Scott as a research vessel during the National Antarctic Expedition in 1901. Daily 1–4.45.
Dr. Johnson's House (17 Gough Square, Fleet Street, E.C.4). Dr. Johnson lived here from 1748–1759 and toiled over his great Dictionary. Manuscripts, autographs, first editions, etc. Weekdays, 10.30–5.
Guildhall (King Street, Cheapside, E.C.4). Civic Hall of the Corporation

Tower of London

of London. The Great Hall, restored after war damage, is used for the annual election of the Lord Mayor and Sheriffs and for many civic and political gatherings. Library, museum, art gallery. Weekdays 10–5.

Keats House and Museum (Wentworth Place, Keats Grove, N.W.3). Keats wrote the ode 'To a Nightingale' in the garden here. Weekdays 10–6. Keats Memorial Library in adjoining library.

Kenwood (Hampstead, N.W.3). The mansion is fine example of work of Robert Adam. Iveagh Bequest of furniture and pictures. Extensive gardens, concerts. Weekdays from 10, Suns from 2. To NE are the beautiful Highgate woods. To SW is Hampstead Heath (320 acres) with extensive views.

Lancaster House (St. James's, S.W.1). Presented to the nation by late Lord Leverhulme for housing the London Museum and for provision of a centre for Government hospitality. The main museum collections have been moved to Kensington Palace, and Lancaster House is now used for International conferences and by visiting Government guests. Open Easter–Dec on Sats, Suns and Bk Hols, 2–6.

Law Courts (Strand, W.C.2). Monastic Gothic style building of the Royal Courts of Justice. Central Hall with fine rose window in the gable. The public galleries of the courts are open Mon–Fri, 10–4. In roadway is Temple Bar, marking an ancient portal to the City of London.

Madame Tussaud's (Marylebone Road, N.W.1). Famous waxwork exhibition of famous and infamous people. 10–5.30 (6.30 Apr–Sep). Adjoining is the Planetarium.

Mansion House (Bank, E.C.3). The official residence of the Lord Mayor with fine Corinthian portico. Fine Egyptian Hall. Alternate Sat afternoons on written application.

Old Bailey (Newgate Street, E.C.4). Central Criminal Court on site of old Newgate Prison. Public gallery, weekdays 10.15 and 1.45. Conducted parties on days when courts not sitting at 11 and 3.

Planetarium (Marylebone Road, N.W.1). A projector throws a realistic reproduction of the ever-changing night sky as seen from any point on the earth's surface on to a hemispherical ceiling. Presentations on the hour from 11, Suns from 1.

Post Office Tower (Maple Street, W.1). Britain's tallest building (580 ft with 40 ft mast). At top is restaurant which revolves once in every 20 minutes. Viewing platforms, lifts. Daily.

Public Record Office (Chancery Lane, W.C.2). Fine Gothic building and repository of National records since time of Norman Conquest. Museum, Mon–Fri, 1–4. Search rooms, 9.30–5.

Royal Exchange (Bank, E.C.3). The present building, the third on the site, was designed by Tite and opened in 1844. A gilded grasshopper, crest of Sir Thomas Gresham who founded the Exchange in 1568, surmounts the clock tower. Interior court, daily from 10. The Guildhall Museum is temporarily housed here, 10–5.

Royal Mint (Tower Hill, E.C.3). Produces coins, official medals and seals for U.K., Commonwealth and many foreign countries. Applications to see coining processes to Deputy Master at least six weeks in advance.

Somerset House (Strand, W.C.2). Head office of Inland Revenue, the Probate Registry where Wills are kept and may be inspected, and office of the Registrar General of Births, Deaths and Marriages. Weekdays, 9.30–4.30. The East Wing is occupied by King's College, University of London.

Stock Exchange (Throgmorton Street, E.C.2). Visitors' Gallery from which floor of House may be observed, Mon–Fri, 10–3.15. Films are shown at regular intervals describing activities of the Stock Exchange.

Syon House (London Road, Brentford). Home of His Grace the Duke of

The London Planetarium

Northumberland, noted for its magnificent Adam interior. Portraits and furniture. Apr–Oct, Mons–Fris only 11–1, 2–4.30.

Tower Bridge (E.C.3). Famous two-tier bridge with raised footway (142 ft, now closed) and twin bascules or leaves which are raised to allow passage of large vessels.

Trinity House (Trinity Square, E.C.3). Rebuilt 1953, and headquarters of Corporation of Trinity House, the General Lighthouse Authority for England and Wales.

University of London (Woburn Square, W.C.1). Buildings designed by Charles Holden include the Senate House; the Tower (210 ft); and various schools and institutes.

U.S. Embassy (Grosvenor Square, W.1). Mammoth new embassy completed in 1960 on west side of Grosvenor Square, one of London's finest squares. On N side is Franklin D. Roosevelt Memorial.

Wallace Collection (Manchester Square, W.1). Collection of treasures and works of art bequeathed to the nation by Lady Wallace. Lord Hertford resided in Paris where he assembled most of the French works of art of 17/18c which give the Collection its special character. Weekdays, 10–5, Suns, 2–5.

Zoological Gardens (Regents Park, N.W.1). The London Zoo occupies an area of about 31 acres in the northern part of Regent's Park. Summer from 9, winter from 10.

Inns of Court and Chancery

The four great inns of court were originally founded for the education and lodging of law students, to one or other of which all barristers are 'admitted'.

Inner and Middle Temple (Fleet Street, E.C.4). The Inner Temple Hall was rebuilt after war damage and dates from 1955. The Middle Temple Hall similarly damaged has been restored to its ancient 16c splendour. In the courtyard is the fountain immortalized by Charles Dickens in 'Martin Chuzzlewit'.

Lincoln's Inn (Chancery Lane, W.C.2). Another great Inn of Court with powers of 'calling to the bar'. The Old Hall dates from 1506. The New Hall and library were built in 1845. The library is largest law library in London.

Gray's Inn (Gray's Inn Road, W.C.1). Occupies large area from Holborn to Theobald's Road. The Hall, chapel and library have been rebuilt after war damage.

Staple Inn (Holborn, E.C.1). Though long connected with the law, it owes its name to an earlier use, when it served as a custom house where wool was weighed and dues collected.

London's Green Heart

No other city possesses so many parks and open spaces as does London. Besides the great parks under the control of the Crown, like Hyde Park, Kensington Gardens, St. James's, and Regent's Park, there are many under the management of the G.L.C. and the total area amounts to over 7,000 acres. It is possible by just crossing the road at Hyde Park Corner to walk from the Westminster corner of St. James's Park in an almost direct line for nearly three miles through parks and gardens abounding in magnificent trees and wild bird life.

Parks and Gardens

Alexandra Park (Wood Green, N.22). The grounds of Alexandra Palace with lake. Fair, roller skating, racecourse.

Battersea Park (Queens Road, S.W.11). One of the largest of South London's pleasure grounds, adjoining south bank of the Thames. Old English Flower Garden. Festival Gardens section with funfair. Open-air concerts and music.

Bushy Park (Teddington). A royal demesne of 1099 acres noted for its deer. Famous Chestnut Avenue is magnificent in May. Diana fountain.

Green Park (Westminster, S.W.1). Triangular space of 53 acres between Constitution Hill and Piccadilly. The Queens Walk on eastern side was named after Queen Caroline, wife of George II. The iron gateway on Piccadilly side is memento of the old Devonshire House, town residence of Duke of Devonshire.

Hampstead Heath (Hampstead, N.W.3). With its broken heights, grassy glades, lakes and furze-covered expanses, one of the most natural and bracing of London's open spaces. Far-reaching views. To SE is Parliament Hill. To NE is Kenwood and, beyond, the beautiful Highgate Woods.

Holland Park (Kensington, W.8). Former grounds of the Jacobean mansion. Woodland area. Dutch garden, Iris gardens, open-air concerts. Yucca garden with Scottish country dancing.

Hyde Park. With an area of 340 acres and joined on the west by Kensington Gardens (275 acres) this is London's finest lung. The Serpentine is artificial sheet of water (41 acres) with boating and swimming lido. Rotten Row is reserved for horse riding. Bandstand. Teahouse and restaurant.

Kensington Gardens. Appropriated from the old Hyde Park by Queen Caroline. The Serpentine is crossed by pretty five-arched bridge with picturesque views. The Round Pond is a paradise for juvenile yachtsmen and proud owners of model craft. The Broad Walk leads to Kensington Palace on west side. The statue of Peter Pan beside the Long Water is by Sir George Frampton, R.A.

LONDON

Kew Gardens (Kew). Three hundred acres of lordly park with every species of tree, shrub and flower labelled for the visitor's interest. The prime function of the Royal Botanic Gardens is the correct identification of plants, but for most people the gardens are a delight of verdent lawns, flower displays, lake and ponds, palm house and conservatories, museums and classic temples. Gardens, daily from 10. Hot-houses from 1, museums from 10.

Parliament Hill (N.W.3). Wide expanse (270 acres) with extensive views southward over London. Highgate Ponds are in NE portions. There is lido, athletics track, swimming, entertainment.

Regents Park (N.W.1). One of the largest of London's parks having with Primrose Hill to the north an area of 670 acres. Laid out by John Nash for the Prince Regent. Around the park runs the two-mile Outer Circle road. The Inner Circle road encloses the Queen Mary's Gardens with beautiful floral displays. Open-air theatre. Ornamental lake with boating. To N is the London Zoo.

Richmond Park (Richmond). First enclosed by Charles I, extends to 2,358 acres and between 10 and 11 miles in circumference. Large herds of deer roam the park. Woodland garden. Golf course. Pen Ponds (18 acres) are favourite with skaters when conditions permit. The White Lodge is used by the Lower School of the Royal Ballet. Pembroke Lodge is now restaurant; it has fine gardens. Polo near Roehampton Gate on Tues and Thurs evenings and Sat afternoons in season.

St. James's Park (S.W.1). One of the oldest and most beautiful of London's parks. The lake extends nearly the entire length and is haunt of many varieties of wild fowl, including white pelicans. Lunch-time and evening band concerts.

Oxford Street

Shopping Centres

Regent Street, W.1. Laid out by architect Nash in 1813, but his buildings have been replaced by marble and concrete palaces that make the street the finest shopping thoroughfare in the world. Many famous companies have premises here, stores, shops and agencies, i.e. Liberty's, Dickens & Jones, Hamley's, Galleries Lafayette, Fifth Avenue, Austin Reed, Swan & Edgar.

Oxford Street, W.1. Busy thoroughfare extending from Marble Arch to Tottenham Court Road thronged throughout the day by shoppers to the great stores, including Selfridge's, John Lewis's, Marks & Spencers, Marshall & Snelgrove, Bourne & Hollingworth, D. H. Evans, Waring and Gillows and many others.

Bond Street, W.1. Running between Oxford Street and Piccadilly both portions, Old and New, make up London's most fashionable shopping street. Many famous shops, notably jewellers, milliners and art galleries.

Piccadilly, W.1. One of London's most attractive thoroughfares said to derive its name from the pickadils, or ruffs, worn in the early Stuart period. Extends westward from Piccadilly Circus for nearly a mile to Hyde Park Corner. The eastern portion only is occupied by shops including Simpson's, Fortnum & Mason, Hatchards.

Knightsbridge, S.W.1. Fashionable shopping quarter for furniture dealers, jewellers, antique shops and the famous store of Harrods.

Kensington High Street, W.8. Favourite shopping quarter of many small but specialist shops and the larger stores of Barkers and Derry & Toms.

Markets

Billingsgate Market (Lower Thames Street, E.C.3). Principal fish market of London. Best visited from 8 a.m.

Covent Garden (W.C.2). Chief wholesale market in London for fruit, vegetables and flowers. On W is St. Paul's Church, built by Inigo Jones in 1633. On E side is Royal Opera House.

Leadenhall Market (Gracechurch Street, E.C.3). For vegetables and poultry, etc. Stands on site of ancient Roman basilica or town hall of Londinium. Weekdays 9–5.

London Silver Vaults (Chancery Lane, W.C.2). The largest collection of silver in the world, displayed by many individual merchants. Mon–Fri, 9–5.30, Sats, 9.30–12.30.

New Caledonian Market (Bermondsey Square, S.E.1). Open Fri, 8–1.

Petticoat Lane (Middlesex Street, E.1). Famous open-air market, Sun mornings 9–12.

Portobello Road Market (W.11). Vegetables, fruit, flowers daily except Suns. Antiques Sats, 9–6.

Smithfield Market (E.C.1). Ancient jousting ground outside City walls, now Central Meat Market and poultry, fish and vegetable markets. Weekdays.

Spitalfields Market (E.1). Fruit, vegetables and flowers, among the largest and most modern markets of its kind in the world. Weekdays.

Museums

British Museum (Great Russell Street, W.C.1). Vast National storehouse famous for its collections of sculpture, prints, drawings and books. Notable Greek and Roman antiquities. Elgin Marbles. The famous Reading Room (ticket-holders only) accommodates 500 readers. The library has statutory right to a copy of every book published in the U.K. Weekdays 10–5, Suns 2.30–6.

Commonwealth Institute (Kensington High Street, W.8.) Modern building with tent-like roof sheathed in copper. The galleries house colourful display devoted to countries and peoples of the Commonwealth. Films, temporary exhibitions. Weekdays 10–5.30, Suns 2.30–6.

Geffrye Museum (Kingsland Road, E.2). Small but interesting collection of furniture and domestic objects from Elizabethan times to present day. Reading room. Tues to Sats, 10–5, Suns 2–5.

Geological Museum (Exhibition Road, S.W.7). Regional geology of Great Britain is demonstrated by exhibits including rocks, fossils and minerals, relief models, photographs. Exhibits of useful rocks and minerals of the world. Daily 10–6, Suns 2.30–6.

Guildhall Museum (Royal Exchange, E.C.3). Extensive collections of articles of archaeological and civic interest bearing on the history of the City. Many Roman relics. Weekdays, 10–5.

Horniman Museum (Forest Hill, S.E.23). Ethnographical collections from all parts of the world, musical instruments, natural history collection, reference library. Concerts and lectures in winter months. Daily 10.30–6, Suns 2–6.

Imperial War Museum (Lambeth Road, S.E.1). Commemorates the effort and sacrifice of men and women of British Commonwealth in two World Wars. The galleries contain naval, military and air service relics and souvenirs of all campaigns in which British Forces have been engaged since August 1914. Reference library. Photographic library. Film library. Daily 10–6, Suns 2–6.

London Museum (Kensington Palace, W.8). Originally at Lancaster House but since removed to Kensington Palace pending new premises to be built. Collections illustrate the history, social and domestic life of London in all periods. Daily from 10, Suns from 2.

National Maritime Museum (Greenwich S.E.10). Illustrates sea affairs from Tudor times to the present day. The Queen's House is the oldest

Victoria and Albert Museum

Italianate house in England (1618–35). In west wing is notable marble rotunda. Library; medal and seal rooms. Navigation room. Weekdays, 10–6, Suns 2.30–6. To S is Greenwich Park. Nearer the river is Royal Naval College where the Chapel and Wren's Painted Hall are open daily, 2.30–5 except Thurs and in winter, Suns. In dry dock near Greenwich Pier is the Cutty Sark, the last survivor of the famous tea-clippers. Weekdays, 11–5, Suns 2.30–5.

Natural History Museum (Cromwell Road, S.W.7). Part of British Museum and principal centre in British Commonwealth for general study of natural history. National collections of recent and fossil forms of animal and plant life, rocks and minerals, and meteorites from outer space. The elaborate sculptural ornamentations is of interest. Daily, 10–6, Suns, 2.30–6.

Science Museum (Exhibition Road, S.W.7). National Museum of Science and Industry, illustrating their development through the years. Many working models. Daily, 10–6, Suns 2.30–6. Lectures, films. Library in Imperial Institute Road.

Soane Museum (Lincoln's Inn Fields, W.C.2). The private house built in 1812 by Sir John Soane, architect. Collections of architectural significance, including 26,000 drawings from 16–19c. Egyptian and Roman antiquities. Tues to Sats, 10–5. Closed in Aug and Bk Hols.

Victoria and Albert Museum (South Kensington, S.W.7). Museum of Fine and Applied Art of all countries, styles and periods. It includes Architectural Details, Arms and Armour. Art of the Book, Carpets, Costumes, Drawings, Embroideries, Furniture, Glass, Gold and Silversmiths Work, Ironwork, Ivories, Jewellery, Lace, Lithographs, Miniatures, Musical Instruments, Oil Paintings, Pottery and Porcelain, Tapestries and Woodwork. Weekdays, 10–6, Suns, 2.30–6.

Wellington Museum (Apsley House, Hyde Park Corner, W.1). Town residence of Duke of Wellington built 1771–78. Museum contains Spanish, Dutch and Flemish paintings together with many personal relics of the First Duke of Wellington. Weekdays 10–6, Suns 2.30–6.

Art Galleries

Courtauld Institute (Woburn Square, W.C.1). University of London's galleries containing pictures bequeathed to the University. Works by Botticelli, Bellini, Veronese. Collection of 19c French paintings. Mons–Sats, 10–5, Suns, 2–5.

National Gallery (Trafalgar Square, W.C.2). Unequalled as a representative collection of the various schools of painting with over 2,000 paintings. Especially rich in Italian and Dutch schools. Weekdays, 10–6, Suns, 2–6.

National Portrait Gallery (St. Martin's Place, W.C.2). Over 5,000 portraits of famous British men and women of the past. Paintings, drawings, busts and miniatures. Weekdays from 10, Suns from 2.

Royal Academy of Arts (Piccadilly, W.1). Founded in 1768, its members are elected from among the most distinguished artists practising in Britain. The Summer Exhibition has been held each year since 1769. Daily (May–Aug) 10–6, Suns 2–6.

Tate Gallery (Millbank, S.W.1). Contains the National Collections of British Painting, Modern Foreign Paintings, and Modern Sculpture. Especially notable for examples of Blake, Turner, Stevens, Sargent and the Pre-Raphaelites. Weekdays 10–6, Suns 2–6.

Concert Halls

Albert Hall (Kensington Gore, S.W.7). One of the largest concert halls in the world with seating capacity of nearly 7,000. The magnificent organ comprises some 10,000 pipes.

Central Hall (Storey's Gate, S.W.1). Imposing square block in Renaissance style. The dome is third largest in London.

Royal Festival Hall (Waterloo Bridge, S.E.1). Built in 1951 as outstanding example of contemporary architecture and acknowledged among finest concert halls in the world. Smaller theatres and music rooms have since been added.

Royal Festival Hall

Churches

All Hallows by the Tower (Byward Street, E.C.3). Founded in 675 by
the first abbess of Barking Abbey. The Guild Church of Toc H.
All Souls (Langham Place, W.1). Built in 1824 by John Nash to complete
his design for Regent Street. Unusual spire.
Brompton Oratory (Brompton Road, S.W.). Italian Renaissance style,
opened by Cardinal Manning in 1884. Has great tradition in sacred music.
Fashionable wedding church.
St. Andrew Undershaft (St. Mary Axe, E.C.3). Deriving its name from
a long shaft or Maypole which used to be set up opposite the south door,
and which the Puritans declared an idol, and caused to be burnt. In north
side is alabaster monument to Stow (d. 1605) chronicler of London, with
quill pen in hand.
St. Bartholomew the Great (Smithfield, E.C.1). The oldest church in
London next to the chapel in the Tower. Fine Norman building founded
by Rahere in 1123.
St. Bride's (Fleet Street, E.C.4). Rebuilt by Wren, after Great Fire, in
1680. Museum with Roman relics. The church has close associations with
the Press.
St. Clement Danes (Strand, W.C.2). Wren church built 1681. Restored
and reconstructed 1958 as central church of the Royal Air Force. The
annual service at which oranges and lemons are distributed to children is
held at end of March. The bells ring out the tune of the nursery rhyme
every third hour.
St. George (Hanover Square, W.1). Small but attractive church by John
James, a pupil of Wren, completed in 1725. Fashionable wedding church.
St. George's Cathedral (Lambeth Road, S.E.1). Roman Catholic cathedral rebuilt 1953–8 but to designs of the original church by Pugin.
St. James (Piccadilly, W.1). Built by Wren 1680–84 with fine interior,
restored after war damage. In Garden of Remembrance is impressive figure
of 'Peace' by Alfred Hardiman, R.A.
St. Margaret's (Westminster, S.W.1). Mother church of the City of
Westminster and parish church of the House of Commons. Fashionable
wedding church.
St. Martin-in-the-Fields (Trafalgar Square, W.C.2). The Royal Parish
Church, Buckingham Palace being within the parish. George I was at
one time a churchwarden. Nell Gwynne buried here.
St. Paul's Cathedral (Ludgate Hill, E.C.4). Wren's masterpiece, begun
in 1675 and completed 1710, built in Portland stone. Length 515 ft;
width 250 ft; height to top of cross 365 ft; diameter of inner dome 112 ft.
The golden ball is 6 ft in diameter.
Savoy Chapel (Savoy Street, W.C.2). Queen's Chapel of the Savoy
originally part of the old palace erected in the Manor of Peter of Savoy in

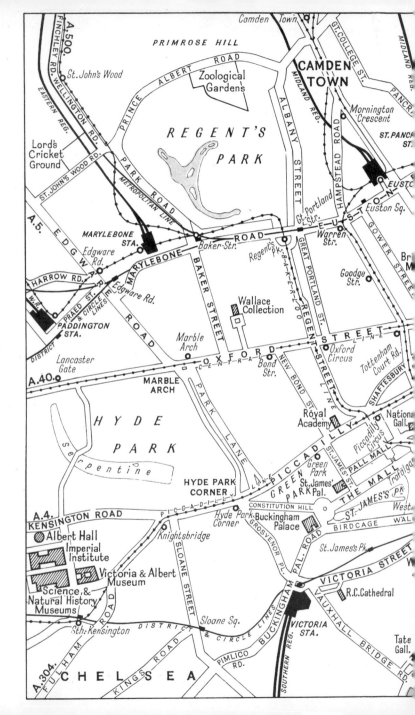

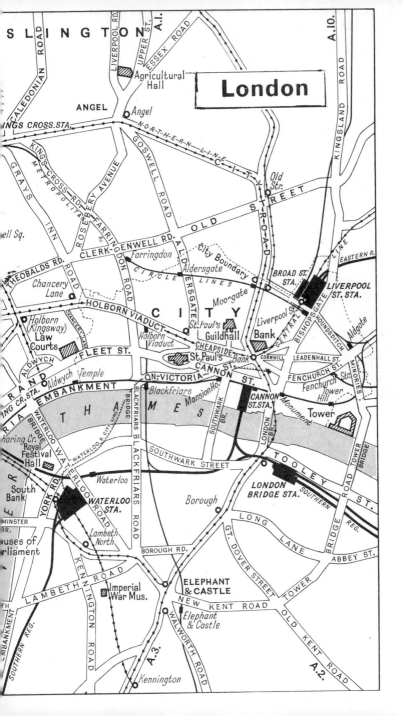

1241 and now disappeared. Private chapel of her Majesty the Queen by right of her Duchy of Lancaster.

Southwark Cathedral (London Bridge, S.E.1). Recently restored but one of London's oldest buildings. Portions of Norman nave incorporated. The Choir and Lady Chapel built about 1207.

Temple (The Temple, Fleet Street, E.C.4). Joint property of the Inner and Middle Temple. The Round Church, built by the Knights Templars, contains remains of the effigies of nine knights. Norman porch.

Westminster Abbey (Parliament Square, S.W.1). Edward the Confessor is usually regarded as the founder. William the Conqueror was crowned here as has almost all monarchs since. The burial place of kings and queens. Length 513 ft; breadth 200 ft; western towers 225 ft.

Westminster Cathedral (Ashley Place, S.W.1). Roman Catholic Cathedral. Vast structure of brick and stone in Early Byzantine style. Campanile, 273 ft (to cross 284 ft); length 360 ft; width 156 ft.

Memorials

Albert Memorial (Kensington Gardens, S.W.7). Designed by Sir Gilbert Scott on model of Eleanor cross. Memorial to Prince Regent after Great Exhibition of 1851.

Cenotaph (Whitehall, S.W.1). Designed by Sir Edward Lutyens, R.A. and commemorating those who died in the two World Wars. Scene of annual Armistice Day ceremony (Nov).

Charles I (Whitehall). Equestrian statue cast in 1633. All mileage distances from London are calculated from this spot.

Cleopatra's Needle (Victoria Embankment, W.C.2). Towed here by sea from the great temple of Heliopolis. Of red granite with inscriptions, the obelisk weighs 180 tons and is $68\frac{1}{2}$ ft high.

Duke of York Column (Carlton House Terrace). Granite pillar 124 ft high commemorating second son of George III.

Eros (Piccadilly Circus, W.1). At London's hub, graceful aluminium statue, part of memorial fountain to Lord Shaftesbury.

Monument (King William Street, E.C.4). Fluted Doric column of Portland Stone (202 ft) by Wren commemorating the Great Fire of 1666. 311 steps to caged balcony. Weekdays, from 9. Suns in summer from 2.

Nelson Column (Trafalgar Square, W.C.2). Granite corinthian column surmounted by statue of Nelson. Total height 170 ft 2 in. Four colossal lions by Landseer crouched around the base.

Nurse Cavell (St. Martins Place, W.C.2). Work of the late Sir George Frampton, R.A. It bears her fateful words: "Patriotism is not enough; I must have no hatred or bitterness for anyone".

Richard I (Old Palace Yard, S.W.1). Marochetti's fine statue of Richard Coeur de Lion.

Roosevelt Memorial (Grosvenor Square, W.1). Statue of Franklin D. Roosevelt, unveiled by Mrs. Roosevelt in 1944.

The Post Office Tower

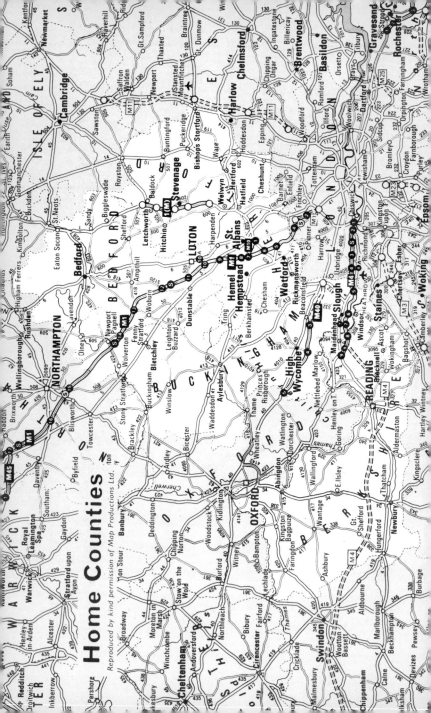

Home Counties

Reproduced by kind permission of Map Productions Ltd.

Home Counties

of Bedfordshire, Berkshire, Buckinghamshire and Hertfordshire

Bedfordshire

One of the smallest of the English counties, largely devoted to farming and market gardening for the London market. In the north is the broad level valley of the River Ouse, while to the south are the breezy downs above Dunstable. North of Luton are the Barton Hills, outliers of the Chiltern Hills. Foremost among many stately homes with their wooded parklands is Woburn Abbey. the magnificent home and deer park of His Grace the Duke of Bedford.

Berkshire

A county dominated by the River Thames and the Berkshire Downs. The Thames forms some eighty miles of the northern boundary and in its winding course the wooded banks provide some delightful scenery. The Downs, the highest chalk hills in England, rise to a height of 1,000 feet at Walbury Hill and Inkpen Beacon, with vast open landscapes. To the south are numerous heaths and commons. Reading is the county town but chief tourist attraction is undoubtedly Windsor, with its great Royal castle and unending river activity.

Buckinghamshire

Small county of varied scenery, mainly agricultural with emphasis on market gardening for the London market. Several major roads cross the county allowing speedy access to London. Hertford is the county town and Letchworth and Welwyn are examples of modern garden cities. The city of St. Albans with important Roman remains and its great Norman cathedral are of prime interest. Among many stately homes are Hatfield House, Knebworth House and Gorhambury. Of literary interest is Shaw's Corner, the home of George Bernard Shaw, at Ayot St. Lawrence.

HOME COUNTIES
Hertfordshire

A beautifully rural and mainly agricultural county ideal for walking. The Chiltern Hills, alternately wooded or bare expanse, run south-west across the southern section providing good views. In the valleys are many small churches and attractive cottages of flint and thatch. The River Thames forms the southern boundary amid a particularly beautiful stretch of the great river. The northern portion of the county is typically Midland in character with the low-lying meadows and undulating land of the Ouse valley and the Vale of Aylesbury. Aylesbury, a famous old dairy farming centre, is the capital town.

Of Special Interest

Ascott (Wing, 3m SW of Leighton Buzzard). 19c mansion with fine furniture, pictures and oriental porcelain. Large grounds with rare trees and bulbs (NT). Apr–Sept, Weds, Sats, and Bk Hols, and Suns in Jul–Aug, 2–6.

Buscot Park (3m NW of Faringdon). Adam-style house, later altered, with fine furniture and paintings. Extensive gardens with lake. (NT). Mar–Oct, Weds, 2–6; additionally first Sat and subsequent Suns in Apr–Sept.

Claydon House (3½m SW of Windsor). Stone-faced West Wing contains series of magnificent rococo state rooms with wood carving. Florence Nightingale's bedroom and museum (NT). Mar–Oct, daily except Mons, 2–6.

Cliveden (4m N of Maidenhead). 19c mansion overlooking fine reach of Thames. Furniture, tapestries, gardens (NT). Apr–Oct, Weds and Sats, 2.30–5.30. Gardens daily except Mons and Tues, 11–6.30.

Donnington Castle (1m N of Newbury). Barbican of 14c castle with extensive Civil War earthwork defences. (AM standard hours).

Dunstable Downs (2m S of Dunstable). Magnificent views with popular gliding activities. (NT). Nearby Whipsnade Zoological Park.

Hatfield House (Hatfield). Magnificent house built by first Earl of Salisbury, with portraits and relics of Elizabeth I. Park and gardens. Separate admission for park and house, mid Apr–Sept.

Hughenden Manor (2m N of High Wycombe). Former home of Benjamin Disraeli with furniture and books (NT). Daily except Mons, 2–6. Closed Jan.

Ivinghoe Beacon (1½m E of Ivinghoe). Magnificent Chiltern viewpoint (700 ft) on NT land freely accessible. Pitstone windmill is prominent in view.

Knebworth House (Knebworth, 3m S of Stevenage). Tudor mansion with associations with Earls of Lytton. Gardens. May–Sept, Sats, Suns and Bk Hols, 2.30–5.30.

Luton Hoo (2m S of Luton). Fine country mansion housing magnificent Wernher collection of art treasures. Park and gardens. Apr–Sept, Mons, Weds, Thurs, Sats, 11–6, Suns 2–6. For gardens see announcements.

Savill Garden (Windsor Great Park, Englefield Green). Magnificent garden and floral display in woodland setting. Mar–Oct, daily, 10–6.

Uffingham Castle and White Horse (2m S of Uffington). Iron-age camp surrounded by rampart and ditch. Below, cut in hillside turf, is figure of horse, probably of contemporary date. (AM any time).

Verulamium (St. Albans). Excavated remains of Roman city wall. Museum (open).

Waddesdon Manor (6m NW of Aylesbury). House (1880–9) in French style with furniture made for French royal palaces, Savonnerie carpets and Sevres and Dresden china. Pictures, library. Extensive parkland and gardens (NT). Apr–Oct, daily except Mons and Tues, 11–6.

West Wycombe Park (2½m W of High Wycombe). Rebuilt house about 1765 in Adam manner, with notable painted ceilings. Pictures, tapestries, furniture. Fine park with lake (NT). Jul–Aug, daily except Mons, 2.15–6.

Windsor Castle (Windsor). Restored Norman castle and Royal Residence. Precincts daily from 10 a.m. State Apartments etc. weekdays from 11 a.m. and Suns in summer from 1.30 p.m.

Woburn Abbey (Woburn, 8m NW of Dunstable). Palatial mansion of Duke of Bedford with state apartments and pictures. Large park with wild life. Daily throughout the year.

Wrest Park (1m E of Silsoe). Extensive 18c gardens with Thomas Archer Pavilion (1709) and Banqueting House (1735). (AM). Gardens only Apr–Sept, Sats, Suns and Bk Hols, from 2 p.m.

Cliveden

Resorts and Centres of Interest

Abingdon (Berks). Picturesque old town on River Thames, 8m S of Oxford by river. Bathing pool, fishing, boating, golf, tennis, bowls. The striking arcaded County Hall, dating from 1677, houses Borough museum. Medieval gabled houses, Tudor and Georgian buildings. Restored remnants of Benedictine abbey of AD 955 include a gateway, the Checker Hall with its rare chimney and the rebuilt Long Gallery, Guildhall (Art Gallery). St. Helen's Church has 13c tower and later spire and is remarkable in having five aisles.

Aldermaston (Berks). Attractive brick-built village in Kennet valley. Church with Norman doorway and 14c wall painting. Atomic Energy Research establishment.

Amersham (Bucks). Growing town in valley of River Misbourne with wide main street of attractive Tudor and Georgian houses. Old inns include the 16c half-timbered Kings Arms and the 17c Crown. The old market hall (1682) is supported on arches over an open area with an old lock-up. The church has magnificent 17c east window.

Ampthill (Beds). Pleasant country market town with some attractive Georgian houses. Ampthill Park is now a Cheshire Home, but much of the parkland is public. Houghton Park House (AM standard hours) is ruined Jacobean mansion believed to be the 'House Beautiful' in Bunyan's *Pilgrim's Progress*.

Ascot (Berks). Renowned for its famous racecourse on Ascot Heath and venue for the Gold Cup race in 'Royal Ascot' week (June) and other meetings. To NE is Windsor Great Park. Golf.

Aylesbury (Bucks). The county town and busy centre of industry and commerce. The 13c church has Norman font and Elizabethan monuments of interest. County Museum. 18c County Hall. The King's Head Hotel preserves a 15c hall (NT). 6m NW is Waddesdon Manor.

Ayot St. Lawrence (Herts). Village 3m W of Welwyn, known for Shaw's Corner (NT), the house of George Bernard Shaw 1906–50. Not far is the Lullingstone Silk Farm, a live exhibition of new silk production (open in summer).

Bedford (Beds). Municipal borough and administrative centre for the county. Boating on River Ouse. Associations with John Bunyan (1628–88), his statue stands at north end of the High Street. The Bunyan Meeting House displays many of his relics. 4m E is the 16c Willington Dovecote (NT) lined with 1500 nesting boxes.

Berkhamsted (Herts). One time thriving town at time of William the Conqueror but now pleasant residential centre amidst large areas of heath and common land. Well-known public school. Interesting remains of large motte-and-bailey castle dating from 11c (AM standard hours). $3\frac{1}{2}$m N is Ashridge College where the gardens are open on summer weekends, 2–6. 6m NE is Little Gaddesden Manor House.

Luton Hoo (Wernher Collection)

Bishops Stortford (Herts). Modern town on River Stort 31m NE of London, and birthplace of Cecil John Rhodes. There is Commonwealth Centre and Rhodes Memorial Museum.

Bourne End (Bucks). Small village on one of the best sailing reaches of the Thames (sailing week in June). Good river fishing. 2m E is Cliveden (NT). 3m NE is Burnham Beeches.

Bracknell (Berks). Former villages of Bracknell and Easthampstead now being developed as New Town to reduce pressure of population and industry in Greater London area. To S is Caesar's Camp, a small Iron Age hill-fort. Nine Mile Ride runs east-west across the district.

Bray (Berks). Quaint village resort on south bank of River Thames a mile south-east of Maidenhead. Ferry, weir, lock. Boating, fishing. St. Michael's Church, 13c with massive tower, has fine old brasses and monuments and picturesque lych gate dating from 1448. Monkey Island is 1m downstream.

Buckingham (Bucks). Quiet but busy market centre and ancient county town, a distinction now lost to Aylesbury. There are a number of pleasant 18c houses and inns. Handsome Georgian Town Hall. The parish church on a hill-top is 18c. The Old Gaol is castellated 18c structure near the market square. 3m NW is Stowe with its famous public school.

Chalfont St. Giles (Bucks). Pretty village visited on account of Milton's Cottage where John Milton lived in 1665. It is museum with Milton relics. 2m S is Jordans, a charming old Meeting House in grounds of which rest remains of William Penn, founder of Pennsylvania.

65

Chorleywood (Herts). High-class residential area with extensive common (golf), a popular week-end picnic spot.

Combe (Berks). Village 6m SE of Hungerford in depression between Sheepless Hill (876 ft), Combe Hill (936 ft), and Walbury Hill (959 ft). Walbury Camp is prehistoric camp on highest chalk down in southern England. On Combe Hill is old gibbett.

Cookham (Berks). Historic village on beautiful stretch of River Thames. The river scenery upstream past Quarry Woods and downstream past Cliveden is unsurpassed by any other stretch of the Thames. Village green, known as the Moor, with picturesque houses and famous old hotels (King's Arms, Bel, and Dragon). Art gallery. Winter Hill (NT) is fine viewpoint (225 ft).

Datchet (Bucks). Thames-side village opposite Windsor, with attractive Green. Many houseboats. The Thames has formed a 'beach' and there is a seaside atmosphere.

Dunstable (Beds). Prosperous industrial and residential town at crossing of the two ancient highways of Icknield Way and Watling Street. The famous Dunstable Downs (NT) a little to the west of the town, give fine viewpoints and provide interest in the local gliding activities. To south is Whipsnade Zoological Park, a branch of London Zoo.

Elstow (Beds). A plaque on a cottage marks the site of Bunyan's birthplace. The Norman church, with a detached tower, has memorial windows to him, and the 16c half-timbered Moat Hall has museum of Bunyan relics.

Eton (Bucks). Ancient town on River Thames famed for its public school founded by Henry VI in 1440. Across the river is Windsor with its Royal Castle. Steamers, boating, fishing. Annual regatta. The College Chapel, begun in 1441, is oldest building and has similarity to the chapel of King's College, Cambridge. The Lower School, opposite, is the original schoolroom.

Faringdon (Berks). Old market town in Vale of White Horse with houses built of local limestone. The Market Hall (17c) stands on stone columns. The church has Norman nave and some monuments and brasses to the Astor and Pye families. Faringdon House dates from 1780. A tower built by Lord Berner (1936) stands on Faringdon Hill, a splendid viewpoint. 2m SW is Great Coxwell with its huge stone tithe barn (NT).

Hambleden (Bucks). Thames-side village clustered round Tudor manor house and a church, a cruciform building containing many interesting monuments and pictures. Nearby on the river is the course of the famous Henley Regatta.

Harwell (Berks). Large village in cherry orchard district 6m S of Wantage. Atomic Energy Research Establishment is 2m away.

Harpenden (Herts). Attractive old-world town midway between Luton and St. Albans with large common from which there are extensive views. The parish church is modern but retains a 15c tower.

Hatfield (Herts). Small village of Georgian houses and old inns. A new town is being developed to the south-west. Hatfield House, historic home of the Cecils, in its great park, was built 1607–11 by 1st Earl of Salisbury who had exchanged Theobald's Park with James I for the Manor and Palace at Hatfield. The Earl demolished part and built the present lovely Jacobean house of red brick. Adjoining gardens is portion of old palace of the Bishops of Ely, where Elizabeth I was imprisoned during the reign of Mary Tudor. The Salisbury Chapel contains notable memorials.

Hemel Hempstead (Herts). New town among wooded ridges of the Chiltern hills at confluence of River Gade and River Bulbourne, 6m W of St. Albans. 1m N is Piggotts End, a 500-year-old 'hall' house with notable wall paintings (open).

Hertford (Herts). County town on River Lee with slight remains of Norman castle and notable Norman church. A number of old houses of 16c date remain. Lombard House, where lived Chauncey, the county historian, is 17c.

High Wycombe (Bucks). Second largest town of the county and a growing industrial and residential centre. 18c pillared Guildhall with cupola. Parish church has some good stained glass. Furniture-making industry, a museum illustrates past and present aspects. To N is Hughenden Manor (open) former home of Benjamin Disraeli. To W is West Wycombe with West Wycombe Park (NT). On hill-top is church and mausoleum built by Sir Francis Dashwood in 1762. Some hill-side caves are open to the public.

Hitchin (Herts). Busy market town at foot of Chiltern Hills near northern boundary of the county. Fine parish church of 13–14c date with good screenwork. The Sun Hotel is well-known coaching inn. Library and museum. Golf. The Biggin almshouses are of interest as also several old houses in Tilehurst Street and Bridge Street.

Hungerford (Berks). Market town on River Kennet. Fishing, sports club, annual Hocktide ceremony second Tuesday after Easter. Bear Inn has Elizabeth I and William of Orange associations. Gothic St. Lawrence Church was built 1814 and has embattled tower.

Hurley (Berks). Pretty Thames-side village. Boating, fishing, swimming pool, golf. Picturesque weir. Old Bell Inn is 12c. On Bucks bank is Hurley-ford Manor.

Leighton Buzzard (Beds). Market town on River Ousel. The fine market cross dates from 15c. Much of the parish church dates from 13c. 5m N is Woburn Park.

Luton (Beds). County borough and industrial town of large manufactures including motor vehicles. The ancient industry of hat-making still prospers. Municipal airport. Wardown Park, with boating lake and sports facilities, lies in centre of town. The mansion in the Park houses the museum and art gallery. Stockwood Park is large public park. St. Mary's Parish Church is one of the largest parish churches in England. 2m S is Luton Hoo, the magnificent mansion of Sir Harold Wernher. 11m N is Wrest Park, Silsoe, with its notable garden layout.

Maidenhead (Berks). Popular Thames-side resort with graceful 18c bridge connecting with Taplow. There is boating, fishing, a regatta, towpath walks and golf. Art collection (Tues and Thurs). A mile upstream is Boulter's Lock in particularly beautiful stretch of the river.

Marlow (Bucks). Bright clean-looking town on River Thames, 6m upstream from Boulters' Lock. Exceptionally spacious High Street and attractive houses in and around. Picturesque suspension bridge dates from 1836 and provides grand views up and down river. The weir makes pretty picture but is rather dangerous. All Saints' Church was rebuilt in 1835.

Medmenham (Bucks). Thames village of picturesque old cottages and a church with traces of Norman work and two early 15c brasses. Medmenham Abbey is sham ruin built by Sir Francis Dashwood some three hundred years ago on site of former Cistercian monastery.

Newbury (Berks). Prosperous agricultural town on River Kennet. Good shops, swimming pool, golf, tennis, bowls, cinema, concerts, racecourse. Ancient Cloth Hall (museum) reflects Newbury's importance in clothmaking industry established by 16c John Winchcombe. The red-brick St. Bartholomew Hospital dates from 1618. Donnington Castle (AM standard hours) is 1m N. Sandleford Priory is 2m S.

Olney (Bucks). Small but busy market centre in north of county with long main street of stone houses. The church with graceful broach spire dates from 14c. The Cowper Memorial Museum is in house once home of William Cowper. The famous annual Pancake race which takes place on Shrove Tuesday was first run in 1445.

Pangbourne (Berks). Thames-side village with pretty thatched cottages and some modern development. Towpath almost to Basildon. Several 17c black and white houses, including Swan Hotel. The pretty Hartslock Wood marks the southern end of the Chiltern Hills.

Reading (Berks). Prosperous industrial, residential and University town and county headquarters at meeting of the River Kennet with the Thames. The bridge over the Thames connects with Caversham. There is boating and swimming in rivers and baths, fishing, regatta. Hunting, golf, tennis and bowls. Museum and Art Gallery, Blagrave Street, and Museum of English Rural Life in Whiteknights Park. Forbury Gardens and Prospect Park are delightful public parks. The University buildings are set in Whiteknights Park. The former Benedictine Abbey was founded in 12e. Here Henry I was buried in 1136 and John of Gaunt married in 1359. St. Mary's church was rebuilt 1550 with material from old abbey.

Rickmansworth (Herts). Much sought after residential area but with several items and activities of possible interest to visitors. There are several golf courses and the mansion of the Moor Park Clubhouse is open to the public at certain times. An earlier mansion nearby was the home of

The Thames at Caversham Bridge

Catherine of Aragon and of Anne of Cleves. Fishing for coarse fish and trout in River Colne. Water ski-ing at Aquadrome.

St. Albans (Herts). Historic cathedral city 21m N of London. Pleasant residential town though modern industrial development increases. The ancient city is the Verulamium of the Romans, excavations having revealed the theatre site and parts of the Roman Wall (museum). The restored Cathedral, with one of longest naves (275 ft) in England, is mixture of Norman, Early English and Decorated styles. Close to River Ver is Ye Olde Fighting Cock's tavern, claiming to be oldest licensed establishment in England. 2½m W is Gorhambury Park.

Sandhurst (Berks). Residential town well-known for its Royal Military Academy (grounds and chapel open). National Army Museum. Ambarrow Hill (NT) is nearby pine-clad hilltop.

Slough (Bucks). The largest town in Buckinghamshire. Large residential and industrial centre on Great West Road. Trading estate. Community centre.

Sonning (Berks). Quiet Thames-side village with old bridge. Golf. Towpath upstream to Reading through exceptional scenery. Picturesque mill among trees on Oxfordshire bank. Parish church, on site of Saxon cathedral, has interesting brasses.

St. Albans Cathedral

Stoke Poges (Bucks). Small town with associations with Gray who is buried in churchyard. His monument (NT) was designed by James Wyatt. To W is Burnham Beeches.

Streatley (Berks). Thames resort opposite Goring in gap between Chilterns and Berkshire Downs. Landon Chase (NT) and Lough Down (NT) overlook the village and give views of the Thames valley and the Chilterns. Golf. Towpath to Moulsford, popular with anglers, artists, and boating enthusiasts.

Taplow (Bucks). Attractive Thames-side village with boating and fishing. The church is modern and has fine stone screen. Boulter's Lock on the Berkshire side is well-known boating spot.

Tring (Herts). Small town below Chiltern Hills in western part of county. Zoological museum is branch of British Museum. Tring Park was long the seat of Rothschild family. Tring Reservoirs (fishing) are National Nature Reserve. 3m N is Ivinghoe Beacon (views).

Uffington (Berks). Attractive village in Vale of White Horse of thatched houses and one old church. Thomas Hughes (1822–96) author of 'Tom Brown's Schooldays' was born here. On slope of White Horse Hill (856 ft) is prehistoric White Horse cut in the chalk. Uffington Castle is site of Iron-age hill fort. The Ridgway is ancient trackway across high ground. Along the Roman Icknield Way towards Ashbury is Wayland Smith's Cave (AM), a prehistoric dolmen.

Wallingford (Berks). Busy agricultural centre on River Thames. Swimming pool, boating, golf. The bridge is graceful 14–arched structure. The

17c Town Hall has some Gainsborough and other masters' works. Of the former Saxon castle extensive earthworks remain.

Wantage (Berks). Old town situated between Berkshire Downs and Vale of White Horse, birthplace of King Alfred in AD 849. Swimming baths, sports clubs, cinema, museum. King Alfred statue in market place. Bear Inn is old hostelry. Annual fairs in May, September and October.

Ware (Herts). Pleasant town on River Lee 24m N of London. Boating and fishing. The grounds of a former friary are now public with various sports facilities. Swimming pool. The 13–15c parish church with battle-mented tower is imposing.

Wargrave (Berks). Thames-side resort 3m upstream from Henley. The church, rebuilt after a fire in 1914, retains its original old brick tower. Shiplake is 1m upstream where River Loddon comes in to join the Thames. Tennyson was married in Shiplake Church in 1850.

Watford (Herts). The largest town in Hertfordshire at confluence of River Gade and River Colne 15m NW of London. Popular shopping centre. The River Colne flows through the attractive Oxhey Park on the town's southern boundary. Cassiobury Park is considerable open space with sports facilities.

Windsor (Berks). Royal borough and prosperous town on south bank of River Thames. The picturesque bridge links with Eton and its famous college on the Buckinghamshire side. Steamer trips, boating, angling, swimming baths. Theatre. Racecourse. Royal Windsor Horse Show in Spring. Windsor Castle, founded by William the Conqueror, is chief residence of the British Sovereign. The Round Tower (230 ft) stands on the original Norman mound. The Castle Precincts, State Apartments, Queen Mary's Dolls' House, Albert Memorial Chapel, Round Tower, Curfew Tower and St. George's Chapel are open to the public. Home Park (500 acres) adjoining castle has spectacular Long Walk and Frogmore House used by members of the Royal family. In the Royal Mausoleum rest the bodies of Queen Victoria and the Prince Consort. Windsor Great Park (4000 acres) extends further south, is beautifully wooded and has splendid gardens (polo on Smith's Lawn in summer). The magnificent Savill Gardens near Englefield Green are open in summer. The 17c Guildhall in Windsor High Street was completed by Wren (paintings and exhibition). To S of Windsor Great Park is Virginia Water, an artificial lake. The ruins were brought here from Tripoli in 1827.

Woburn (Beds). Small town of pleasant 18c houses well-known for the adjoining Woburn Abbey in its great deer park. The magnificent home of the Duke of Bedford, with art treasures and historic rooms, and a popular Zoo Park, are open to the public.

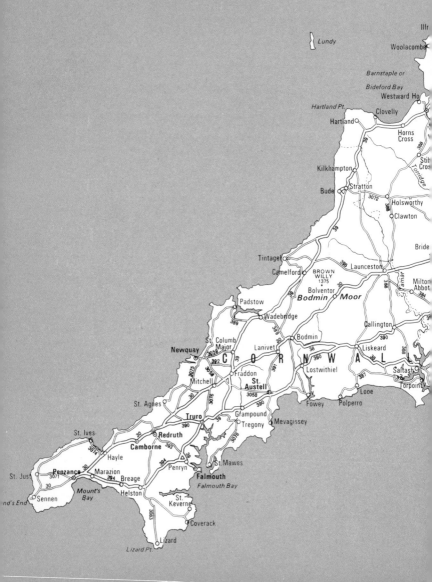

West Country

Reproduced by kind permission of Map Productions Ltd.

West Country

Cornwall—Devon—Somerset

Cornwall

With an area of 1,357 square miles and a population of 353,000 Cornwall is the extreme south-western county of Britain. Apart from its eastern boundary where a 45-mile stretch of the Tamar river separates it from Devon, it is surrounded by the sea. The western and northern shores are pounded by a relentless Atlantic Ocean, the southern shore by quieter waters of the English Channel. The interior is for the most part barren and bleak with Brown Willy on Bodmin Moor the highest point at 1,375 ft. The county abounds with Prehistoric antiquities, notable among which are the Iron Age village of Carn Euny at Sancreed, Chysauster village, Madron, and the inscribed stone of St. Cleer. The county town is Bodmin, but most of the administrative function is carried out at Truro, a city dominated by its cathedral. Important inland centres are Launceston, Wadebridge, Redruth and Camborne. Almost the entire coastline is one long holiday playground interspersed with picturesque resorts the largest among which are Newquay, St. Ives, Penzance and Falmouth.

Devon

A county of scenic beauty, hilly and well-wooded. A rugged northern coastline of splendid cliffs and sandy bays; a contrasting south coast with characteristic red cliffs; secluded valleys; the barren moorland of Dartmoor; high-hedged lanes. Clotted cream and cider. The county of Raleigh and Drake. But above all the choice of thousands of British holidaymakers year after year. Capital is Exeter, a cathedral city and university town with some industrial importance with brewing, cloth manufacture, engineering and paper-making. Other important towns include Plymouth and the great naval harbour of Devonport, Newton Abbot, Tiverton, and the ancient market boroughs of Barnstaple and

Bideford. Principal holiday centre is Torbay (a local authority consortium of Torquay, Paignton and Brixham). Other south coast resorts include Dartmouth, Salcombe, Exmouth, Teignmouth. On the north coast Ilfracombe, Clovelly, Lynton and Lynmouth attract many thousands of visitors.

Somerset

A south-western county bordered on the north by the Bristol Channel. The central area is low lying and marshy but to the north are the Mendip Hills (Blackdown 1,068 ft.) with the famous Cheddar Gorge and to the west the wooded Quantock Hills (1,260 ft.). The Exmoor plateau includes the famous Doone country near Oare. The county town is Taunton and other major towns include Bath, Bridgwater, Frome and Wells. Well-known holiday resorts include Minehead and Weston-super-Mare.

Of Special Interest

Anthony House (2m NW of Torpoint) (NT). Beautifully preserved manor house built between 1711 and 1721. The panelled rooms with portraits and old furniture. Gardens. Apr–Sept, Tues, Weds, Thurs and Bk Hol Mons 2–6.

Arlington Court (7m NE Barnstaple) (NT). Chichester mansion of 1822 with collection of pewter, seashells and model ships. Large grounds with lake. Apr–Sept, daily except Sats, 11–6.

Barrington Court (3m NE Ilminster) (NT). Beautiful Tudor mansion built by Lord Daubeny in 1514–1520. Converted stable buildings date from 1670. Summer, Weds.

Bath Abbey—Assembly Rooms, Pump Room, etc. See page 79.

Bicton Gardens (East Budleigh). Le Notre gardens with magnificent pinetum. Narrow gauge railway and museum. Afternoons Apr–end of Jun. 11–6 Jul, Aug, Sept.

Bradley Manor (Newton Abbot). (NT). Rebuilt 15c small fortified manor house though much altered. 13c undercroft, 15c Great Hall. Meadows and riverside walks. Thurs, 2–5, Apr–Sept.

Buckland Abbey (6m S of Tavistock) (NT). Modified 13c monastery purchased by Sir Francis Drake in 1581. Now naval and Devon folk museum. Medieval tithe barn. Shrub and herb gardens. Easter to end Sept,11–6 and Sun afternoons. Wed, Sat and Sun afternoons in Winter.

Cadhay (Ottery St. Mary). A fine specimen of Elizabethan domestic architecture. Spring and Summer, Bk Hol Suns and Mons, also Weds, Thurs in August, 2–6.

Claverton Manor (Bath). The American Museum in Britain. Exhibition of American decorative arts, and gardening of 17c, 18c and 19c. Manor built by Sir Jeffry Wyatville in 1820. Apr–mid Oct, daily except Mons.

Cleeve Abbey (Washford). Well preserved 12/13c Cistercian house with fine refectory and timber roof, beautiful tracery and wall paintings. Gatehouse and dormitory of note. Open 9.30–4, 6, or 7. Sundays from 2.

Clevedon Court (Clevedon) (NT). Restored 14c house with chapel and 18c terraced garden. House of Elton family. Museum. Glass. Apr–Sept, Weds, Thurs and Suns, 2–30–5.30.

Compton Castle (4m W of Torquay). Fortied manor house built between 1320–1520. Courtyard, great Hall, chapel and kitchen. Apr–Oct, Mons, Weds, Thurs, 10–12, 2–5.

Cotehele House, Calstock (NT). Medieval house of grey granite (1485–1539) set in beautiful gardens. Furniture, tapestry and exquisite needlework. Apr–Sept, daily except Tues, 10–6. Oct–Mar, Weds, Sats and Suns, 2–6.

Cothay Manor (Greenham). Beautiful 15c house in remote situation. Great Hall, minstrels' gallery, oratory, solar. Yew hedges. June–Sept, Thurs, also Weds in Aug. Some Suns.

Glastonbury Abbey, and Tribunal. See page 81.

Glendurgan Gardens, Helford river. (NT). Grounds with fine trees and shrub, water garden and maze. Apr–Sept, Mons and Weds, 10.30–4.30. Also Fris in Apr and May.

Godolphin House (5m NW of Helston). House of early Tudor date with Elizabethan additions. Unique colonnaded front. One time home of Earls of Godolphin. Thurs, May–Sept, 2–5. Also Tues, Aug–Sept.

Killerton Gardens (7m NE Exeter) (NT). Lovely displays of colour in Spring and Autumn. Daily.

Lanhydrock (2½m SE of Bodmin). (NT). Restored 17c mansion with good gatehouse. North wing only open Apr–Sept, Weds and Sats, 2–6.

Lytes Cary (2½m SE Somerton) (NT). Typical Somerset Manor house of 15c, and 14c chapel. Home of Lyte family. Mar–Oct, Weds and Sats, 2–6.

Montecute House (4m W of Yeovil) (NT). Magnificent house of Ham Hill stone built 1588–1600. Fine panelling, furniture, tapestries, glassware. Notable Jacobean garden. Easter–end Sept. Daily except Tues, 11–6. Mar, Oct, Nov, Weds, Sats, Suns, 2–6. Closed Dec–Feb.

Muchelney Abbey (1½m S of Langport). Remains of medieval Benedictine abbey. (AM standard hours). Priests House (NT Easter–Oct, Weds, Sats, Suns, 11–6).

Nunney Castle (Nunney). Moated 14c structure with large round towers at the angles. (AM standard hours).

Pendennis Castle, Falmouth. Henry VIII coastal defence built c. 1543 and later enlarged. AM standard hours.

Penfound Manor, Poundstock. A part-Saxon manor house with Norman, Elizabethan and Stuart additions. Easter–Sept, Mon–Fri, 2–6.

Powderham Castle (Kenton, Exeter). Medieval home (built c 1390) of Earls of Devon. Fine furniture and family portraits. Deer park. June–Sept. Daily except Sats, 2–6.

Prior Park (Widcombe). Georgian mansion dating from 1735. State apartments. Palladian bridge. May–Sept, Tues, 3–6, Weds, 2–6. Also Mons and Thurs in Aug, 2–6.

Restormel Castle (1½m N of Lostwithiel). Remains of 12c castle but little of this period exists other than earthworks. (AM Standard hours).

St. Michael's Mount, Marazion. (NT). Lofty isolated rock, with causeway from Marazion, and crowned by castellated mansion of the St. Aubyns. Conspicuous square tower, pretty chapel and fishermen's houses. Weds and Fris, also Mons, Jun–Sept.

Saltram House (3½m E of Plymouth) (NT). Remains of large Tudor house with Georgian additions. Two rooms added by Robert Adam are among best examples of his work, Period furniture, paintings. Landscaped gardens. Apr–Sept, daily except Tues, 2–6.

Sharpitor (Salcombe) (NT). Overbecks museum of local interest and 6 acres of gardens. Museum Apr–Oct, daily except Sats. Gardens throughout the year.

Tapeley Park Gardens, Instow. Italian style gardens and lovely woodlands. June–mid-Sept, daily except Mons and Sats, 2–6.

Tintagel Castle, Trevena. Ruins of Norman stronghold set on majestic cliffs. (AM standard hours).

Tintinhull House (5m NW of Yeovil). (NT). 17c manor house with fine garden. Apr–Oct, Weds, Thurs, Sats and Bk Hol Mons, 2–6.

Torre Abbey, Torquay. 18c mansion with furniture and paintings. Remains of abbey founded 1196. Italian rock and water gardens. Daily.

Trelissick Gardens (4m S of Truro). (NT). Fine rhododendrons, camellias and hydrangeas and views over Fal estuary. Mar–Oct, Weds, Thurs, Fris and Bk Hol Mons, 10–5.

Trengwainton Gardens (2m W of Penzance) (NT). Fine collections of shrub particularly magnolias and rhododendrons. Walled garden. Mar–Sept, Weds, Fris, Sats and Bk Hol Mons, 11–5.

Trerice (3m SE of Newquay) (NT). Small Elizabethan house, rebuilt 1571, with contemporary fireplaces and plasterwork. Apr–Sept, Weds, Suns, 12–5.30.

Tresco Abbey Gardens (Isles of Scilly). Exceptional terraced gardens of sub-tropical plants. Valhalla museum of shipwreck figureheads. Daily except Suns, 10–4.

Resorts and Centres of Interest

Barnstaple (Devon). Ancient and prosperous market town near head of Taw estuary. Facilities for various sports with golf at nearby Saunton and Westward Ho! Annual fair in September. Sandy beaches and fine surfing at Saunton, Croyde and Woolacombe. The more placid shore at Instow is ideal for children. Arlington Court (NT) is 7m NE.

Bath (Som). Famous spa and city on River Avon since Roman times. The Roman Baths are among the best of Roman relics in Europe. Pump Room. The fine sixteenth-century Abbey Church is on site of Benedictine monastery at which Edgar was crowned in 973. Many fine eighteenth-century houses. The unique Pulteney Bridge (1770) over the Avon is lined with shops. The 400 ft. high Beechen Cliff overlooks the city. Ancient earthworks in the district include the Iron Age hill fort on Solsbury Hill (NT).

Beer (Devon). Coastal village with fishing, boating and bathing (shingle beach) overlooked by 400 ft chalk cliff of Beer Head. Nearby stone quarries.

Bideford (Devon). Market town and port on river Torridge with trout and salmon fishing. Ancient bridge. Urban district includes *Northam*, *Appledore* with narrow streets and colour-washed cottages, and *Westward Ho!* a bracing resort and golfing centre, with magnificent sands (wind yachts) backed by the famous Pebble Ridge.

Bodmin (Corn). County town and touring centre on fringe of the extensive Bodmin Moor. St. Petroc's Church (1469–71). *Lanhydrock House* (NT) is 2½m S. Good views from Brown Willy (1,375 ft) and Rough Tor (1,312 ft).

Boscastle (Corn). Old world village with narrow rocky harbour (NT) winding inland between rugged cliffs. Excellent sea fishing but best bathing at Bossiney. Good walks in Valency Valley. On Tintagel Head is the famous castle while in the nearby village is the Old Post Office building (NT) and the stone built King Arthur's Hall.

Bridgwater (Som). Busy little town and river-port on the River Parret. Manufacturing centre and market for produce from rich surrounding countryside. Blake's House, reputed birthplace of Admiral Robert Blake, is now the Borough Museum.

Bude (Corn). Popular Atlantic coast resort with surfing from the glorious sandy beaches the main attraction. Bude has golf, tennis and bowls. Stratton, 2m, is tiny market town within borough. Widemouth Bay to the S also has fine sands. Beyond *Millook*, among wooded hills, is *Poundstock* with old frescoes in its church and a fine old Guildhouse. *Penfound Manor* reputed oldest inhabited manor house in Britain *(open).*

78

Budleigh Salterton (Devon). Quiet resort at mouth of river Otter 5m. E of Exmouth. A long pebble beach provides safe bathing, sea and river fishing are good, and there is tennis and golf. Bicton Gardens are at Otterton, 3m N whilst at East Budleigh 3m NW is Hayes Barton, birthplace in 1552 of Sir Walter Raleigh.

Burnham-on-Sea (Som). Small Bristol Channel resort with long stretch of sand. Good centre for the Mendip and Quantock Hills. The ancient hill-fort Brent Knoll is nearby.

Chard (Som). A lovely old town in hilly country. Birthplace of John Stringfellow who made the first power-driven model aeroplane. The 18c Court House and 15c parish church are of note. Good views from nearby Windwhistle Hill (733 ft) and Snowdon Hill (709 ft).

Cheddar (Som). Small town at foot of the magnificent Cheddar Gorge in a giant cleft of the Mendip Hills, clothed with shrubs and trailing creepers. Caves in the hillside reveal remarkable stalactites and stalagmites. Famous for its cheese, though little is made here.

Clevedon (Som). A tree-lined resort on the higher reaches of the Bristol Channel. The bay is rocky and grass and trees grow down to the water's edge. Good views from the town's seven hills. Clevedon Court (NT) has been home of the Eltons since 1790.

Clovelly (Devon). Quaint cliff-edge village of steep, stepped and cobbled street descending to tiny quay and rock strewn beach. The Hobby Drive winds through idyllic wooded combes for 3m. Buck Mills to the east has quiet bathing beach.

Combe Martin (Devon). Holiday village between Ilfracombe and Lynton facing Bristol Channel. The main street straggles for 1½m through wooded combe on edge of Exmoor. A shore of sand and shingle beneath the Hangman Hills. At 6m is Arlington Court (NT).

Dartmoor (Devon). Rocky tableland, 365 sq. miles in extent, and largest area of moorland in Southern England, now a National Park. Attractive villages form good centres for moorland walks. Of antiquities there are many examples of cromlechs, stone crosses and circles.

Dartmouth (Devon). Ancient port and holiday resort overlooking land-locked estuary of River Dart. Excellent sea and river fishing, sailing, bowls, tennis. A Car ferry crosses to Kingswear opposite and there are river excursions to and from Totnes. The old Butterwalk has some restored 17c houses and a nautical museum. Above the town is the Royal Naval College whilst below is Dartmouth Castle (AM).

Dawlish (Devon). Tiny seaside town with long sandy beaches beneath rose-red cliffs.

Dunster (Som). Attractive village 3m SE of Minehead. Its broad main street, 17c Yarn Market, ancient inn and warm pink stone church are overlooked by well preserved castle home of the Luttrells.

Exeter (Devon). Historic capital city and university town on River Exe, fine shopping centre and starting point for excursions on Dartmoor and for the S Devon coast. The magnificent twin-towered Cathedral dates from 12c and is famous for its long west front and exquisite choir screen. The Guildhall (1330) has beautiful Elizabethan portico. See Tucker's Hall (1471), Rougemont Castle (Norman remains), Museum and Art Gallery. At Kenton 8m SE is Powderham Castle in lovely deer park.

Exmouth (Devon). Pleasant resort on estuary of River Exe with good sands and wide variety of amusements and sports. Sea bathing and open-air pool. Boating and yachting. A-la-Ronde, a circular house built in 1798, with a shell gallery is 2m N.

Falmouth (Corn). Historic sea-faring town with two fronts, the oldest part facing north-east and rambling along the western bank of the Penryn river, the modern portion with seashore of golden sands, gardens and pleasure grounds. The magnificent natural harbour is guarded by *Pendennis Castle* built as coastal defence by Henry VIII. All sports including golf. *Penjerrick Gardens* 3m SW have a noted collection of sub-tropical plants, while a mile further is *Glendurgen* (NT) a beautiful garden close to the Helford river inlet.

Across the estuary is picturesque *St. Mawes* with castle contemporary to that at Pendennis. Over the Percuil river is St. Anthony-in-Roseland and St. Anthony's Head (240 ft) with its lighthouse. At Madron is Chysauster Iron Age site.

Fowey (Corn). On the W bank at the mouth of the lovely Fowey river, this picturesque little port is another of the county's deservedly popular coastal resorts. There is excellent bathing from the sandy shore at Readymoney Cove. *St. Chatherine's Castle* (1540) a former defence of the harbour, is in ruins. Across the harbour is picturesque *Polruan* and the steep hillside at *Bodinnick* with Pont Pill creek between. The ancient town of *Lostwithiel* with a fine nine-arched bridge lies seven miles up the Fowey river. A mile north is *Restormel Castle* (AM) and in another mile *Lanhydrock House* (NT).

Glastonbury (Som). Market town and borough, traditionally the site of the first Christian church in Britain, founded by Joseph of Arimathea in 1c, and the Avalon of Arthurian legend. Remains of its ancient abbey include 12c chapel, great church and the Abbot's Kitchen. In High Street are the interesting George Inn and the Tribunal (AM), a former courthouse. The two excavated lake villages in the vicinity are believed to have been inhabited 150 years before the Romans occupied Britain, and models can be seen in the local museum. Glastonbury Tor (NT) (520 ft) is crowned by the tower of the 13c St. Michael's Church.

Honiton (Devon). Busy market town of one long street with many pleasant Georgian houses in a number of which the famous lace is still made.

Ilfracombe (Devon). Principal among the north coast resorts with shingle and sand bathing beaches. Covered sea-water bath. Golf and various sports and entertainment. Picturesque harbour, gardens, zoo. Torrs Walks is beauty spot at W end of town. Lee is a pretty village 3m westward

Lynmouth

in Borough Valley. There are fine walks in vicinity of Morte Point (NT).

Ilminster (Som). Busy market town at foot of Blackdown Hills. In the church are brasses of Nicholas Wadham who founded Wadham College, Oxford, and his wife.

Isles of Scilly. Archipelago of some hundred and fifty islands, islets and rocks, though only five are inhabited. St. Mary's, Tresco, Bryher, St. Martin's and St. Agnes. Mild climate, flower-scented air and exhilarating Atlantic breezes. Many sandy bathing beaches, golf on St. Mary's, boating and fishing. On Tresco are the beautiful Abbey Gardens.

Kynance Cove (Corn). Glorious sands, colourful serpentine rocks, intriguing caves, a blowhole, varying sea views all go to make up one of the most popular coves on the whole Cornish coast.

Land's End (Corn). The westernmost point of England terminates a promontory of granite cliff. Offshore is Longships Lighthouse and further out to the S is Wolf Rock. A mile NE is *Sennen Cove* (sand) with good bathing and surf-riding.

Launceston (Corn). Former capital of the county and the Norman "Dunheved". Tennis, golf and fishing in the River Tamar. The remains of its 12/13c castle (AM) include fine cylindrical keep.

Liskeard (Corn). Old market town and centre for Bodmin moor. St. Cleers' Well, Trethevy Quoit, Minions, Hurlers, and Cheesewring are among antiquities nearby.

WEST COUNTRY

The Lizard (Corn). Great rugged tableland jutting seaward to form the southernmost point of England. Nestling among colourful cliffs are numerous lovely little coves and fishing villages of stone built whitewashed cottages. Cadgwith with its crabs and lobsters, Coverack with miniature harbour and lifeboat-station, and Mullion Cove among lichen covered cliffs have long been popular. Kynance Cove with firm tide washed sands and serpentine rocks is entrancing. *Helston* is a busy market town and touring centre, well-known for its annual "Flora" or "Furry" day (May 8th) when the inhabitants dance through the streets and in and out of the houses.

Looe (Corn). East and West Looe are linked by a stone bridge which spans the mouth of the river Looe. The twin towns have developed into one of Cornwall's most popular resorts and there is little room to spare in the high season. Every sports facility, including an 18-hole golf course is available. Shark fishing is popular.

Lynton and Lynmouth (Devon). Lynmouth, with picturesque little harbour at mouth of the East and West Lyn rivers, and hill-top town of Lynton (cliff lift connects the two) combine to make one of the most popular tourist venues in southern England. Shingle and rocky foreshore. Exmoor Museum. The steep Countisbury Hill rises eastward. 1¾m upstream is glorious Watersmeet.

Mevagissey (Corn). Small harbour resort and fishing port, sand and shingle beach. Good sands and bathing at nearby Polstreath, Portmellon and Pentewan.

Minehead (Som). Popular Bristol Channel holiday resort flanked by the rolling Exmoor hills. A wide explanade and sea wall sweeps round the bay. Excellent sands and all holiday amenities. Of interest are the 15c St. Michael's Church and Quirke's Almshouses (1630).

Newquay (Corn). Principal N coast resort with bathing and surfing from magnificent sandy beaches. All entertainment and sports including golf. *Trerice* is NT property 3m SE. Sandy beaches and dunes also at Crantock (2m) and Holywell Bay (3m).

Newton Abbot (Devon). Market centre of large agricultural and cider-making district in midst of scenery of diversified beauty. Bradley Manor (NT) (½m) on river Lemon.

Okehampton (Devon). Town on northern edge of Dartmoor. Golf, swimming pool, entertainment. Convenient for walks over some of wildest parts of Dartmoor, for Yes Tor and High Willhays, two of the highest points.

Ottery St. Mary (Devon). Pleasant town near river Otter with fine 14c church ranking next to Exeter cathedral in architectural merit in the county. Birthplace of S. T. Coleridge, poet. 1m W is Cadhay, a notable Elizabethan manor house (1550).

Padstow (Corn). Popular holiday harbour town at mouth of Camel river. Excellent sands on north shore at Rock (ferry). Sailing, golf. Trevose, Harlyn Bay and Treyarnon popular for surfing.

Paignton (Devon). Now part of the local government consortium of Torbay. Popular seaside resort of extensive sandy beaches, full entertainment, golf, sailing, tennis and bowls. Kirkham House dates from 15c. Oldway mansion (1874) now used as civic headquarters. Torquay is 3m N.

Penzance (Corn). Busy sheltered town on the shore of Mounts' Bay with extensive views. Mild climate, good sea-fishing, boating and bathing from shingle and sand. On the SW side is *Newlyn* a colourful fishing village beloved by artists. Along the coast is *Mousehole* another typical fishing village with small sandy beach, and *Lamorna Cove* with its tiny jetty and trout stream.

Eastward in Mounts Bay is *Marazion* with a causeway uncovered at low tide to *St. Michael's Mount* (NT). The castle, ancestral home of the Lords of Levan dates from the 14c. Antiquities in the district include *Lanyon Quoit* (NT) a Stone Age long barrow, and *Chysauster,* an early British settlement of stone houses dating from the 1st and 2nd centuries.

Perranporth (Corn). Atlantic coast resort noted for its vast stretches of golden sands and dunes. Popular surfing centre, tennis, golf, and entertainment. Cliff walks. Droskyn Point to S with grand rock scenery, caves and pools.

Plymouth (Devon). Historic city at mouth of river Tamar, now considerably rebuilt after war damage. Naval base and holiday resort. The statue of Sir Francis Drake on Plymouth Hoe marks the spot where he finished his famous game of bowls. Sutton Pool was departure point of the 'Mayflower'. At Plympton, 4m E, is Saltram House (NT).

Watergate Bay, Newquay

WEST COUNTRY

Polperro (Corn). One of the most picturesque Cornish fishing villages nestling in cleft in steep cliffs to the west of Looe. Smugglers' museum. Magnificent cliff walks.

Porthcurno (Corn). Beautiful cove, golden sand, grand cliffs. Unique open-air Minack theatre on cliff top.

Porthscatho (Corn). Quiet village with bathing, fishing and boating. Nare Head (NT) gives fine views across Gerrans Bay.

Port Isaac (Corn). Harbour and water-edge fishermen's cottages make a quaint scene. Mackerel and lobster fishing. Bathing at Port Gaverne with shingly beach and attractive rock scenery.

St. Austell (Corn). Centre of the china clay industry with little harbour of Charlestown 2m away on St. Austell Bay. Bathing beaches at Carlyon Bay, Crinnis, Par, Pentewan and Porthpean.

St. Ives (Corn). Colourful resort with fishing harbour and extensive sands. Artists studios rub shoulders with picturesque fisherman's cottages, antique shops and modern boutiques, inns and cafes. In 1½m is Carbis Bay with magnificent sands. Lelant (golf) is attractive village on estuary of river Hayle. Westward is wild cliff scenery with many walks.

St. Mawes (Corn). Delightful sailing resort at mouth of Percuil river. The castle (AM) is contemporary with Pendennis across Falmouth harbour.

Salcombe (Devon). South of Dartmouth, this small sheltered resort provides some of the best sailing off the Devon coast. Good bathing both N towards Torcross and Slapton Sands and W towards Hope Cove and Bigbury-on-Sea. The rocky coastline provides splendid walks, particularly in region of Bolt Head (NT).

Seaton (Devon). Pleasant resort at mouth of River Axe close to Somerset border. Pebbly beach and high cliffs.

Selworthy (Som). Enchanting scene of thatched cottages, latticed windows and gabled porches. The church is handsome Perpendicular structure. At nearby *Allerford* is ancient pack-horse bridge.

Sidmouth (Devon). Holiday haunt midway between the estuaries of the Exe and Axe rivers. Beach of shingle with sand at low tide. There is good rock scenery at Ladram Bay, 3m.

Taunton (Som). County town and prosperous market centre. Though modern in appearance, the town is one of the oldest in England, reputed to have been founded in 710. Earliest building is the Norman Castle of which remnants of the keep and Great Hall (County museum) remain. The tower of St. Mary Magdalene Church (163 ft) is a good example of Perpendicular.

Teignmouth (Devon). Popular holiday resort at mouth of River Teign. Extensive sands, pier. Excellent sailing, sea and river fishing. There are some pleasing Georgian houses. Ferry to Shaldon across estuary of Teign. The Ness Headland gives extensive views.

84

Cockington Village

Torbay (Devon). Local government consortium of Torquay, Paignton and Brixham. Torquay spreading over hills behind the sheltered bay ranks as one of the loveliest of the county's holiday resorts. Miles of sandy beaches are backed by two-tiered promenade, luxury hotels and modern flats. Palm trees flourish in near sub-tropical climate. Inner and outer harbours shelter many yachts and pleasure craft. The grounds of Torre Abbey are very splendid. Cockington is picturesque village. Compton Castle at Marldon 4m W. The new borough includes Paignton and Brixham, which see.

Truro (Corn). County headquarters, cathedral city and small port at head of Truro river. The cathedral, of Cornish granite, built between 1880 and 1910, in Early English style has a notable reredos and beautiful baptistry. Golf, tennis, bowls. The river excursion to Falmouth (11m) passes delightful scenery.

Wadebridge (Corn). Market town on Camel estuary, good centre for coast resorts. 500 years old bridge. Fishing, tennis and bowls. Nearby antiquities include Giants Quoit at Pawton, and the prehistoric hill fort of Castle Killibury (2m).

Watchet (Som). Busy little seaport town with harbour and paper mills. Shingle beach, sandy stretches and rock pools. Sea fishing, bowls and tennis.

Wells (Som). Lovely city by the Mendips of ancient cathedral with majestic west front, ancient gateways, a street of 14c houses, a 15c Deanery, and moated Bishop's Palace.

Weston-super-Mare (Som). Bracing Bristol Channel resort of mild climate, firm sands, endless variety of entertainment and sport.

Yeovil (Som). A market town on the river Yeo. Swimming pool, library and museum. The 14c parish church has some good brasses.

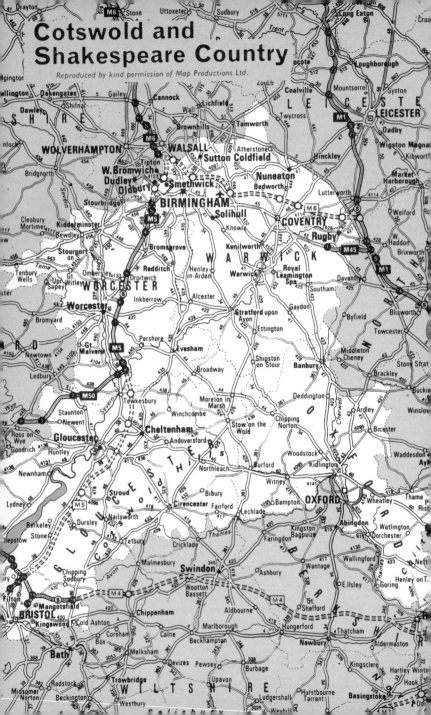

Cotswold and
Shakespeare Country

Reproduced by kind permission of Map Productions Ltd.

Cotswold and
Shakespeare Country

The counties of Oxfordshire, Warwickshire, Gloucestershire and Worcestershire

Oxfordshire

An inland county, for the most part in the Thames basin, that great river forming its southern boundary for a little over 70 miles. The steep scarp of the Chilterns extends in the SE while to the W are low spurs of the Cotswold hills. The Evenlode, Windrush, Cherwell and Thame are tributaries of the Thames, and along their banks are many picturesque villages. The university city of Oxford is the county town and apart from its academic claims to fame has many buildings of historic or architectural interest. Of historic homes, the county is especially rich, with a long list undoubtedly topped by the magnificent Blenheim Palace at Woodstock.

Gloucestershire

A beautiful county embracing the Cotswold Hills, the Severn vale and the wooded Forest of Dean. The Cotswolds, seldom climbing beyond 1000 ft, roll across the county from SW to NE. The valleys are rich and fertile. Lovely towns and villages of the local grey stone are famous and much-pictured. The Severn Vale stretches from Tewkesbury, where Severn and Avon meet, to the county town of Gloucester, not the reserved cathedral city one might expect, but a busy thriving inland port. The Royal Forest of Dean, N of the Severn, preserves much of its oak-wooded beauty. The county is richly endowed with superb churches, many built by 15c wool merchants, fine castles, handsome stately homes and Roman relics of various kinds.

Warwickshire

A county in the heart of England. Close to Britain's industrial hub with the great cities of Birmingham and Coventry in the N, its main river, the

Avon, meanders through an agricultural land with pleasant small towns and villages of charming houses and delightful gardens. Though boasting no great grandeur of scenery, in the field of historical heritage the county has no equal. The feudal fortresses of Kenilworth and Warwick are both picturesque and of great interest, and of stately homes Charlecote, Compton Wynyates, Coughton and Ragley are among the finest in the land. Prime centre for the visitor however, is Stratford-upon-Avon, a mecca for pilgrims to Shakespeare's birthplace.

Worcestershire

A county of rich and varied beauty. It includes the unique and beautiful Malvern Hills, with the six townships that go to make up Malvern, the valley of the Severn, Teme and Avon rivers, the fruit-growing Vale of Evesham, Bredon Hill, the Clent and Lickey Hills, the ancient city of Worcester, the equally ancient Droitwich, celebrated for its brine baths, and many delightful villages and hamlets distinguished by their 'black and white' half-timbered mansions, houses and cottages.

Shakespeare's Birthplace

Of Special Interest

Arbury Hall (4m W of Nuneaton). Unique Gothic style country house, home of Newdegate family since 16c. Gardens. East–Oct, Suns and Bk Hol Mons and Tues, 2.30–6.

Aston Hall (2m N of Birmingham). Jacobean house with period rooms. Weekdays 10–5. Suns in summer only, 2–5.

Badminton House (Great Badminton, 5m E of Chipping Sodbury). Home of Duke of Beaufort in Palladian style. Paintings. Stables and kennels. Jun–mid-Sept, Weds, 2.30–5.

Berkeley Castle (Berkeley). 12c castle of the Berkeleys. Scene of murder of Edward II. Furniture, paintings, tapestries. Terraced gardens. Apr–Sept, daily except Mons, 2–5.30. Suns only in Oct.

Blenheim Palace (Woodstock). Magnificent home of Duke of Marlborough. Fine China, paintings, tapestries and furniture. Gardens, park and lake. Model railway. Apr–Oct, Mons, Tues, Weds and Thurs. Additionally weekends, Aug–Sept, 1–6.

Bredon Tithe Barn (3m NE of Tewksbury). 14c barn at 132 ft long, the second largest in England. (NT). Weds and Fris, 2–5.

Charlecote Park (5m NE of Stratford). Historic home of the Lucy family. Deer Park. Museum in 16c gatehouse. (NT). Apr–Sept, daily except Mons, 11.15–5.45.

Chastleton House (5m W of Chipping Norton). Jacobean manor house built by Witney wool merchant in 1603. Furnishings. Topiary garden. Daily except Weds, 10–1, 2–6, Suns, 2–5.

Chedworth Roman Villa (3m NW of Fossebridge). One of best preserved Roman villas in England. Mosaic pavements. (NT). Daily, except Mons, 10–1, 2–7. Close in Jan and early Oct.

Clopton House (1m N of Stratford-upon-Avon). Home of Clopton family since 13c. Furniture, pictures, 15c chapel. Daily, 10–5.

Compton Wynyates (10m W of Banbury). The Warwickshire seat of Marquess of Northampton, an early Tudor Manor house. Topiary garden. Easter, then Apr–Sept, Weds, Sats, and Bk Hols, 2–6. Suns, June–Aug.

Deddington Castle (6m S of Banbury). Extensive earthworks of castle on which Piers Gaveston was seized prior to his execution. (AM any time).

Dodington House (2m SE of Chipping Sodbury). Regency house with fine staircase. Gardens. Easter and May–Sept, Weds, Thurs and Suns, 2–5.30.

Dyrham Park (7½m N of Bath). 17c Bath stone house, panelled rooms, furniture, pictures, tapestry. (NT). Easter-Sept, daily except Mons, 2–6, Mar, Oct and Nov, Weds, Sats, Suns. Closed Dec–Feb.

Farnborough Hall (5m N of Banbury). Mid-18c house with some 17c details. Grounds with temples. (NT). Apr–Sept, Weds and Sats, 2–6.

Hanbury Hall (2½m E of Droitwich). Wren-style red brick house built 1701. Fine hall, staircase, Long Room with plasterwork (NT). May–Sept, Weds, Sats and Suns, 2–6.

Hartlebury Castle (2m E of Stourport). Restored 15/18c home of Bishops of Worcester. Staterooms. Easter–Sept, Suns and Bk Hols, 2–6.

Harvington Hall (4m SE of Kidderminster). Tudor and later moated house. Daily, except Mons, 2–6.

COTSWOLD AND SHAKESPEARE COUNTRY

Hidcote Manor Garden (4m NE of Chipping Campden). Formal gardens, rare trees, shrubs, bulbs, roses. (NT). Easter–Oct, daily except Tues and Fris, 11–8.

Kenilworth Castle (Kenilworth). One of the most extensive castles in Britain. 12c keep, 13c curtain walls and towers. Magnificent great hall and apartments. (AM standard hours).

Mapledurham House (4m NW of Reading). Pure Tudor with grand facade and wings at either end. House of Blount family. Easter–Sept, Sats and Suns, 2.30–5.30. Also Bk Hols.

Minster Lovell Hall (3m NW of Witney). Remains of 15c manor house erected by 7th Lord Lovell. (AM standard hours).

North Leigh Roman Villa (5m SW of Woodstock). Villa in excellent preservation revealing tessellated pavements, large bath, hypocaust, etc. (AM standard hours).

Packwood House (Hockley Heath, 10m NW of Warwick). Timber-framed Tudor House in park and woodlands. Yew garden. Furniture, tapestries. (NT). Apr–Sept, daily except Mons and Fris, 2–7. Oct–Mar, Weds, Sats, Suns, 2–5.

Ragley Hall (2m SW of Alcester). Home of Marquess of Hertford built 1680. Magnificent Great Hall and elegant rooms. Paintings, china, works of art. Gardens, park and lake. Mid Apr–Sept, daily except Mons and Fris, 2–6.

Rousham House (Steeple Aston, 8m W of Bicester). 17/18c house, pictures, furniture. Fine garden by William Kent. Jun–Aug, Weds and Bk Hols, 2–6, Suns, gardens only.

Shakespeare Trust Properties. (See Stratford-upon-Avon).

Slimbridge, Wild Fowl Trust (12m W of Stroud). World's largest collection of wildfowl. All the year, weekdays from 9.30, Suns from 12.00.

Snowshill Manor (2½m S of Broadway). Tudor house with collection of musical instruments, clocks and toys. Terraced garden (NT). Easter and May–Sept, Weds, Thurs, Sats, Suns, Bk Hol Mons, 11–1, 2–6. Sats and Suns in Apr and Oct.

Spetchley Park (3m E of Worcester). Extensive deer park. Lake with wildfowl. Apr–Sept, Suns and Bk Hols, 11–dusk.

Sudeley Castle (Winchcombe, 7m NE of Cheltenham). Dignified stone building in beautiful setting, terraces and lovely gardens. May–Sept, Weds and Thurs, Bk Hol weekends, alt. Suns, May–June, all Suns in Aug and Sept, 2–5.

Upton House (Kineton, 7m NW of Banbury). House, paintings, porcelain, terraced gardens (NT). July–Sept, Weds and Sats, 2–6. Oct–June, Weds only.

Westonbirt Arboretum (3m SW of Tetbury). Fine tree-scapes, many rare specimens. Daily, 10–8.

Resorts and Centres of Interest

Alcester (Warws). Market town on western boundary of county on River Alne. 17c Town Hall. The embattled and pinnacled church has some good brasses. Coughton Court (NT) 2m N contains Jacobite relics. Ragley Hall, seat of Marquis of Hertford, is 2m SW.

Atherstone (Warws). Market town on Watling Street near Leicestershire boundary. Some 18c houses. Outside Red Lion Hotel is old milestone marking 100-mile mark from London. Ancient Shrovetide football still played through streets.

Bampton (Oxon). Old village famous for its Morris dancers who at Whitsun attract many visitors to the streets. St. Mary's Church is fine building with Norman to Decorated work and high spire.

Banbury (Oxon). Industrial town and agricultural centre on River Cherwell close to northern edge of county. The original Cross of nursery rhyme fame was pulled down by the Puritans in 1602. The famous Banbury cakes are still sold locally. Several old houses with ornamental plasterwork. 16c Reindeer Inn. 3m W is Broughton Castle (Apr–Sept, Weds, 2–6) seat of Lord Saye and Sele.

Bibury (Glos). Famous Cotswold village on River Coln (trout fishing). Old mill house, Swan Inn, 17c manor house, Norman church and Arlington Row (NT) an exquisite row of stone-built cottages are all notable.

Bicester (Oxon). Small market-town in fox-hunting country. Several old houses of 16c. The church is 12c with later additions. There is wall monument to Thomas Grantham (d.1718). The site of the former Roman station of Alchester is 2m S.

Birmingham (Warws). County borough and next largest city after London. With population of over a million people, there are admirable facilities for entertainment and sport. Redevelopment is leading to dramatic transformation of city's appearance. Bull Ring is most modern shopping and business centre. The Cathedral Church of St. Philip was consecrated in 1715. The City Museum and Art Gallery in Congreve Street, the Museum of Science and Industry, Newhall Street, the Natural History Museum, Cannon Hill Park, and Barber Institute of Fine Arts in University Road are all notable collections. The University is at Edgbaston 1m from city centre. Nearby are the Botanic Gardens, Queen Elizabeth Hospital, Oratory of St. Philip Neri, Cannon Hill Park with zoo and arts centre, and the county cricket ground. Birmingham Airport is at Elmdon, 7m on Coventry road.

Bladon (Oxon). Village on SE edge of Blenheim park, Woodstock. In churchyard are graves of Sir Winston Churchill and his parents. To SE are earthworks of Round Castle.

Bourton-on-the-Water (Glos). Cotswold village on River Windrush. Low stone bridges join wide grass verges on either bank. Trout fishing. Model village. Birdland botanical garden and aviary. Museum of witchcraft.

Bredon (Worcs). Old village 3m N of Tewksbury. Boating and fishing in Avon. The 14c tithe barn (NT) is second largest in England. To NW is Bredon Hill (960 ft) with Kemerton Camp, ancient British fort on summit.

Bristol. County borough, historic city and busy port on River Avon 6m from Bristol Channel. The University was founded in 1909. Restored Cathedral retains part of Norman monastic church. 14c St. Mary Redcliffe is largest parish church in England. Modern Council House overlooks College Green and Lord Mayor's Chapel. Cabot Tower on Brandon Hill. Galleries and museums include City Art Gallery and Museum; Georgian House; Red Lodge; Chatterton House. Broadmead, Horsefair and Haymarket are modern shopping thoroughfares. The City Centre is broad space attractive with flowers. Dignified buildings in business area include The Exchange, Corn Street, where are four brass 'nails' on which money payments were made. John Wesley's chapel was first Methodist chapel in the world. St. John the Baptist surmounts the last remaining city gate. Charles Wesley's House, Charles Street, was the hymn writer's home (1749–1771). Entertainments in Colston Hall, Theatre Royal, Hippodrome and cinemas. At Clifton are the famous Downs, Brunel's Suspension Bridge over the Avon gorge, Clifton College and Bristol Zoo.

Broadway (Worcs). A famous showplace and principal Worcestershire village of northern Cotswolds. Stone-built houses and wide grass-bordered street. Lygon Arms is 17c. Parish church is modern but St. Eadburgha's dates from Norman times. SE is Broadway Beacon (1,924 ft) with its lone 18c tower. 3m S is Snowshill Manor (NT).

Burford (Oxon). Picturesque town in Windrush valley with sloping main street of stone-built houses. Large church with Norman west door. Other buildings include 15c almshouses and 16c Grammar School.

Cheltenham (Glos). Pleasant town of elegant Regency buildings and imposing modern houses. One time fashionable mineral spa but now residential and touring centre. Natural alkaline water available at Town Hall and Pittville Pump Room. Horse-chestnut trees line the principal promenade. Pittville Park with lake, Pittville Gardens, Imperial Gardens and Montpellier Gardens with floral displays in season. Good sports facilities. Art gallery and museum. Well-known schools. Racecourse at Prestbury. At Southam, to the S, is fine tithe barn. Nearby Cleeve Hill (1,000 ft) is highest point in Cotswolds. To E is Belas Knap, a Neolithic long barrow.

Chesterton (Warws). Straggling village with 15c church notable for monuments of the Peyto family, ancestors of Lord Willoughby de Broke.

NW is Windmill Hill with unusual stone windmill (1632) designed by Inigo Jones. Further W is Roman Fosse Way with site of ancient camp.

Chipping Campden (Glos). Former wool-centre and typical Cotswold town 9m from Evesham. The 14c church with 120 ft tower is notable for fine brasses and medieval embroidery collection. Old buildings include Grevel's House, 17c Market Hall (NT) and picturesque almshouses. Nearby is Dovers Hill (754 ft NT) scene of famous Cotswold Games. Ebrington, 3m E, is village of thatched cottages. 4m NE is Hidcote Bartrim with Hidcote Manor Garden (NT).

Chipping Norton (Oxon). Picturesque town on southern slopes of valley carved by tributary of the Evenlode river. Town Hall in Classical style. Perpendicular church with unusual hexagonal porch. Row of 17c almshouses in local stone. 4m N are the Rollright Stones (AM) famous prehistoric stone circle. 6m NW is Chastleton village with fine barn and Jacobean Chastleton House (open). 3m SW is Churchill, birthplace of Warren Hastings.

Chipping Sodbury (Glos). Old Cotswold market town with wide main street. 15c church with lofty tower. Horton Court (NT. Weds 2.30–6.30) is 3m NE. Dodington House is 2m SE. Badminton House 5m E. Dyrham Park (NT) is 4m S.

Cirencester (Glos). Attrative town, a touring and hunting centre. Sports facilities include swimming bath, bowls, tennis and squash, and clubs for football, cricket and hockey. Golf (2m). The broad market place is dominated by fine church with unique three-storeyed south porch. Corinium Museum, Park Street, preserves important finds of the Roman period. Cirencester Park (polo) with 3,000 acres, belongs to Earl Bathurst. A magnificent yew hedge protects house on its eastern side.

Clent Hills (Worcs). Range of bold hills (NT) SE of Stourbridge. Highest point Walton Hill (1,036 ft). Ancient camp site on Wychbury Hill, near Hagley.

Clifton Hampden (Oxon). Pretty Thames-side village among trees with modern bridge. Boating, bathing. Plough Inn. Caravan site. To N is wooded Nuneham Park.

Courton (Warws). Village on Birmingham–Alcester road which here follows the line of the Roman Ryknild Street. 15/16c church with rare bread cupboard, brasses and tombs of the Throckmortons. Their family seat, Coughton Court (NT open), is fine early 16c mansion noted for its Jacobite relics.

Coventry (Warws). Great manufacturing city and county borough on River Sherbourne 19m SE of Birmingham. The walls and tower of the ancient cathedral destroyed by bombs are dwarfed by the huge modern Cathedral designed by Sir Basil Spence and completed in 1962. The wartime bombing destroyed the city centre which has been rebuilt as highly modern traffic-free precinct. New buildings include the Art Gallery and

Museum, Civic Theatre, Colleges of Art and Technology and swimming baths. There are theatres, cinemas and provision for all sports including four golf courses. The Lady Godiva statue now stands in Broadgate, and a figure of 'Peeping Tom' is to be seen above a shop in Hertford Street. Old buildings include: Holy Trinity Church with spire rising to 231 feet; medieval St. Mary's Hall (AM); restored 14c spire (204 ft) of Christ Church; 15c St. John's Church; and fragments of old city wall may be seen behind Bond's Hospital.

Dorchester (Oxon). Charming village on River Thame close to junction with Thames. Picturesque old inns and houses. Abbey church has famous Jesse window, Norman font and shrine to St. Birinus, first bishop of Dorchester (634).

Droitwich (Worcs). Inland spa well-known for its brine baths used for treatment of rheumatic diseases. Droitwich Park has facilities for bowls, tennis and a unique sea-water swimming pool. Golf, hunting. There are some old half-timbered houses. R.C. Church with mosaics of Venetian tesserae. At Hampton Lovett, 2m N, is church with monument to Sir John Pakington, original of Addison's 'Sir Roger de Coverley'.

Dudley (Worcs). Iron and steel working centre. Famous zoo, sports, entertainments. Remains of 13c castle and older 12c priory. Wren's Nest Hill is nature reserve to NW.

Edge Hill (Warws). Long ridge, 5m long, between northern slopes of which and Kineton was fought bloody battle of Edge Hill in 1642 between the King and Parliamentary forces under Lord Essex. Edgehill Tower marks position of army of Charles I on morning of battle. Upton House (NT open).

Evesham (Worcs). Market town on River Avon and centre of fertile Vale of Evesham in fruit and vegetable growing district. 1m outside town is obelisk commemorating Simon de Montfort, killed in Battle of Evesham, August 4, 1265. Few remains of former abbey include Abbot Reginald's Tower (c. 1135) and fine Bell Tower. All Saints Church with some good glass, and St. Lawrence's Church with good fan tracery, share the same churchyard. The Abbey Almonry is now museum. Annual Horse Show in August.

Fairford (Glos). Old market town where John Keble, poet, was born. Good trout fishing in River Coln. Old Mill and several stone and half-timbered houses of interest. The church has wonderful stained glass.

Forest of Dean (Glos). Ancient Royal forest between rivers Severn and Wye offering very fine woodland scenery. On Speech House Hill, traditional centre of forest, is Speech House, now hotel, but formerly headquarters and court house of the ancient Forest Verderers.

Gloucester (Glos). County town and city on east bank of River Severn. Fine Cathedral with pinnacled central tower consists of Perpendicular exterior built around former Norman abbey church. Tomb of Edward II near high altar. The magnificent east window is largest ancient stained

Gloucester Cathedral

glass window in existence. Three Choirs Festival every third year. Folk Museum, Westgate Street, in house of Bishop Hooper, burned at stake 1555. His memorial is in the Square. Museum of Gloucester Regiment. City Museum with Roman relics. 15c New Inn has galleried courtyard. Sports facilities at Spa Field.

Goring (Oxon). Lovely resort on attractive stretch of Thames with boating, fishing, golf. Norman church has some good brasses. Opposite Goring is Streatley in Berkshire.

Henley-on-Thames (Oxon). Well-known riverside resort famous for its Royal Regatta held first week in July each year. Boating and coarse fishing. Golf, bowls and tennis. The picturesque Marsh Lock is 1m upstream.

Holt Fleet (Worcs). Picturesque riverside resort 6m N of Worcester with good fishing. Church shows Norman work. Of castle only 14c square tower remains (May–Sept, Thurs 10–1, 2–5).

Ilmington (Warws). Village on northern slopes of Cotswold hills with Ilmington Down (854 ft). Thatched stone houses, 11c manor house and restored church. Foxcote is 18c stone-built house with garden (open) and lake. Mern Hill (637 ft) 3m NW with Neolithic earthworks gives fine views over Vale of Evesham.

Kenilworth (Warws). Small county town with fine castle built in time of Henry I (AM). A few foundations remain of abbey founded by Geoffrey de Clinton in 1122. St. Nicholas Church (13c) has Norman doorway and marble monument by Westmacott. Stoneleigh Abbey, home of Lord Leigh, is 2m E.

Kineton (Warws). Small old-world town of old stone houses and church dating in part from time of Edward II but mainly rebuilt 1775. At Little Kineton are kennels of the Warwickshire Hunt. 3m SE is Edge Hill (700 ft) with fine views. In vicinity is Upton House (NT).

Leamington (Warws). Midland resort town on River Leam known for its medicinal waters. Good touring centre. Regency and early Victorian houses and tree-lined avenues are a feature of the town. The Royal Pump Room and Baths built over a spring provides modern hydrotherapy and physiotherapy services; swimming bath. Pump Room Gardens and Jephson Gardens, either side of the Victoria Bridge, are splendid riverside retreats with floral displays in season. All Saints Church (1843) has handsome pinnacled tower. Concerts at Pump Room and Town Hall (festival in June), cinema, sports facilities. Golf at Whitnash. Museum, Art Gallery and Library, Avenue Road. At 2m W is Warwick.

Lechlade (Glos). On quiet reach of River Thames with boating and fishing. In the churchyard Shelley wrote his 'Summer Evening'. The New Inn is over 600 years old.

Malvern (Worcs). Comprises six stone-built townships at northern end of Malvern Hills, together forming attractive inland resort. Entertainments and sports facilities. Priory Park with Winter Gardens and Festival Theatre, boating and sports. Priory church especially rich in 15c glass. Malvern College is well-known public school. At Malvern Wells above church is Holy Well, one of springs that first made Malvern famous. Chief heights of adjacent Malvern Hills, all giving widespread views are: North Hill (1307 ft), Worcestershire Beacon (1,395 ft) on which is St. Ann's Well, Sugarloaf (1,214 ft) and the Herefordshire Beacon (1,114 ft) with ancient British camp. At Guarlford the church bell hangs in a tree. At Madresfield, 2m NE, is moated seat of Earl of Beauchamp.

Mapledurham (Oxon). Delightful Thames-side resort at foot of Chilterns noted for beautiful scenery. Old mill, picturesque weir. Mapledurham House was long home of the Blount family. ½m upstream in beautiful reach of the river is Hardwick House.

Meriden (Warws). Scattered village 4m W of Coventry claiming to be in exact centre of England. Cyclists' National Memorial and medieval cross on the green. Church shows Norman masonry. To W is Forest Hall (1788) headquarters of the Woodmen of Arden. Archery meetings in summer.

Lower Slaughter

Naunton (Glos). Cotswold village on River Windrush. 15c pigeon house with over one thousand nest-holes.

Northleach (Glos). Market town and former wool trade centre. 17c almshouses. Church with 100 ft tower, battlemented and pinnacled roof and fine S porch. 1m NE is Hampnett where is unspoiled Norman church and tithe barn.

Oxford (Oxon). Historic University city and county town set between River Thames (here also known as Isis), and River Cherwell. Angling, boating and bathing. Launch excursions. Golf and other sports. Cinema, theatre. 'Eights' week in May. The University comprises over twenty colleges, halls and institutions, the oldest being University College (1249). The colleges, their chapels and grounds are generally open to visitors. University Botanic Garden is oldest of its kind in England. The Ashmolean Museum contains priceless collection of antiquities. The University Museum has important geological and mineral collections. The Pitts Rivers Museum serves University Department of Ethnology. The Museum of the History of Science has fine collection of scientific equipment. The Bodleian Library, with over three million books and manuscripts, carries statutory right to a copy of all copyright publications in Britain. 18c Radcliffe Camera is now Reading room. The Norman chapel of Christ Church is the city's cathedral and St. Mary the Virgin is University church. St. Michael-at-the-Northgate has Saxon tower once serving as a town defence. The Sheldonian Theatre was designed by Wren. Other buildings include the Divinity School, Clarendon Building (1772) and Rhodes House (1929).

Painswick (Glos). Attractive town of narrow streets on northern slopes of Cotswold hills. Early 15c church with famous churchyard yews. Painswick Beacon (922 ft) is good viewpoint (golf) with Kimsbury Camp, old hillfort, on summit. Haresfield Beacon (NT view indicator) 714 ft is 2m W.

Pershore (Worcs). Small town on River Avon in district noted for its plum orchards. Boating and coarse fishing in Avon. Famous Abbey church of 13c choir, Norman south transept and 14c tower. Elmsley Castle is attractive village 4m SE at foot of Bredon Hill.

Rugby (Warws). Prosperous industrial town well-known for its public school, founded 1567, at which Rugby Football originated in 1823. Important railway junction with railway and engineering works and other large industrial concerns. Important cattle market. Golf, tennis and other sports. Hunting centre for several packs. To SE, near Hillmorton, is G.P.O. wireless station.

Shottery (Warws). Picturesque hamlet 1m from Stratford-upon-Avon, and famous for home of Shakespeare's wife. Anne Hathaway's Cottage (open) is fine old timber-framed and thatched building, oldest parts of which are 15c. Other old cottages, dovecote and pigeon house.

Steeple Aston (Oxon). Hillside village overlooking River Cherwell 4m S of Deddington. Church with Norman font and good woodwork. 1½m S is Rousham House with its fine garden.

Stroud (Glos). Cloth manufacturing town. In Stratford Park are gardens and facilities for sports. Lypiatt Park, 2m E, has Gunpowder Plot associations. At Bisley is church with Norman font. Over Court is fine mansion once owned by Elizabeth I.

Stow-on-the-Wold (Glos). Northern Cotswold hill-town with lofty church with 14c tower. Old market cross and stocks. Picture gallery and museum. Fair in October.

Stratford-upon-Avon (Warws). World renowned market town where William Shakespeare (1564–1616) was born, lived and died. Boating and fishing on River Avon, annual regatta. Golf, tennis and bowls. Racecourse. Cinemas, theatre, Festival Club. 'Birthday' Celebrations on 23rd April and annual 'Mop' Fair in October. Holy Trinity Church contains the tomb and monument of Shakespeare and register entries of his baptism and burial. Properties of the Shakespeare Birthplace Trust open to the public include: Shakespeare's Birthplace, Henley Street; Hall's Croft, Old Town (home of his daughter Susanna and Dr John Hall); New Place, Chapel Street, where Shakespeare died: Nash's House (New Place Museum); Anne Hathaway's Cottage Shottery (1m); and Mary Arden's House, Wilmcote (3m). The Royal Shakespeare Theatre (1932) is in Waterside. Adjoining is the Library, Art Gallery and Museum. The Guild Chapel (1269) was founded for members of the Guild of the Holy Cross. Adjoining is original half-timbered Guild Hall and above it the Grammar School where Shakespeare attended. The Town Hall was built in 1767. Harvard House was maiden home of mother of John Harvard,

founder of Harvard College, U.S.A. Mason Croft (Shakespeare Institute) was once home of Marie Corelli.

Sutton Coldfield (Warws). One-time medieval market town now developed into modern residential municipal borough 7m N of Birmingham. Several golf courses and facilities for other sports. Sutton Park has lakes for boating, fishing and bathing. Rectory Park has large sports field and was scene in 1856 of first cricket game played by the Free Foresters Cricket Club. 13c parish church and Vesey Memorial Gardens. Barr Beacon (700 ft) to W is good viewpoint.

Tewkesbury (Glos). Ancient town at confluence of Avon and Severn rivers 10m N of Gloucester. Coarse fishing, sailing and boating. Norman Abbey Church with massive tower and seven-fold arch in west front. Chapels, chantries and tombs of medieval date. The Black Bear (1308) is reputed oldest inn in county.

Thame (Oxon). Old market town on River Thame with wide main street and notable old buildings from 15c. Church with high central tower, and Prebendal House with restored chapel, both date from 13c. Fine old inns. Thame Park is 1½m S. In Rycote Park, 3m W, is beautiful chapel (open daily).

Warwick (Warws). County town with boating and fishing on River Avon. Sports facilities in St. Nicholas Park. Racecourse. County Museum in Market Place. Annual fair in Oct. The 14c castle is seat of Earl of Warwick. In grounds is building housing the celebrated Warwick Vase. The

Collegiate Church of St. Mary was mainly rebuilt in 1704. The 15c Beachamp Chapel contains the grey Purbeck marble tomb of Richard Beauchamp (1382–1439). Of the town's former gateways, the E and W Gates remain, the latter with ancient chapel over. Lord Leycester's Hospital (open) is quaint half-timbered building from time of Henry VI. Oken's House is a Doll museum.

Waterperry (Oxon). Quiet village on River Thame 7m E of Oxford. Georgian manor house is now Horticultural School (occasionally open in Gardens Scheme). The church in grounds shows some Saxon and Norman work.

Watlington (Oxon). Quiet town of narrow streets and picturesque houses and 17c market hall. Church rebuilt in 1877 except for its 15c tower. Watlington Hill (NT) is large expanse of down and copse on Chilterns 1m SE.

Wilmcote (Warws). Village 3m NW of Stratord-upon-Avon famous for Mary Arden's House, home of Shakespeare's mother (open). In garden is square stone dovecote with 637 nesting holes. Old buildings house a museum of old farm implements.

Winchcombe (Glos). Quiet town of old houses, historic inns and church noted for its many gargoyles and battlemented tower. George Inn with medieval gallery. Ancient stocks in front of Town Hall. Sudeley Castle is 1m S and Hailes Abbey (AM and NT) 2m NE.

Witney (Oxon). Market town on W bank of River Windrush busy with blanket making and light engineering. Pillared Buttercross incorporates part of old market cross and the Blanket Hall (1721) has a curious clock. At Cogges, 1m SE, the church (1100), vicarage and manor house (c. 1250) are of interest.

Woodstock (Oxon). Small town, a Royal manor in Saxon times, with main street lined by stone houses. Edward, the Black Prince was born in the borough. S and W is magnificent park and lake with Blenheim Palace (open). Further S is Bladon in the churchyard of which lies Sir Winston Churchill.

Wootton under Edge (Glos). Old Cotswold market town on high ground. 14c church with lofty pinnacled tower and good brasses. Ancient Tolsey in High Street. Edward Jenner, discoverer of vaccination, educated at Grammar School and Isaac Pitman was schoolmaster here. To S is Newark Park (NT).

Worcester (Worcs). County town on River Severn. Angling, boating, bowls, tennis and golf. County cricket ground off New Road. Racecourse on Pitchcroft. Worcester Royal Porcelain Factory and Museum (open). City Library, Museum and Art Gallery. Restored Cathedral with central tower. Three Choirs Festival every third year. Interesting churches and buildings include Trinity House; St. Helen's Church originating from 680; The Commandery, an almshouse founded in 1085; Guildhall with Queen Anne facade; and numerous 16c timbered houses.

Welsh Borders

Cheshire—Shropshire—Herefordshire

Cheshire

The northernmost county of the region and predominantly agricultural, producing the famous cheese. Architecturally it is famous for its 'magpie' or black and white buildings, wonderful examples of which are to be found in almost all towns and villages. The county town is Chester, an important city with a wealth of interest and beauty. There are both seaside and riverside resorts. The Wirral peninsula, between the Mersey and Dee estuaries, has a sea frontage of good sand and New Brighton, Hoylake and West Kirby are popular resorts. The River Dee provides opportunity for boating and fishing. Picturesque scenery is to be found along the River Dane and in the Goyt Valley. There are notable churches showing Norman work. Tatton Park, Lyme Park and Little Moreton Hall are but three of the many stately houses and gardens open to the public.

Shropshire

Shropshire, also known as Salop, is the largest of our inland counties. It is bounded on the N by Cheshire, on the S by Herefordshire, the E by the Black Country and to the W by Wales. The River Severn flows through the heart of the county. North of the river the land is flat with small lakes or 'meres' around Ellesmere. To the S are hill ranges and wooded valleys. Shrewsbury is the county town and, with Ludlow, is famous for beautiful half-timbered buildings. Both towns are good touring centres as also are Church Stretton and Ellesmere. There are numerous small and friendly towns and villages of dignity and beauty. The county has much to offer the sportsman and summertime pursuits include golf, tennis, bowls, sailing and gliding. National Hunt meetings are held at Ludlow, while motorcycle scrambles and hill climbing are popular.

Welsh Borders

Reproduced by kind permission of Map Productions Ltd.

Herefordshire

This county forms the southern portion of the region, being bounded on the N by Shropshire, the W by the Welsh mountains, on the E by Worcestershire and Gloucestershire, and on the S by Monmouthshire. The River Wye, a famous salmon fishing river, flows through the county via Hereford and Ross to reach its supreme loveliest at Symonds Yat. With the exception of Hereford, the county town, there are few large towns, but each and every village or hamlet with its distinctive black and white houses and old inns is a delight to the eye. There are numerous prehistoric remains and much evidence of Roman occupation, and many abbeys, castles and manor houses reflect bygone days.

Of Special Interest

Adlington Hall (5m N of Macclesfield). 15c Great Hall, Elizabethan 'black and white' portion and 18c S front. Easter–Sept, Sats, Suns and Bk Hols, 2.30–6.

Arley Hall Gardens (Northwich). Topiary garden and flowering shrubs. The house (Viscount and Viscountess Ashbrook) not shown. Gardens. May–Sept, Sats, Suns and Bk Hols, 2.30–7.

Attingham Park (4m SE of Shrewsbury). House designed by George Steuart for first Lord Berwick. Remarkable interior decoration. Extensive park. NT. State rooms. Easter–Sept. Weds, Thurs and Bk Hols, 2–6.

Beeston Castle (2m W of Banbury). 13c stronghold on steep hill, almost impregnable. (AM Standard hours.)

Benthall Hall (4m NE of Much Wenlock). 16c stone house, carved staircase, plasterwork. Shrub garden. NT Easter–Sept, Tues, Weds, Sats, Bk Hol Mons, 2–6.

Berrington Hall (3m N of Leominster). Built in 1778 by Henry Holland with fine plasterwork. Choice trees and plants in Capability Brown grounds. NT. Easter–Sept, Weds, Sats and Bk Hols, 2–6.

Bramall Hall (Bramall, 2m S of Stockport). 15c half-timbered mansion. Daily except Thurs, Apr–Sept, 10–1, 2–7. Oct–Mar, 11–4.

Brockhampton (2m E of Bromyard). Large estate of typical Herefordshire farmland and woods. Lower Brockhampton is small half-timbered moated manor house of c. 1400. NT. Mons, Weds, Fris, Sats, 10–6. Suns, 10–1.

Buildwas Abbey (11m SE of Shrewsbury). 12c Cistercian abbey in fine setting on river Severn. (AM Standard hours.)

Burford House Gardens (1m W of Tenbury Wells). Close to river Teme, beautiful gardens of shrub and herbaceous plants. May–Sept, daily, 2–5.

Chester Castle (Chester). The Agricola Tower of the 19c castle contains museum of Cheshire Regiment. Apr–Oct, daily except Mons, 10–12.30 and 2–6.

Croft Castle (5m NW of Leominster). Welsh Border castle of 14c or 15c origin of ancient walls and round corner towers of pink stone. Fine Georgian-Gothic staircase and ceilings. NT. Easter–Sept, Weds, Thurs, Sats, Suns and Bk Hols, also Sats, Suns in Oct, 2.15–6.

Dorfold Hall (1m W of Nantwich). Jacobean gabled house c. 1616. Panelling, plasterwork and furniture. May–Sept, Mons, 2–5.

Eastnor Castle (2m E of Ledbury). Early 19c house built by first Earl of Somers. Furnishings, armour, pictures. June–Sept, Suns and Bk Hols, 2.15–6.

Eye Manor (4m N of Leominster). Built 1680. Fine interior plasterwork, furniture, pictures, arts and crafts. Easter–Sept, Suns, Weds, Thurs, Sats, Bk Hol Mons and Tues, 2.30–5.30. Also Sats, Suns only in Oct.

Gawsworth Hall (3m SW of Macclesfield). Fine 'black and white' building. Former home of Mary Fitton, supposed 'dark lady' of Shakespeare's sonnets. Tilting ground. Pictures, armour and furniture. Grounds. Apr–Oct, Weds, Sats, Suns, 2–7.

Goodrich Castle (3m SW of Ross). Important example of military architecture, 12c–14c, in beautiful Wye Valley setting. One time residence of Earls of Shrewsbury. (AM Standard hours).

Haughmond Abbey (3½m NE of Shrewsbury). Extensive remains of Augustinian canons' house. Chapter house, infirmary hall and abbots' lodging well preserved. (AM Standard hours).

Hodnet Hall Gardens (6m SW of Market Drayton). Notable 60–acre landscape gardens. Apr–Sept, daily 2–5, Suns and Bk Hols, 12–6.30.

Lilleshall Abbey (4½m S of Newport). Abbey of Augustinian canons. Remains of 12/13c church and claustral buildings (AM Standard hours).

Little Moreton Hall (4m SW of Congleton). Wonderful example of 'black and white' building, moat, long gallery, great hall and chapel. NT. Mar–Oct, daily except Tues, 2–8 or dusk.

Lyme Park (6½m SE of Stockport). Elizabethan house with elaborate rooms and saloon. Gardens and deer park. (NT). Mar–Nov, 1–6.15. Park and Gardens, 8–dusk.

Shipton Hall (6m SW of Much Wenlock). Elizabethan manor house. Fine interior, stable block. May–Sept, Thurs, 2.30–5.30.

Tatton Park (3½m N of Knutsford). Late 18c house by the Wyatts. Pictures, furniture and silver. 54-acre garden and 2,000-acre park with lake. NT. Apr–Oct, daily except Mons, 2–6. Park also Nov–Mar.

Wenlock Priory (Much Wenlock). Ruins of Cluniac Priory of 1080. Also Priors' lodge with two-storeyed gallery. (AM always open).

Wilderhope Manor (7m E of Church Stretton). 16c limestone house, 17c plasterwork, in wooded country. Now a Youth Hostel. Apr–Sept, Weds, 2.30–5.30.

Gawsworth Hall

Resorts and Centres of Interest

Acton Burnell (Salop). Attractive small town with notable E.E. church and ruined 13c fortified manor house (weekdays and Sun afternoons).

Alderley Edge (Ches). Residential town below Alderley Edge (NT 650 ft) a fine viewpoint embracing the Cheshire plain and the Pennines. 2m S is Nether Alderley where is Alderley Old Mill (NT) and notable church.

Atcham (Salop). River Severn village where modern bridge carries the Holyhead road. The church shows Saxon and Norman work. Attingham Park (NT) is remarkable for its interior decoration.

Birkenhead (Ches). County borough on W bank of River Mersey opposite Liverpool with which it is linked by ferry and the Mersey Tunnel. The extensive docks form part of the Port of Liverpool. Parish church built 1822 in grounds of ruined 12c priory (open). Adjoining the borough in the N is Wallasey with the popular resort of New Brighton.

Bishop's Castle (Salop). Small borough in picturesque and hilly Clun Forest district. The steep, winding streets show some old timbered houses. There are fragments of an old castle and the timbered 'House on Crutches' (1573) is of interest.

Bosbury (Here). 4m SW of Ledbury. Picturesque half-timbered houses and an ancient church, its 12c tower standing 80 feet away from the main building. Parts of ruined palace of Bishops of Hereford are incorporated in old farm buildings.

Bredwardine (Here). Delightfully situated on River Wye with old six-arched bridge, ancient church containing curious carvings and only foundations of its castle. Fine views from Bredwardine Hill and Merbach Point (1,000 ft). On Merbach Hill is King Arthur's Stone, a cromlech 18 ft long. On the river 2m SE is Moccas, an old village with notable Norman church.

Bridgnorth (Salop). The River Severn divides this busy town into Low Town and High Town, the two being connected by an exceptionally steep funicular railway. The church was built by Telford in 1794. Many black and white half-timbered buildings. Restored N Gate (museum). A steeply sloping tower is only remnant of a Norman castle.

Bromyard (Here). Small market town of winding streets and a number of half-timbered houses. Norman church. 2½m E is Lower Brockhampton (NT). Good walking centre for Frome Valley and neighbouring Downs.

Buildwas (Salop). Old village on River Severn noted for the picturesque ruin of the Cistercian Buildwas Abbey (AM). To E is Coalbrookdale with fine scenery.

Burwarton (Salop). Pleasant village SW of Bridgnorth. 3m NW is Brown Clee Hill (1,790 ft) with fine views over Wenlock Edge.

The Dee at Chester

Chester (Ches). Historic county town and cathedral city, the former Roman city of Deva, on the River Dee. Holiday resort and good touring and shopping centre. Entertainment and sports facilities including golf and racing on the Roodee by the river. Zoological gardens at Upton. The walls, of red sandstone, mainly medieval, link many ancient towers and gateways. The 14c cathedral originates from a Benedictine abbey and is notable for its monastic remains. St. John the Baptist Church dates from the late 11c. The Castle (AM Regimental museum) was mainly rebuilt in 18/19c. St. Mary's Church contains old monuments. The Wishing Steps were built in 1785. The famous Rows are a distinctive feature and consist of double tiers of shops with raised pedestrian footways. A vast Roman amphitheatre is in process of excavation and many Roman relics are to be seen in the Grosvenor Museum. The River Dee provides good boating and excursions are run to Heron Bridge, Eccleston Ferry and Ironbridge.

Church Stretton (Salop). Small holiday town in pleasant wooded dale at foot of the Long Mynd (1,696 ft). The Welsh Border hills hereabouts come within an Area of Outstanding Beauty.

Claverley (Salop). Norman to Perpendicular church with 12c murals. 15c vicarage. 1m NE is Ludstone Hall, noted Jacobean mansion with moat.

Clun (Salop). Welsh border town. Church has picturesque old lych-gate. Massive square keep of Norman castle remains. Clun Forest to W. 4m SE is Hopton Castle, a typical Shropshire village of half-timbered houses and retaining a fine keep from its Norman castle.

Condover (Salop). Small town with several interesting houses and 17c church with some Norman work. Condover Hall (School for Blind) is stonebuilt 16c mansion (open in Aug). 3m SE is Pitchford Hall.

Congleton (Ches). Busy market town on River Dane (boating). Several picturesque old buildings and inns. 5m S is Mow Cop (NT) with 18c sham ruins.

Craven Arms (Salop). Livestock centre in beautiful well-wooded valley of the River Ommy. To S is Stokesay Castle a fine medieval fortified manor (open daily).

Diddlebury (Salop). Hamlet in Corvedale 5m NW of Craven Arms. The church shows herring-bone work.

Dinmore Hill (Here). Well wooded viewpoint (NT) 6m from Hereford overlooking the Lugg Valley. Dinmore Manor is 16c house with detached 12/14c chapel (chapel and gardens Apr–Sept, 2–6).

Eardisland (Here). Lovely little village of black and white houses clustering near bridge over River Arrow. St. Mary's Church is old stone building with 12c nave. Adjoining is the quaint Pigeon House. Staick House is charming old timbered house (14c). Leominster is 5m W.

Eardisley (Here). The 13/14c church has finely sculptured Norman font. Black and white houses. Traces of British and Roman encampments in the parish.

Ellesmere (Salop). Small dairy farming centre with many picturesque features. The 19c church preserves a 15c Oteley chapel and many early monuments. Adjoining the town are a series of lakes or 'meres' on some of which fishing and boating are available. A branch of the Shropshire Union Canal extends into the town and is used for boating.

Fownhope (Here). River Wye village 5m SE of Hereford with some old black and white houses, ancient inn and church with a Norman tower. The old village stocks and whipping post are preserved.

Gawsworth (Ches). Attractive old village with church with yews, fishponds, half-timbered 15c rectory and Tudor Old Hall. 3m SE is Bosley.

Goodrich (Here). Village on W bank of River Wye 5m SW of Ross-on-Wye. The church has some good glass. The castle (AM) is of great interest. Wordsworth associations. Below the village is Kerne Bridge with barn the only remnant of Flanesford Priory founded in 1346.

Habberley (Salop). Well situated village 2m S of Pontesbury. Small Early English church. Fine views.

Heath (Salop). Tiny village 3m SE of Munslow close to Brown Clee Hill. The little church is exquisite example of Norman architecture.

Hereford (Here). The county town and a cathedral city on the River Wye set among wooded vales, green fields and orchards. There are various entertainments, and sports facilities include boating, bowls, tennis and golf. Racecourse. Three-Choirs music festival every three years. Parts of the old city walls may still be seen. The Old House (furniture and loan exhibitions) is good example of Jacobean residence. The cathedral, a mixture of many styles, contains a rare Mappa Mundi, a medieval map of the world. The chained library is the largest of its kind in the world. The Bishop's Palace retains Norman timber pillars. City library, museum and art gallery. The Red Coat Hospital is picturesque old almshouse. Dinedor Hill, 2½m SE gives fine views. About 2m along Abergavenny road is Belmont Abbey.

Hoylake (Ches). Popular Wirral resort with sandy beach and good bathing. Long sunny parade. Parks and gardens with facilities for tennis, putting and bowls. Famous golfing centre. To S beyond Hilbre Point is West Kirby, another popular resort.

Kilpeck (Here). Village 9m SW of Hereford. The church is remarkable example of Romanesque architecture with profusely ornamented S doorway of symbolic carving and zig-zag moulding. The castle site of earthworks and two portions of its walls gives extensive views.

Kington (Here). Small town in hilly scenery in Radnor Forest. Old church with Norman tower. The picturesque Stanner Rocks are 3m SW.

Ledbury (Here). One of the county's chief towns and birthplace of John Masefield, Poet Laureate. A number of black and white houses, particularly the Old Market House in the main street. The church has detached tower with spire and contains many interesting memorials. 2m E is Eastnor Castle (q.v.).

Leominster (Here). Quaint old borough, 12½m N of Hereford in Lugg Valley at junction of that river with River Pinsley. The Priory Church is unusual in that it has three naves. In it is preserved one of the few perfect

Shrewsbury

ducking stools left in England. 3m N is Berrington Hall (NT). 4m S is Hampton Court a fine castellated mansion and home of Viscount Hereford. 6m NW is Croft Castle (NT). Yarpole (5m N), Eyton (2m NW) and Kingsland (4m NW) have all beautiful churches of note.

Ludlow (Salop). Picturesque old town on River Corve and River Teme (fishing) in charming district. Good sports facilities including golf and horse-racing. The castle is important feature and the ruins include one of the five round churches built by the Templars. Timbered black and whilte buildings of note include the Readers' House and the Feathers Hotel. Of old inns there are the Angel and the Bull, and St Giles Hospital, Lane's Hospital, the Tolsey and Ludford House are noteworthy. 4m E is Whitton Court, an Elizabethan mansion with terraced garden (Apr–Sept, Thurs and Suns, 2–6).

Mordiford (Here). At junction of Rivers Lugg and Wye in charming scenery. In churchyard is an ancient cross.

Much Wenlock (Salop). Charming market town below Wenlock Edge 8m NW of Bridgnorth. There are many half-timbered houses and some of the streets are narrow and winding. The Guildhall has good oak panelling and the old stocks are preserved. Wenlock Priory dates from 1080 (AM Standard hours).

Munslow (Salop). 6m NW of Craven Arms. Village of half-timbered houses and inns. The church has Norman work and some good early glass. 2m S is Diddlebury, a Corvedale hamlet where the church shows Saxon work.

Nantwich (Ches). Town noted for its cheeses and brine baths. There are notable old almshouses and some picturesque black and white buildings. St. Mary's Church is cruciform building with central octagonal tower. Churche's Mansion (1577) is fine example of Elizabethan merchant's house. 5m SE is Doddington Hall. 1m W is Dorfield Hall, a Jacobean gabled house (open).

New Brighton (Ches). Popular Wirral resort on west bank of estuary of River Mersey and part of county borough of Wallasey. Promenade, pier and many facilities for entertainment and sport. Firm sands. One of the largest sea-water swimming pools in the world. Golf.

Oswestry (Salop). Old market town and industrial centre set between pastoral lowlands to the E and the hilly Berwyns to the W. The church several times rebuilt is mostly 19c.

Pitchford (Salop). Quiet village 3m SE of Condover. Pitchford Hall dating from 16c is elaborate half-timbered mansion.

Richard's Castle (Here). Village 4m SW of Ludlow where castle (fragments) was one of first to be built in England. Pleasing half-timbered houses. Church with detached tower.

Ross-on-Wye (Here). Small town on high ground on left bank of River Wye close to the county's SE borders with Gloucestershire and Monmouthshire. Splendid centre for Wye Valley excursions. Boating. Golf at Gorsley, 5m E. The Market Hall is red sandstone building erected in time of Charles II. The 13c church overlooks the town. In churchyard is old plague cross. 3m SW is Goodrich Castle (AM).

Rushbury (Salop). Pleasant Ape Dale village below Wenlock Edge 3m E of Hope Bowlder. Old packhorse bridge.

St. Weonards (Here). Old village with fine church where Myners Chapel has some 16c glass of note.

Shifnal (Salop). Old town on main Holyhead road and once a busy coaching station. Featured in Dickens 'Old Curiosity Shop'. A number of half-timbered houses and inns.

Shrawardine (Salop). Pleasant small village 7m NW of Shrewsbury close to River Severn. 17c church and timbered houses. Shrawardine Pool is bird sanctuary.

Shrewsbury (Salop). Ancient county town showing some old narrow streets and picturesque half-timbered houses. It is situated on a hill surrounded on three sides by the looping River Severn. Four bridges of note cross the river. Parts of the pink sandstone castle were converted to residential use by Telford in 18c and are now used by local council. The old Council House has picturesque half-timbered gateway (17c). The old Market Hall in the Square was built in 1596. The Abbey church is sole remains of extensive 11c Benedictine monastery. Opposite is an ornate 14c canopied pulpit. St. Mary's church with graceful spire is noted for its stained glass including a Jesse window of 1345. The town walls include a 14c tower (NT). There is a museum, library and art gallery. Boating and regattas. Floral fete. Park and recreation ground. Popular excursions are to Haughmond Abbey (4m NE), Attingham (NT 4m SE), Buildwas Abbey (11m SE), Wroxeter (6m SE), and Condover Hall (5m S). 10m S lies the Wrekin (1,330 ft) from which there are magnificent widespread views.

Symonds Yat (Here). Famous beauty spot in bend of River Wye 6m N of Monmouth. The actual Yat rock is 500 ft high and commands a magnificent view in every direction. Good centre for boating trips and rambling in beautiful riverside scenery.

Tong (Salop). Small village associated with Dickens 'Old Curiosity Shop' as being where Little Nell died. 15c church with many monuments and brasses. 3m E. is Boscobel House (AM Standard hours).

Vowchurch (Here). Delightful village in picturesque Golden Valley, SE of Hay-on-Wye. The church has some good woodwork.

Weobley (Here). Attractive old village of half-timbered houses and buildings—some dating from 15c—a 14c church and earthworks of an old castle. Good walking centre.

West Kirby (Ches). Wirral holiday resort facing SW across the wide estuary of the River Dee. Sandy beach. Marine lake. Swimming baths. The Grange and Caldy Hills are preserved as open spaces. The Hilbre Islands are the haunt of seals and many birds.

Wigmore (Here). Village of half-timbered cottages amid the well-wooded Mortimer Forest. Slight remains of Wigmore Abbey.

East Anglia

Essex—Norfolk—Suffolk

Mountains apart, East Anglia has enough diversity to satisfy every type of holidaymaker, from a bracing coast and a network of inland lakes to an undulating and wooded countryside punctuated with homely villages and mellow old towns. Complementing the landscape, captured on the canvases of Constable and Gainsborough, are the many historic buildings —'pargeted' cottages, flush-flint parish churches and great Tudor houses.

Essex

London has spilled over into the SW corner of Essex. Outside this area, beyond the great forest of Epping, there remains the Essex of farmland and stream, village and market town. Between the sophisticated holiday resorts in the S and NW are the hauntingly desolate marshlands and the yachting centres on the creeks and inlets of the many deep estuaries, the home of hosts of wading birds and wildfowl.

Norfolk

Near-islanded by sea and river, Norfolk displays a landscape of wide horizons and cloud-filled skies that inspired one of the greatest schools of painting in England. Elements in the scene are high heaths and fir forests, marshes and reed-fringed broads, wheatfields and purple-heathered moorlands, sea-saltings and dune-backed beaches overlooked by resorts both big and small. With its cathedral towns, Dutch-like ports, ancient manor houses and reed-thatched cottages, urban Norfolk is no less varied.

111

Suffolk

Primarily agricultural, Suffolk has suffered less from industrialisation than any other county. Undulating rather than hilly, the domesticated countryside is characterised by cornfields, heathlands, wooded valleys— and few large towns. The constantly-eroding coastline with its broad estuaries is accessible only in places, for there is no continuous coast road. Yet winding byways abound. It is to the unhurried tourist on these that Suffolk reveals its unspoilt charm.

Of Special Interest

Audley End (Essex, 4m NE Newport). Great Jacobean house (AM) built by Earl of Suffolk in 17c. Altered by Vanbrugh in 1721. Fine collection of paintings and furniture. Miniature railway. Refreshments. Apr–Oct, Tues–Suns, 11.30–5.30, also Bk Hols.

Blicking Hall (Norfolk, 1½m NW Aylsham). House with Dutch gables (NT) built 1616–28 and altered in 18c. State rooms, 130-ft gallery, paintings and tapestries. Formal gardens and lake. Easter Sat–first Sun in Oct, Weds, Thurs, Sats and Bk Hols, 2–6.

Bradwell Lodge (Essex, 7m NE Southminster). Small Georgian mansion with Adam wing, Apr–Sept, Weds and Sats and Bk Hols, 3–6. Nearby (2m) is church of St. Peter on the Wall, built by St Cedd in 654.

Bressingham Gardens (Norfolk, 2½m W Diss). Five acres of informal gardens with 5,000 species of hardy plants. Miniature railway. Collection of restored railway engines and road vehicles. Last Sun in May–first Sun Oct, Thurs and Suns, 1.30–6.30. Refreshments.

Fritton Old Hall (Suffolk, 7m SW Yarmouth). Gardens with rare shrubs and plants, woods, lake (fishing, boating), May–Oct, daily.

Gosfield Hall (Essex, 2½m W Halstead). Imposing Tudor mansion restored and added to in 19c with fine gallery, all year, Weds, Thurs, 2–5.

Grimes Graves (Norfolk, 7m NW Thetford). Flint mines (AM) made by neolithic man, who sank shafts of up to 40-ft depth from which galleries led off in all directions. Two of the 16 shafts already excavated accessible.

Haughley Park (Suffolk, 8m E Bury St Edmunds). Elizabethan manor built in 1620 on E-plan in an extensive park, May–end Sept, Tues, 3–6.

Helmingham (Suffolk, 7m N Ipswich). Tudor manor in deer park, built by the Tollemache family. Ringed by moat over which drawbridge still drawn up nightly.

Heveningham Hall (Suffolk, 8m N Framlingham). Exceptional Palladio-style house designed by Sir Robert Taylor in 1779 in parkland landscaped by Capability Brown. Apr–Oct, Thurs and Suns, 2–5.30, Sat also in Jun–Sept and Tues–Suns in Aug. Refreshments.

Holkham Hall (Norfolk, 3m W Wells next the Sea). Palladian mansion by Sir Thomas Coke. Built 1734–59 on H-plan, with four wings to central section.

Heveningham Hall

Lavishly decorated interior planned to give vistas of connecting rooms. Jun–Sept, Thurs, 2–5, Jul–Aug, Mons and Thurs, 2–5.

Ickworth (Suffolk, 4m SW Bury St. Edmunds). Oval-shaped house (NT) planned by fourth earl of Bristol in 1792 to contain art collection but completed only in 1830. Interior notable for Regency and French furniture and fine collection of paintings, silver and objets d'art. Easter Sat–first Sun October, Weds, Thurs, Sats, Suns, 2–6.

Ingatestone Hall (Essex. 7m SW Chelmsford). Brick-built house dating from c. 1545. Portraits, armorial china and rare 16c virginal in long gallery, over 3m documents in archives in NW wing. Apr–Oct, Tues–Sats, 10–12.30 and 2–4.30.

Layer Marney Tower (Essex, 8m SW Colchester). Large 16c gatehouse, May–Sept, Sats, 2–6.

Leiston Abbey (Suffolk, 4½m N Aldeburgh). Remains of abbey (AM) founded 1182 and transferred to this spot 200 years later. Early 16c gatehouse with turrets.

Norfolk Wild Life Park (Gt. Witchingham, 12m NW Norwich). One of Europe's largest game parks. Licensed restaurant. All year, daily, 10.30–6.30 or sunset.

Norton Gardens and Petsenta (Suffolk, 9m E Bury St. Edmunds). Animals, birds and flowers in natural setting. Children's playground. Refreshments. Daily, 2–dusk.

Oxburgh Hall. Stoke Ferry (Norfolk, 7m SW Swaffham). Moated 15c house with large gatehouse (NT) set in extensive parklands, Easter Sat–first Sun Oct, Weds, Thurs, Sats and Suns, 2–6.

Paycocke's House, Coggleshall (Essex, 6m E Braintree). Early 16c home of Tudor woolmaker (NT), with exceptional panelling and carved timbers.

Sandringham (Norfolk). In absence of Court, church and gardens open May, Jun and Sept, Weds and Thurs, 11–5, Jul and Aug, Tues–Fris, 11–5.

Stansted Wildlife Park (Essex, 4m NNE Bishop's Stortford). Britain's largest private bird sanctuary, daily, 11–sunset.

Waltham Abbey Gatehouse and Bridge (Essex). 14c gatehouse (AM). Undercroft museum in nearby abbey church.

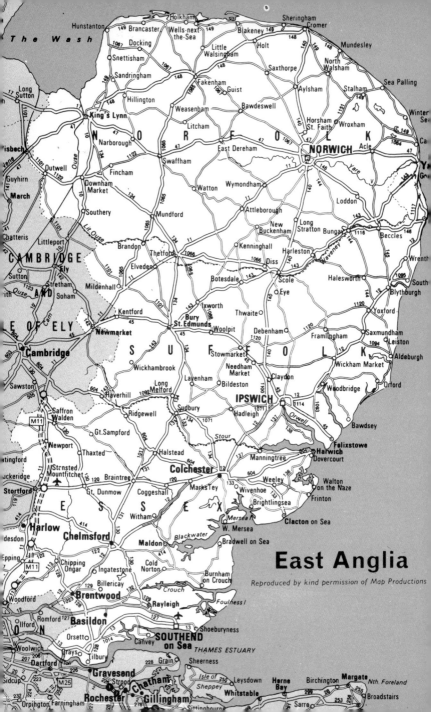

Resorts and Centres of Interest

Aldeburgh (Suffolk). 15c port, 18c watering place and now developing a reputation as a music centre. English Opera Group festival held annually since 1948. Early 16c two-storey moot hall with external stair to upper floor hung with ancient maps and prints; all year. Mons–Sats 10.30–12, 2.30–5, Suns 2.30–6.

Beccles (Suffolk). Popular angling and boating centre on river Waveney. 14c church with adjacent bell tower and interesting Georgian houses. Open air swimming pool.

Blakeney (Norfolk). Remote village, one-time seaport now 2m from sea over salt marshes. Fishing and wild fowling. Yacht club. Boat trips to Blakeney Point, wild bird and rare plant reserve (NT).

Brightlingsea (Essex). On creek in Colne estuary. Yachting, boating, fishing and bathing from firm sand and mud. On first Monday after St Andrew's Day annual 400-yr-old ceremony when town swears allegiance to mayor of Sandwich in memory of its former links with Cinque Ports. Church contains fine brasses and interesting sculpture. Timbered Tudor house, Jacob's Hall.

Broads, The. 'Meres' or lakes (flooded peat diggings) in flat marshlands of Norfolk and Suffolk increasingly popular for boating, sailing and fishing. They are linked by around 100m of navigable waterways, the three main rivers being the Bure, Yare and Waveney, which enter Breydon Water before flowing into the sea at Yarmouth. Other important Broads are Oulton, Hickling, Horsey and Barton. (See Potter Heigham, Caister on Sea, Gt Yarmouth, Horning and Wroxham).

Bungay (Suffolk). Market town in Waveney valley. Ruined 12c castle (AM) built by the Bigod family. Many attractive 18c red brick houses built after catastrophic fire in 1688. Butter Cross (1689) in market place and Norman Holy Trinity church with 16c and 17c woodwork.

Burnham on Crouch (Essex). On crouch estuary, one of East Coast's most popular yachting centres also notable for its oyster beds, boat and yacht building and abundance of wild fowl.

Bury St. Edmunds (Suffolk). Chief town of W Suffolk and the place to which the body of the saint was brought after his martyrdom by the Danes at Hoxne. Many 17c houses. Two parish churches, St. Mary's, with an interesting interior, and St. James's, now a cathedral. In market place, 12c Moyses Hall, now museum with rare exhibits. Angel Corner, fine Queen Anne house containing Gershom-Parkington collection of clocks and watches, daily except Suns 10–1 and 2–5. Angel Hotel, where Dickensian characters of Pickwick and Sam Weller stayed. Guildhall of 15c with ornamented doorway and Cupola House, 17c, with cantilevered second floor, are noteworthy. Hengrave Hall (3m NW) mansion enclosing interior courtyard, built by Sir Thomas Kytson in 1530, with hammer-

115

beam ceiling and minstrel's gallery in banqueting hall, twin-turreted gatehouse and main entrance with Renaissance carving; now convent school, open by appointment.

Caister on Sea (Norfolk). Seaside resort convenient for the Broads. Largest parish church in England. Gatehouse and 100 ft tower, remnants of Caister Castle, now housing vintage car collection, May–Oct, daily 10–6, St. George's Fishermen's hospital (AM), early 17c.

Canvey Island (Essex). In Thames estuary, approached by bridge from Benfleet. Two miles of sandy beaches along S coast. Dutch Cottage Museum (8m W) with collection of model ships, Whitsun to last weekend in Sept, Wed, Sats and Suns, 2.30–5.

Castle Acre (Norfolk). Village with main street spanned by 13c gateway of ruined 11c motte and bailey fortress. Of Cluniac priory (AM) c. 1090, the sacristy, prior's lodging (11c) with 14c murals, and 15c gatehouse remain. Near priory is St. James's church, 13–15c, with 15c paintings on rood screen and perpendicular font-cover retaining some original colouring.

Castle Hedingham (Essex). 5m NW Halstead. Quaint old village with good examples of Georgian and medieval houses. Keep with walls 11 ft thick only remnant of 12c castle built by the powerful de Vere family, May–Sept, Tues, Thurs and Sats, 2–6.

Castle Rising (Norfolk). Once a port, now an inland village. The castle (AM), built by Earl of Sussex in 1150 on some of the most spectacular earthworks in Britain not yet fully excavated, is encircled by moat and 64 ft high rampart; well-preserved keep. Nearby Bede House, founded 1614 as home for twelve spinsters; the women sometimes wear a Jacobean costume of high-peaked black hat and red cloak.

Chelmsford (Essex). County town with remarkable shire hall (1791). Original square tower of cathedral houses 17c library. Victorian house in park contains Chelmsford and Essex museum of historical, archeological and anthropological specimens, Mons–Sats 10–5, Suns 2–5. Interesting villages nearby are Writtle and Springfield (the deserted village of Oliver Goldsmith).

Clacton (Essex). One of Britain's most popular seaside resorts, with well-organised range of entertainments and miles of safe, sandy beaches. Day excursions to France. Annual events include fishing festival, carnival, regatta and beauty and amateur talent competitions.

Colchester (Essex). First Roman town in Britain (Camulodunum), still part-encircled by wall designed to protect rebuilt city following its sacking by Boadicea in AD 61–2. N of wide High Street, 11c Norman castle (AM) with walls up to 30 ft thick housing museum rich in Roman relics, daily 10–5. Suns (Apr–Sept) 2.30–5. Georgian mansion ('Hollytrees') contains period furniture and medieval antiquities, Mons–Sats, 10–5. Albert Hall gallery of paintings, many by local artists. Norman St. Botolph's priory (AM), ruined during 12-week siege of the town by Royalist forces in 1648. Famous oyster fisheries in estuary of Colne, the river on which Colchester stands (annual oyster feast in late October). Gun Hill Place, Dedham (5m NE) has 30-acre garden of azaleas and rhododendrons, with aviary and lake, mid-Apr–early May, Jun–early Sept, 2–7.

Cromer (Norfolk). Family resort with cliffs and firm sands. Angling, crab and lobster fishing. Golf course adjoins lighthouse, open weekday afternoons. Zoo. Horse-riding (excellent bridle paths). Cromer lifeboat station guards dangerous sandbanks of Sheringham Shoal and Haisboro offshore. Birdland, on main coast road, with extensive collection of British and other birds. Small resorts nearby, all with sandy beaches, are Overstrand, Sidestrand and Trimingham.

East Bergholt (Suffolk). Birthplace of Constable. 18c Flatford Mill and house, once owned by the artist's father, appears in the Hay Wain painting. Nearby 17c Willy Lott's cottage, charmingly set beside the millstream (no admittance to interiors). Nayland and Wissingham (6m W) are two attractive villages with interesting churches and old buildings.

Epping Forest (Essex). Acquired as an open space by London County Council (now GLC) in 1878, extensive woodlands covering 6,000 acres. Trees are silver birch, oak, beech and characteristic hornbeam. Many bridle paths. Noted beauty spots include Epping Thicks, The Warren, Long Running, Monk Wood, Connaught Water and, one-time home of the poet Tennyson, High Beech. Two prehistoric caves, at Ambresbury Banks and Loughton Camp.

Felixstowe (Suffolk). Lively and popular holiday resort N of river Orwell, linked by ferry with Harwich. Organised entertainments. Golf course.

117

EAST ANGLIA

Finchingfield (Essex). Claimed to be one of the seven most beautiful villages in England. Charming street winds from village green and duck pond to the church. Guildhall (16c) and roundhouse and windmill (18c). Spains Hall (1m N), seven-gabled house dating from 1570.

Framlingham (Suffolk). Ancient market town with ruins of 12c Bigod castle (AM), home of Mary Tudor in 1553 and rallying point for her supporters when she came to the throne. Castle Street, with striking buildings of 17, 18 and 19c. Dennington church (5m N) contains 15c carved benches, alabaster tomb of Agincourt knight Lord Bardolph, medieval stained glass and lavish 16c screens. Glemham Hall (2m E), grand 17c mansion with 350 acres of grounds; mid-Apr–Sept, Weds and Suns 2.30–6.30.

Frinton (Essex). Select cliff-top resort developed on pattern of regular tree-lined streets. Sandy shore. Good touring centre.

Gorleston (Norfolk). Resort on a sandy but in places steeply shelving beach. Golf course, model yacht pond, Old Tyme Music Hall.

Great Yarmouth (Norfolk). A lively seaside resort backed by Breydon Water, into which flow the rivers Yare, Bure and Waveney. Miles of golden sands. Wide range of organised amusements. Golf course, casino. Coach and boat excursions. Merchants' House (AM) in one of ancient narrow lanes or 'rows' linking Tower Wall and quay. Old Tollhouse of 13c. Maritime Museum, June–Sept, daily except Sats. Fritton Lake (1m S).

Great Yarmouth

Hadleigh (Suffolk). Market town on tributary of Stour. Partly 15c timbered Guildhall with two overhanging storeys, 18c assembly room and musicians' gallery, Apr–Sept, Weds 10–6, Oct–Mar 10–4. Church of 14–15c has 14c font, early 18c organ case and brasses by Charles Regnart (1793) and Eric Gill (1935). Six-storey Deanery Tower of 1495 formerly gatehouse of archdeacon's palace.

Horning (Norfolk). Medieval port on river Bure, now an attractive angling and boating centre for the Broads. Reed-thatched church at Irstead (2m N) is one of the gems of Broadlands.

Hunstanton (Norfolk). Small resort set among sand dunes and creeks ringed by lavender fields. Safe bathing, boating lake, water sports.

Ipswich (Suffolk). Ancient port and market town at head of Orwell estuary. Pleasant Christchurch park near town centre with museum housing works by Constable, Gainsborough and others. Many old houses, among them Sparrowe's house in Butter Market, which dates from 1567. Medieval church of St. Margaret's with painted ceiling and arms of Charles II. Ipswich Museum in High Street (prehistoric and Roman relics), all year, Mons–Sats 10–5, Suns 3–5. Great White Horse hotel in Tavern Street immortalised in Charles Dickens Pickwick Papers. Hintlesham (5m W) has Tudor mansion of 1547 with fine interior panelling, July, 10–6.

King's Lynn (Norfolk). Charming old town formerly a seaport on east bank of river Ouse, renamed after Henry VIII took the manor from the bishop of Norwich. St. Margaret's church in Saturday Market Place by the river has a fine west front and two outstanding 14c brasses below the SW tower. Customs House built 1683. Greenland Fishery in Bridge Street is a timbered house of 1605 once an inn, the name of which recalls the time when the men of Lynn fished for whales off Greenland. Museum and art gallery in Market Street. The Mart fair has been held in the town on Feb 14 for 500 years.

Lavenham (Suffolk). 15c wool-trade town. Exquisite timbered houses overlook 15c church of St. Peter and Paul containing 14c rood screen, carved misericords and statues. Guildhall (NT) built in 1530 by the 15th Lord de Vere, whose effigy is carved on one of the corner posts. Other buildings include 16c Wool Hall and de Vere house.

Long Melford (Suffolk). Dignified little town with stately main street and magnificent Holy Trinity church incorporating stained glass, brasses and monuments. By the green, picturesque 16c almshouse. Melford Hall (NT), 16c turreted manor housing fine collection of furniture, paintings and porcelain, Easter Sun–end Sept, Weds, Thurs and Suns, 2.30–6. Exceptional avenue of lime trees leads to moated Kentwell Hall, built 1564. On S, Melford Place, restored in 18c.

Lowestoft (Suffolk). Important fishing port and holiday resort, with good sands, golf, sea and river fishing. Somerleyton Hall (5m NW), a 16–19c mansion notable for its tapestries, paintings and carvings and the maze and fine trees in its gardens, May 5–Sept 29, Thurs and Suns, 2–6. On S, Oulton Broad.

Maldon (Essex). Picturesque old town on hill overlooking river Blackwater and popular sailing centre. 14c inn. Plume Library, founded 1704. Church of All Saints, 13c, with unique triangular tower. Beeleigh Abbey (1½m W), 12c parts of which are incorporated in private house; extensive library of William Foyle, Mons–Sats, 2–5.

Mildenhall (Suffolk). Small market town beside river Lark at edge of fen country. Church of SS Mary and Andrew, with unique 14c tracery on E window, carved roof and Purbeck marble font. Old market cross and some fine Georgian houses.

Mundesley (Norfolk). One of Norfolk's finest sandy beaches. Golf course. Air beneficial to those suffering from chest or throat complaints.

Newmarket (Suffolk). World-famous horse breeding and racing centre and scene in 1619 of first-ever recorded horse race. National Stud (1½m S), Apr–end Sept, Suns and Bk Hols 2–5, racedays 11–1.

Norwich (Norfolk). Absorbing city, formerly a haven for Flemish, Huguenot and Walloon refugees, who brought with them their crafts and architecture. Norman cathedral, dating from 1096, is one of the finest in existence; Nurse Edith Cavell buried at SE end. 15c Guildhall. Strangers Hall, 14c house with Tudor to Victorian period furniture. Restored 12c keep of Norman castle now museum, all year except Good Fri and Christmas Day.

Orford (Suffolk). Small fishing village on river Ore and a developing holiday centre. 18-sided keep of ruined 12c castle (AM) contains collection of armour. St. Bartholomew church, with 14c nave and tower, has fine font and interesting brasses.

Potter Heigham (Norfolk). Important centre for cruises on the largest and wildest of the Broads. Heigham Sound (2m N), noted for pike and rudd fishing, is linked by White Slea bird sanctuary to Hickling Broad, one of the largest and most shallow. Horsey Mere (NT) is 1m N.

Saffron Walden (Essex). One of England's most picturesque ancient towns, with the largest perpendicular church (1472) in the county. Fine timbered 15 and 16c houses show examples of pargetting (decorative plasterwork).

St Osyth (Essex). Popular holiday centre founded in honour of the saint martyred by Norse invaders in 870. Chapel and abbots' tower of St. Osyth's priory are 13c, May–Sept, 10–7. Gatehouse containing works of art, notably ceramics which include Chinese jade, Aug, 2.30–4.

Sheringham (Norfolk). Charming cliff-top resort with fine sands, good bathing and low rainfall. Upper Sheringham (1m inland), one of prettiest villages in county.

Southend on Sea (Essex). Highly organised and frequently crowded resort, with six miles of sands, longest pier in world, golf, archery, horse-riding and excursions by sea and air. Illuminations Aug–Oct. At airport, historic aircraft museum. Prittlewell Priory Museum, SE Essex antiquities housed in restored 12c Cluniac priory, Apr–Sept, Mons–Sats 11–6, Suns 2.30–6, Oct–Mar, Mons–Sats 11–4.30.

Southwold (Suffolk). Select seaside town, with attractive coloured houses and cottages and a lighthouse on one of the greens. Flint flushwork church of St. Edmund has a tall tower and two-storey S porch. Holton Mill (4m W) is splendid post-mill of 1752 with brick-built roundhouse.

Stoke by Nayland (Suffolk). Delightful village. St. Michael's church, often featured in Constable's paintings, has 17c library, alabaster monuments and interesting brasses.

Sudbury (Suffolk). Ancient market town with charming medieval and 18c buildings. Moot Hall, Chantry and Salter's halls are all 15c, and almost as old are the Bull Inn and Ballingdon Hall across the river Stow. Gainsborough's house, where he was born in 1727, is now an art gallery and museum, Tues–Sats, 10.30–12.30 and 2–5, Suns 2–5.

Thetford (Norfolk). One of the half-dozen cities of 11c England, at the centre of Breckland. Reminders of its Tudor greatness are provided by the King's House, the Bell Hotel and the Ancient House Museum, a 15c timbered mansion containing fine collection of archaeological exhibits. Ruins of Cluniac priory and great castle mound.

Walton on the Naze (Essex). Popular resort on promontory, with calm saltings at rear and gently-shelving sandy beaches to seaward. Boating lake, ten-pin bowling and miniature railway.

Wells next the Sea (Norfolk). Small port and holiday resort popular for sailing, wild fowling and caravanning. Shooting is free on the seaward side of the sand dunes, a mile away.

West Mersea (Essex). A yachting and holiday centre with reputation for boat-building and oysters.

Wivenhoe (Essex). Busy little port and yachting centre at head of Colne estuary. Many pargeted cottages. In local church, 9-ft brasses (Viscount Beaumont and his wife) which may be rubbed for small fee.

Woodbridge (Suffolk). Ancient port on Debden estuary, with 15–18c houses, cobbled lanes dropping down to the quay and historic tide-mill. Three notable inns, King's Head, Angel and Bell, the last with a rare lever weighing machine. Kyson Hill (NT), an attractive stretch of parkland beside the river.

Wroxham (Norfolk). Small town which is one of the main centres on the Broads, with fine views of the winding river Bure. Access to Broads of Salhouse (charge for mooring and fishing), Hoveton Little (Easter–Sept), Ranworth and South Walsham; by river Ant to Barton Broad.

Yoxford (Suffolk). Village of attractive houses ringed by the parklands of three great mansions. Most important is Cockfield Hall, built 1540, with unusual chimneys, crow-stepped gables and fine gatehouse.

Fen Country

Lincolnshire—Rutland—Northamptonshire—Huntingdonshire—Cambridgeshire

All five counties border on the Fenland, which extends W and S of the Wash and covers an area of roughly 70m by 35m. The fens are really a silted-up bay of the North Sea, now intersected by the rivers Witham, Welland, Nene and Great Ouse.

Some efforts to drain the fens were made by the Romans and Normans, but with little success. Large-scale reclamation was first carried out by the Dutch engineer Vermuyden in the 17c. Reclaimed fenland is extremely fertile, and the region has remained predominantly agricultural. Potatoes, sugar beet and other crops are cultivated on a large scale.

A few places have remained relatively untouched, notably Wicken Fen (NT), Chippenham Fen, Quy Fen, and Hayley Wood (NT); and these have been made into nature reserves for the protection of wild life. Naturalists are attracted to the region by the variety of birds and water fowl, fish, insects, and plant life.

On the higher spots monasteries were early established e.g. at Peterborough, Ely, Crowland, Ramsey and Thorney. In succeeding years the area has become rich in historic buildings. There are the superb Cathedrals of Ely, Lincoln and Peterborough; the ancient University of Cambridge, renowned for its learning and the architectural beauty of its colleges; castles such as Kimbolton, Tattershall, and moated Woodcroft with romantic histories; and a vast number of medieval churches. Of the historic country houses, examples are Burghley House, Toseland Manor, and Gainsborough Old Hall. In addition there are innumerable picturesque villages.

Fenland people have always been stouthearted, and tenacious of their liberty and their rights, opposing the drainage enclosure schemes when their land was threatened. Boadicea ruled the Iceni in this region, and Hereward the Wake and Oliver Cromwell were both Fenland men. Prehistoric, Danish and Roman relics abound throughout the whole region.

Cambridgeshire

Cambridgeshire has two outstanding features—the University of Cambridge and the Cathedral of Ely. The county is predominantly agricultural land, intersected by streams and drainage canals, but of late years has shown rapid industrial development. The northern part of the county is separately administered as the Isle of Ely.

The Icknield Way, that ancient trackway through the country of the Iceni, passes SE of Cambridge and is crossed by two lines of prehistoric earthworks—Fleam Dyke and Devil's Ditch.

So flat is the county that even the low hills of Gog Magog afford extensive views of the network of fen waterways, and church spires and towers, as far as Ely.

Huntingdon and Peterborough

The new county was formed in 1965 by amalgamating Huntingdon County with the Soke of Peterborough, Thorney Rural District from the Isle of Ely, and part of Eaton Socon from Bedfordshire.

It is mainly a flat agricultural area, crossed by the rivers Nene and Ouse, and has the largest man-made lake in England—Grafton Water.

The county is rich in picturesque towns and villages, Elizabethan and Georgian houses, and ancient inns; it also possesses a 12c Cathedral and two castles dating from the 13 and 14c.

Lincolnshire

Lincolnshire is the second largest of the English counties, and is still predominantly an agricultural county.

It represents the amalgamation—at the time of the Danish invasions—of the three regions of Lindsey, Kesteven and Holland. Each of these three 'Parts' still has its own Council for the conduct of local affairs, with the exception that Lincoln and Grimsby are independent County Boroughs.

Most of Lincolnshire is notably flat, which explains the abundance of airfields. The 'Cliff' is a narrow ridge of higher land from Grantham to the Humber; along it ran the Roman Ermine Street. Further E are the Wolds. The long coastline that forms the eastern boundary of the county is noted for its clean sandy beaches.

The SE part of Lincolnshire includes a considerable portion of the Fen country, which is particularly fertile. Agricultural industries that have developed in this area include beet-sugar manufacture and canning of fruit and vegetables.

Burghley House

Northamptonshire

This region has a mild climate and a rich soil. It is mostly flat, and wheat, barley, potatoes and sugar beet are extensively grown. Watling Street and Ermine Street cross the county and many earthworks and Roman remains have been found.

In the 11c Northants was part of Tostig's earldom. Later it figured in the Wars of the Roses and the Civil War.

The county was an important footwear centre by 1650. Shoe-making and allied trades still form its most important industry, followed by iron and steel, aluminium, engineering and quarrying.

The many fine buildings include Saxon and Norman churches, Eleanor crosses, and historic country houses.

A remarkable feature of Northamptonshire is that it borders on no less than nine other counties.

Rutland

Rutland is the smallest of the English counties, its area being approximately 150 square miles.

It consists largely of pasture land for sheep and cattle, and has many picturesque stone-built villages with interesting churches. Like Northants, Rutland is a noted fox-hunting county.

Gatehouse, Rockingham Castle

Of Special Interest

Althorp (Harlestone). Medieval mansion with later alterations. Pictures by Dutch and Italian masters, portraits by Reynolds and Gainsborough. Tues, Thurs, Suns, Bk Hols in summer.

Anglesey Abbey (6m NE of Cambridge). Elizabethan mansion created from ruins of 12c abbey. Extensive gardens. NT. Easter–Oct, 2–6, except Mons and Fris.

Aynhoe Park (Aynho). 17c mansion on Norman castle foundations. Contains collection of paintings and Venetian glass. Weds, Thurs, May–Sept.

Burghley House (Stamford). Superb Elizabethan mansion. State apartments, painted ceilings, furniture, tapestries, art collections, and beautiful rose gardens. Apr–Sept, Tues, Weds, Thurs, Sats, 11–5, Suns 2–5.

Castle Ashby (8m E Northampton). Elizabethan mansion in lovely surroundings. Notable furniture, pictures, tapestries, ceilings, staircases and stone-lettered parapet. Gardens. Thurs, Sats, Suns in summer.

Gunby Hall (2½m W Burgh-le-Marsh). Fine house built c. 1700. Oak staircase. Portraits. NT. Wed, Thurs, Fri afternoons in summer.

Kimbolton Castle (8m NW St. Neots). Catherine of Aragon was imprisoned here. Facade rebuilt by Vanbrugh 1708–14. Now a school. Aug, Thurs and Sun afternoons.

Kirby Hall (2m SE Gretton). Built 1570–5. Now mostly ruins, but architecturally significant. Fine gardens (AM Standard hours). Nearby is *Deane Park* with turreted Tudor house and fine park.

Lyddington Bedehouse (AM. 1¾ miles S of Uppingham). Elizabethan manor converted from medieval palace of Bishop of Lincoln. Nearby is *Stoke Dry* Norman church, with wall paintings.

Rockingham Castle (8m N Kettering). Built for William the Conqueror. Norman gateway and towers but present house mainly Elizabethan. Noteworthy furniture and paintings. Thurs, Easter–Sept, and Mons in Aug.

Sawston Hall (6½m S Cambridge). 16c manor house with many Catholic associations. May–Sept, Suns, also Sats Jul–Sept, 2.30–5.30.

Sulgrave Manor (7m NW Brackley). Built 1560, and partly rebuilt 1920. Home of George Washington; contains his portrait and possessions. Daily, except Fris.

Tattershall Castle (4m SE Woodhall Spa). Medieval fortified dwelling, the Keep of original castle. NT. Daily, 9.30–7, Suns, 1–7.

Thornton Abbey (6m SE of Barton-upon-Humber). Shows interesting remains —notably fine Gatehouse—of 12c Abbey. (AM. Open Standard hours).

Resorts and Centres of Interest

Boston (Lincs). A pleasant market town, canning centre, and seaport near mouth of river Witham. The Pilgrim Fathers originally tried to sail from here, and five Boston men later became Governors of Massachusetts. The tall tower of St. Botolph's church (Boston = Botolph's Town) is a landmark and is known as Boston Stump.

Bourne (Lincs). Home of Hereward the Wake, on W boundary of Fens. Roman *Car Dyke* (drainage canal) runs nearby.

Brackley (Nthants). Pleasant old town; prosperous wool centre in 14c. Parish church has interesting 12c features. Magdalen College School (16c) incorporates the chapel of St. John's Hospital, founded 1144.

Cambridge (Cambs). Ancient town on the Granta (now Cam). Still predominantly a University City, modern industrial developments being kept well away from the centre. Over a score of Colleges, three being for women; Peterhouse is the oldest, dating from 13c and Trinity the largest. King's College Chapel is an architectural glory. The picturesque 'Backs' border both banks of the Cam between Bridge Street and Silver Street.

Churches include Great St. Mary's (Parish and University church) and the 12c 'round church' of the Holy Sepulchre. The Fitzwilliam Museum with its Corinthian portico, and Botanic Garden of 40 acres, are equally famous in their respective spheres.

Cleethorpes (Lincs). Adjoins Grimsby, and has developed from a fishing village into a seaside resort attracting a million visitors every summer. Has excellent sands, beautiful gardens, and attractions of sophisticated coast resort.

Corby (Nthants). Thirty years ago was a farming village of 1,500 inhabitants. Now a rapidly developing new town of 42,000 with good modern buildings and spacious streets. Surrounded by ironstone quarries, and has become centre of flourishing steel industry.

Daventry (Nthants). Old town marked for expansion. B.B.C. transmitting station is on prehistoric hilltop camp at Borough Hill; from here in 1925 the first long-wave radio transmitter was installed. Moot Hall contains interesting relics. Charles I stayed at the 'Wheatsheaf' before Naseby.

Ely (Cambs). Name means 'Eel Island'. Here was the last stronghold of resistance by Hereward the Wake against the Normans. The crowning glory is the Cathedral, begun in 1083 on the site of an abbey founded by St. Etheldreda in the 8c. Notable features are central Octagon and Lantern, Bishop's Palace, Prior's Doorway, and Lady Chapel. See also 13c church of St. Mary, South Gatehouse, and Grammar School.

Gainsborough (Lincs). Expanding small town on navigable river Trent. Sweyn, father of Canute, landed here in 1013, and Alfred the Great is said to have married here. The Old Hall should be seen.

127

Geddington (Nthants). Attractive village near Kettering. Has Eleanor Cross (AM 1290) and church with Saxon remains.

Godmanchester (Hunts). Linked with Huntingdon by a fine medieval bridge over the Ouse. The two boroughs were amalgamated in 1961. Originally a Roman posting station, Godmanchester is a pleasant town with half-timbered and thatched houses of 16 and 17c. Church of St. Mary is 13c. and has notable choir stalls.

Grantham (Lincs). Mentioned in Domesday Book; now a thriving town known to all travellers on the A1. Has a magnificent Parish church and a medieval market cross. Ancient inns include the Angel, the George, and the Beehive.

Great Casterton (Rut). Attractive village on the Great North Road. Church dates from 13c. Roman relics of a town and villa have been excavated.

Grimsby (Lincs). Ancient town, said to be first Danish settlement in Britain. First received charter in 1201. Rapid development during last century as a fishing port, and is now largest centre in world for quick-freezing and cold storage. Its commercial docks, together with those of Immingham, make it of great importance as a mercantile centre.

Horncastle (Lincs). Ancient market town on a Roman site. Church has interesting brasses to Dymoke family, hereditary King's Champions, whose seat is nearby at Scrivelsby.

Huntingdon (Hunts). County town, on river Ouse. Long narrow town, mainly Georgian, which was of great importance in the Middle Ages. Oliver Cromwell and Pepys were pupils at the Grammar School, which is now a Cromwellian museum. St. Mary's Church, largely 13c, has interesting carved stalls. All Saints Church, on site of a Saxon Minster, was mainly rebuilt in 15c. Hinchingbrooke House 1m to the W, was the 16c home of the Cromwell family; it has a fine gatehouse and has now become a school.

Irthlingborough (Nthants). Small town of both industrial and agricultural importance. Its Saxon name means 'burgh of the ploughmen'. The medieval bridge over the river Nene stands beside the modern viaduct. Church has a fine 14c detached bell-tower.

Kettering (Nthants). Rapidly developing town on river Ise. Important footwear industry, also clothing, plastics and engineering. In charter of 956 name is given as Cytringan. The Friday market has been held since 1227. Parish church is 13–15c and has tall tower and spire. Elizabethan Grammar School.

Lincoln (Lincs). The 'Lindum Colonia' of the Romans was a fortress at the junction of the Fosse Way and Ermine Street. William the Conqueror built a castle on the steep hill by the river Witham, and close by arose the famous Cathedral that now dominates the City: note the three towers, the fine W front, the Chapter House, and the 13c Angel Choir. Other items of interest are the Castle (AM), High Bridge, the Stonebow

Lincoln Cathedral

(gateway with Guildhall above, AM), the 12c Jews' Houses, and John of Gaunt's Stables (AM NT).

Louth (Lincs). Busy market town whose parish church has 300 ft spire. The 'Pilgrimage of Grace' (revolt in 1536 in defence of the monasteries) began here; after its failure the Vicar was hanged at Tyburn, and many other Lincolnshire people were also executed.

Mablethorpe (Lincs). Was long a favourite quiet resort famous for its golden sands. Now combined with the adjoining Sutton-on-Sea and rapidly developing into a modernised holiday resort.

March (Cambs). Market town in Isle of Ely. The 14c church of St. Wendreda is remarkable for double hammerbeam roof, and for its carved angels.

Northampton (Nthants). County town, Borough and business centre of Northants, on river Nene. Main industry is the manufacture of footwear. Once Roman fortress town dominating the Midlands, and retains many relics of its history. At Hardingstone is a superb Eleanor Cross. Delapre Abbey, now housing the County records, was once a Cluniac nunnery.

Oakham (Rut). County town and centre for fox-hunting (Cottesmore Hunt). Castle has Norman banqueting hall. See also old Grammar School, butter cross, and stocks. At Burley-on-the-Hill (2m) a 17c mansion overlooks the Vale of Catmose. (*Gardens only open*).

Old Fletton (Hunts). Rapidly expanding town adjoining Peterborough. Dominated by brick industry. The church is Norman with Saxon carvings.

Oundle (Nthants). Stone-built market town with fine 17 and 18c houses, picturesque inns, and interesting church with 200 ft crocketed spire, and 14c screens. Oundle School for over 600 boys was founded about 1485.

129

Peterborough (Hunts). A thriving agricultural and industrial centre on the river Nene. Largest town in the county. The magnificent Cathedral, mainly Norman, is built on site of a Benedictine monastery founded 655 and destroyed by the Danes in 870. A second monastery was burnt down on 1116 and a great Norman abbey was erected. After the dissolution of the monasteries this was converted in 1541 into a Cathedral, in which parts of the monastery were preserved. The impressive West Front has three huge recessed arches and a late Gothic porch.

Ramsey (Hunts). Agricultural centre with many outlying villages. Ramsey Abbey founded in 969; destroyed after the Dissolution except for Lady Chapel and Gatehouse. These became part of Abbey House, now a school.

Rothwell (Nthants). Near Kettering. Manufactures footwear and agricultural implements. Noted for one of the largest fairs in the county, held during week following Trinity Sunday. Norman church is interesting for its arcading, stalls, brasses, and remarkable bone-crypt. Elizabethan almshouses and Georgian manor house.

Rushden (Nthants). Prosperous shoe-manufacturing town 5m E of Wellingborough. The church has a fine tower and spire, and a curious 'strainer' arch. Rushden links up with the smaller and less industrialised *Higham Ferrers*, whose 14c church has a very similar tower and spire. By the church is the unusual Bede House founded in 1422. Higham Ferrers is rich in ancient buildings, and has a 13c Market Cross.

St. Ives (Hunts). Picturesque town on river Ouse. Has medieval bridge with bridge-chapel; 14c church; and Elizabethan manor house. Was originally called Slepe, but in 1050 a priory of Ramsey Abbey was set up here and dedicated to St. Ivo.

Skegness

St. Neot's (Hunts). Market town of Saxon origin on river Ouse, occupied with agriculture and light industries. The large market place is flanked by 17c hotels and Georgian buildings. Impressive 15c church with richly ornamented tower.

Scunthorpe (Lincs). Industrial town near river Trent. Local iron ore deposits have made it an important centre of the iron and steel industry.

Skegness (Lincs). The best known of Lincolnshire coast resorts. Has 6m of sandy beach, all modern amenities, and can accommodate 80,000 summer visitors. A few m to the S is the nature reserve at Gibraltar Point.

Soham (Cambs). Here St. Felix founded an Abbey in the 7c. Both this and the abbey at Ely were destroyed by the Danes. In Norman times a causeway was built to link the two towns.

Spalding (Lincs). A fenland town that in Norman times boasted an abbey and a castle. Both have long since disappeared, and the town is now best known as a centre of the bulb-growing industry. Parish church is 13c.

Stamford (Lincs). An attractive town whose records go back to the 7c. Historic buildings and churches, with numerous 17 and 18c residences of architectural interest. Of Brazenose Hall (to which dissatisfied Oxford scholars migrated in 1333) only the gateway still exists. Across the Welland, in Northants, lies the parish of St. Martin, with Burghley House.

Thorney (Hunts). A small island of reclaimed fenland with one village— Thorney. Associated with Hereward the Wake. A monastery was erected in the 7c, destroyed by the Danes in 870, and replaced by a Norman abbey, parts of which still exist. Thorney Abbey dates from the 16c.

Towcester (Nthants). Old town on the site of the Roman *Lactodorum*. The 'Eatanswill' of the Pickwick Papers. Old inns and church with chained books. Easton Neston House is 17c, and was designed by Hawksmoor in the Wren style.

Uppingham (Rut). Pleasant little town situated on high ground amid picturesque scenery. Fames for its public school founded in 1587.

Wellingborough (Nthants). Rapidly expanding industrial town noted for shoe-making and ironworking mainly. Has old parish Church, Public School and Grammar School, and two ancient inns *(Hind* and *Golden Lion)*. Two m to the south, the church of Earls Barton has the finest Saxon tower in England.

Whittlesey (Cambs). A very old market town in Isle of Ely. Possesses two medieval churches—St. Mary's with fine spire, and St. Andrew's —also a Butter Cross and many 17c buildings.

Wisbech (Cambs). Ancient town on navigable river Nene. Centre for flower and fruit produce of fens, with flourishing canning industry. Fine Museum, on site of Norman castle, where King John was told of loss of the Crown jewels. Among the old houses is *Peckover House* (NT); the nearby Church has a double nave.

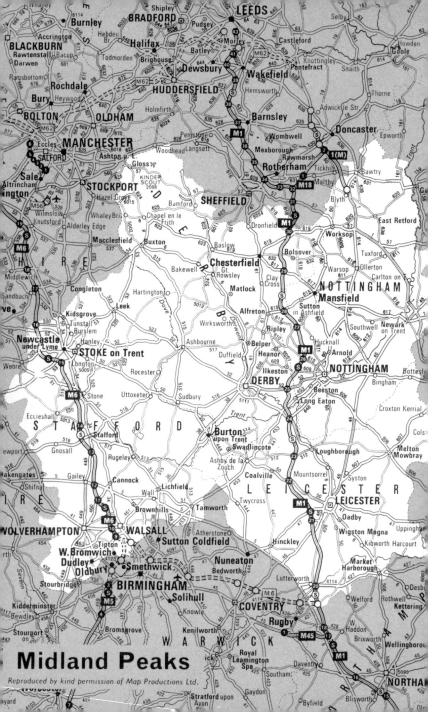

Midland Peaks

Reproduced by kind permission of Map Productions Ltd.

Midland Peaks

Derby—Leicestershire—Nottinghamshire—Staffordshire

Coal-mining and industry have certainly made their mark on the Midlands, particularly in the south, yet there remain in the four shires of Derby, Leicester, Nottingham and Stafford many historic towns and villages set in an unspoilt landscape. As well as many quiet corners this embraces the protected areas of Cannock Chase and the wildly-beautiful Peak District, with its fair share of prehistoric relics as well as stately homes.

Derbyshire

One of the most picturesque regions in England is contained mainly within North Derbyshire, this is the Peak District, an area of craggy hills, steep dales and often-huge underground caverns and one best explored on foot. The E is a district of coal, iron and industry but the flat grazing country in the S gives the county a share in some of the richest dairy farming in England.

Leicestershire

Part of England's central plateau, Leicestershire is divided vertically by the broad valley of the river Soar. On the west is the miniature mountain area of Charnwood Forest, on the E and S the pastoral Wolds. Against a backdrop of scattered woods and rolling grasslands, few counties display so many beautiful village churches, and none so many hunting seats.

Nottinghamshire

The leaf-shaped county of Nottingham, with the river Trent winding northwards along its eastern edge, is surprisingly rural despite its many coalmines and is marked by few large towns. The scenery may not be breathtaking but the county's historical and literary links add to its interest.

Staffordshire

The Black country and the Potteries make Staffordshire one of the most important industrial areas in England, yet five-sixths of the county is still rural. In the north are the beautiful moorlands of the Pennine range, part of widely acclaimed Dovedale, high crags, caves and many bubbling streams, in the S the birchwoods and pine-crowned hills of Cannock Chase, 25 square miles of moorland and deep valleys. In the centre rivers flow gently through undulating dairy-farming country.

Of Special Interest

Arnold Bennett's House (Staffs. Cobridge, Stoke-on-Trent). Home of the writer as a young man and background for some of his novels. Mons, Weds, Thurs and Sats, 2–5.

Baggrave Hall (Leics. 8m NE Leicester). 18c mansion with glorious landscaped gardens including water garden and sunken garden. See local announcements.

Belvoir Castle (Leics, 7m SW Grantham). Fortress high in wolds rebuilt as medieval castle c. 1800 by Wyatt round a large courtyard. Gobelin tapestries, furniture, picture collection containing works by Holbein, Reynolds, Gainsborough and Poussin, armoury, also museum of 17/21st Lancers. Apr–Sept, Weds, Thurs and Sats, 12–6, Suns, 2–7, and Bk Hols, 11–7. Oct, Suns only, 2–6.

Bolsover Castle (Derbys, 6m E Chesterfield). 1615 castle with keep, turrets and battlements (AM) begun by Sir Charles Cavendish, whose son added terraced. buildings in classical style. Panoramic views.

Chatsworth. (See page 143.

Elds Wood (Staffs, 6m NE Market Drayton). Wild woodland garden created from 200-year-old quarry. Mid April–mid June, daily, 2–8.

Haddon Hall. (See page 142).

Hardwick Hall (Derbys, 6m W Mansfield). Magnificent Elizabethan mansion (NT) begun in 1591 by Elizabeth, Countess of Shrewsbury when she was 71 yrs of age. 4 great towers with parapets incorporating initials ES. High Great Chamber with splendid frieze, rambling staircase, furniture, tapestries, portraits and needle-work. Extensive gardens with yew hedges and borders. Easter Sat–end Sept, Weds, Thurs, Sats, Suns and Bk Hols, 2–6 or dusk.

Kirby Muxloe Castle (Leics, 5m W of Leicester). 15c fortified manor house (AM) with moat. Mar, Apr, Oct, weekdays only, 9.30–5.30, May–Sept, 9.30–7, Nov–Feb, 9.30–4.

Melbourne Hall (Derbys, 8m S Derby). 15–18c mansion developed first by Sir John Coke and later by his great-grandson Sir Thomas Coke. Birthplace of Lord Melbourne. Formal gardens with fountains, shell grotto and unique 18c wrought iron bird-cage pergola by Bakewell. Selected Suns Easter–Jul and Oct, 2–6, Jul–Sept daily (except Mons and Fris), 2–6.

Moseley Old Hall (Staffs, 4m NE Wolverhampton). Originally Elizabethan house (NT) where Whitgreave family sheltered Charles II after Battle of Worcester and his secret hiding place and bed can still be seen. Furniture, portraits and

Haddon Hall

family relics. Mar–Nov, Weds, Thurs, Sats, Suns, 2–6. (Bk Hols, incl. Tues following 10.30–12.30 and 2–6 or dusk).

Newstead Abbey (Notts, 4½m S Mansfield). 12c Priory converted into house 1540 by Lord Byron's ancestor Sir John Byron, with 19c Gothic reconstructions. Byron relics, Tudor and Stuart furniture and armour. Landscaped gardens with rare shrubs and trees. Weekdays conducted tours at 2, 3, 4, 5. Suns and Bk Hols half-hourly 2–5.30. Gardens open all year, weekdays, 10–9 or dusk.

Oak House (Staffs, West Bromwich). 15c half-timbered house, Jacobean style furniture and furnishings. Summer weekdays, 11–5 (Thurs, 11–1), Winter 11–4 (Thurs, 11–1).

Revolution House (Derbys, 1½m N Chesterfield). Old inn, now house with 17c furnishings and 1688 Revolution associations. Easter–Sept 30, daily incl. Suns, 11–12.30 and 2–5, and 6–dusk.

Seriby Hall (Notts, 3m SW Bawtry). Gardens, herbaceous borders, magnificent roses and irises. Suns and Bk Hols, May–2nd Sun in Sept.

Spode-Copeland Museum (Staffs. Stoke-on-Trent). The Family museum contains collection of Pottery from early Chinese onwards, the Works museum 18–20c Spode and unsurpassed collection of Blue under Glaze pottery. Mons–Fris, 9–12.30 and 1.30–4. Closed first two weeks in June.

Stanford Hall (Leics, 7½m NE Rugby). 1697 mansion much altered in 1730. Stuart paintings and relics, furniture and family costumes from Elizabethan times onwards. Walled rose garden and lake in grounds. Fishing. Part of stables now house collection of vintage cars and motor-cycles, also replica of Pilcher's 1898 flying machine. Easter–end Sept, Thurs, Sats, Suns, 2.30–6, Bk Hols, 12–6.

Trentham Gardens (Staffs. Stoke-on-Trent). Rose and Italian Gardens, ballroom, boating and heated swimming pool. Fishing.

Twycross Zoo (Leics, 6m N Atherstone). Notable for range of gorillas, lemurs, etc. Aviary and Pets Corner. All year, daily.

Wedgwood Museum and Factory (Staffs, 4m S Stoke-on-Trent). 18–26c ceramics and examples of Josiah Wedgwood's designs. All year except first two weeks in June. By appointment.

Wightwick Manor (Staffs, 3m W Wolverhampton). 19c mansion, collection of pre-Raphaelite works, Morris fabric and de Morgan ware. Terraced gardens. All year, Thurs, 2.30–5,30, Sats, 10.30–12.30 and 2.30–5.30.

Whatton House, Hathern (Leics, 4m NW Loughborough). Family heirlooms in 1800 mansion. Oriental gardens, magnificent herbaceous borders, roses and bulbs. Easter–end Sept and Bk Hols, 2–7.

Resorts and Centres of Interest

Abbots Bromley (Staffs). Delightful village of old timbered houses famed for Horn Dance performed every September. Elizabethan Blithfield Hall (3m SW) with pinnacled doorway and carved staircase, home of Bagot family for 600 years. Adjoining 13c church, with beautiful 15c screen and ancient family monuments, surrounded by orangery, rhododendrons and rose garden; Good Friday–last Sun in Oct, Weds, Thurs, Sats and Suns 2.30–6 and Bk Hols 12–7.

Alstonfield (Staffs). Near Derbyshire border and ringed by magnificent scenery, village with Bronze Age barrows, 15c church containing Saxon relics and, on bank of Dove, Fishing House, 1674, often visited by Izaak Walton. Good angling.

Alton (Staffs). Popular resort above lovely Churnet valley. Alton Towers, neo-Gothic 19c mansion with imposing roofline of turrets, battlements and towers, set in park and pleasure garden with aerial cars, model and miniature railways; Good Friday–last weekend in October. Hawksmoor Nature Reserve (3m N), 200 acres of woods, moors and marshes (NT).

Ashbourne (Derbys). Largely Georgian town in fertile Dove valley on S edge of Peak district. Cruciform 13–14c St. Oswald's church, with 200-ft central spire, 13c font, 19c stained glass and monuments which include memorials to Cockayne family (13–17c) and Thomas Banks famous 18c white marble sculpture of Penelope Boothby. Almshouses of 17c, Green Man inn where Johnson and Boswell stayed. Football match on Shrove Tuesday between northern quarter of town and south.

Ashby de la Zouche (Leics). Pleasant market town centred on broad main street. Remnants of castle (AM) include four-storey Great Tower and kitchen tower above buttery and 52-ft long kitchen. Church of 15c with panelled battlements to pillars of nave arcades, historic sculptured tombs and in E window heraldic glass from ruined castle chapel, as well as unique 13-grooved 'finger pillory' designed to subdue the unruly.

Ashford (Derbys). Old-fashioned town on river Wye; ancient customs still followed include tolling of curfew bell and ceremony of dressing and blessing the wells.

Ashover (Derbys). Pleasant village amid rocky scenery increasingly popular as holiday resort. Parish church of 15c with leaden Norman font, alabaster tomb of 1518 and finely carved screen. Nearby, Pans Gardens with zoo, Darley Dale and Darley Moor.

Bakewell (Derbys). Quaint town delightfully situated on river Wye in Peak national park. Medieval bridge, 17 and 18c stone houses and 12–14c cruciform church with octagonal tower containing 13c font and many monuments to Vernon and Manners families. Bath House with warm springs and swimming pool. Haddon Hall (2m SE), beautifully restored 13 to 15c manor, with panelled hall and terraced rose gardens, romantic

Chatsworth

Dorothy Vernon associations; April–Sept, Tues–Sats, 11–6. Chatsworth (4m NE), one of the great mansions of England designed mainly by Talman and Wyatville, with painted hall, state rooms and theatre gallery containing furniture, sculpture, tapestries and objects d'art; extensive grounds illustrate four periods of garden design and incorporate great cascade and metal weeping willow; house and theatre gallery April–Oct, Weds–Fris, 11.30–4, Sats and Suns, 2–5.30, Bk Hols and following Tues, also Good Fris, 11.30–5.30; gardens daily Mons–Fris, 11.30–4.30, Sats and Suns 2–6, Bk Hols and Good Fris, 11.30–6. Arbor Low Circle (6m SW) at Youlgreave, circle of 50 stones (AM).

Biddulph (Staffs). At the edge of stark Biddulph Moor, with nearby source of river Trent and ancient Saxon burial place marked by unhewn monoliths called Bridestones.

Bradwell (Derbys). Village nestling in rugged scenery close by fantastic underground chambers of Bagshawe Cavern. Brough (1m N), ancient Roman site. To SE, Bradwell Dale.

Breedon on the Hill (Leics). Crescent-shaped village with 18c round-house, formerly local prison. Uphill path to mainly Norman church of SS Mary and Hardulph, with late 16c tombs and effigies and high up in the tower and S aisle fragments of carved Saxon frieze dating from 800.

Brewood (Staffs). Village of timbered houses set in one-time royal forest. Grammar school founded by Edward VI, medieval church with alabaster tombs of Giffard family, and Chillington Hall, seat of Giffards since 12c rebuilt in 18c by Sir John Soane; Jun–Aug, Thurs, 2.30–6.

Buckminster (Leics). High up in Wolds, deightful village of tree-lined roads, cottages and green, with Georgian Hall and park. Church notable for its interior decorated with sculpted heads with 700-year-old tower accessible by staircase inside richly-ornamented eight-sided turret by chancel arch.

Bunny (Notts). Charmingly-odd village evolved by eccentric Sir Thomas Parkyns, 'the Wrestling Baronet', who designed the school, almshouse, cottages and his own weird house Bunny Hall, as well as his own memorial in the 14c church.

Buxton (Derbys). Once an important Roman station built round natural hot springs, now attractive health and holiday resort high up in Peak district. Chief architectural feature is Palladian terrace built by John Carr in 1780 for fifth Duke of Devonshire, together with assembly room (now clinic) and stables (now hospital). St. Anne's church, 1625, with stone-slab roof and bell turret. Opera house, theatre, concert hall, boating lake, golf course, swimming pools. Poole Cavern, large cave on Grin Low Hill extending half-mile underground, with stalactites and stalagmites and museum. Angling in Buxton reservoir. To S, Axe Edge, with panoramic views, and Flash, claimed to be highest village in England (1,515 ft). On SW, Dane Valley, with the astonishing rocky chasm called Lud Church.

Cannock (Staffs). Old town and once-fashionable spa now dominated by coal-mining. Nearby Cannock Chase, area of great natural beauty with many deer marred in S by coal pits. German cemetery of two wars.

Castle Donington (Leics). Pleasant small town on hill in wide Trent valley, with thatched and gabled houses. Old Key House of 1595. Church begun in 13c, with pulpit formed by memorial stones of family group with the figures visible on the inside, fine 15c brass of family of four sons and three daughters. Donington Park (1½m W), former home of Earls of Huntingdon now hotel; park with two herds of deer and famous Chaucer's oak. Nearby beauty spot of King's Mills, with old mill and many islands.

Chapel en le Frith (Derbys). Historic town formerly ringed by royal forest, with ancient inns, stocks, market cross and bell still rung at curfew time. Combs Reservoir (2m W) popular with sailing enthusiasts. Kinder Scout (4m N), with steep Jacob's Ladder climb and Downfall cataract, Snake Pass and Edale Moor.

Castleton (Derbys). Picturesque and popular centre for the most mountainous part of Peak district, renowned for its limestone caverns of Speedwell, Treak Cliff and Blue John, the last-named deriving its title from the beautiful amethystine fluor-spar stone found there; guided tours, some involving strenuous climbs via steps. Ruins of 11c Peveril Castle (AM) on steep rock. Norman parish church of 17c with box pews and old library. Douglas Museum, fascinating miscellany of exhibits. Mam Tor (2m NW), the famous Shivering Mountain. Tideswell (4m S), with cruciform parish church known as Cathedral of the Peak incorporating pinnacled W tower, perpendicular font, 19c stained glass and brass of Bishop Robert Pursglove (d. 1579).

Dukeries (Notts). Area of Sherwood Forest near Ollerton containing at one time mansions of dukes of Portland, Newcastle, Norfolk, Leeds and Kingston, all with extensive parks. Of those remaining, Welbeck, with a maze of underground rooms and passages designed by the eccentric fifth Duke of Portland, is not open to view. Clumber, seat of the Duke of Newcastle, with neo-Gothic church and large lake formed by damming of river Meden, was demolished in 1937, but the grounds are still accessible. Thoresby Hall, seat of Earl of Manvers, was rebuilt for third time on grand theatrical scale by Salvin in 1864; it contains three-storeyed great hall with hammerbeam roof and library with elaborately carved oak mantelpiece 15 ft high; Jun–Aug, Thurs, Sats, 2.30–6, Sept, Weds, Thurs, 2.30–6, Suns, 12.30–6.30, also Good Fris and Bk Hols.

Eastwood (Notts). Unattractive mining village on high windy ridge, but with surprisingly rural views; birthplace of D. H. Lawrence in 1885.

Edwinstowe (Notts). With Ollerton and Clipstone, good centre for 20m by 10m Sherwood Forest, with its silver birches, oaks, beeches and Major Oak, 1,400 years old and with trunk 30 ft across.

Elford (Staffs). Village of quaint cottages in Tame valley, with old hall, and, reached by splendid avenue of lime trees, St. Peter's church, which has 16c tower, 1870 restorations and interesting 15c monuments and effigies.

Buxton

Ellastone (Staffs). Delightful village overlooking river Dove and backed by Weaver Hills. Wootton Lodge (2m W), splendidly sited 17c mansion. House and village featured in George Eliot's *Adam Bede*.

Eyam (Derbys). Village on W side of Derwent Valley which under leadership of rector went into voluntary isolation when plague struck in 1665. Hall of 17c, village green with stocks, lime-shaded 17c church with Saxon font, sundial curiously sited over S door of chancel, 8-ft high Saxon cross and, in churchyard, tomb of rector's wife (plague victim). Carnival with sheep-roasting at end Aug.

Flagg (Derbys). Straggling village which on Tues following Easter is scene of famous point-to-point races.

Gumley (Leics). Set amid hills and dales, one of prettiest villages in county. Path through woodland leads to ancient hall and part-restored 13c church.

Hathersage (Derbys). Old-world village with 14c parish church housing tombs of Agincourt hero Robert Eyre, his wife and 14 children and other relatives. Reputed grave of Robin Hood's Little John in churchyard. Millstone Edge Nick (1½m E), more often called the Surprise by reason of suddenly-revealed beautiful view. Carl Wark (2m E), prehistoric fort. Longshawe Estate (NT) where sheepdog trials are held in Sept. North Lees Hall (1½m N), now farmhouse, associated with Charlotte Bronte's Jane Eyre (by appointment).

Hartington (Derbys). Pleasant town centred on market square, convenient centre for Beresford Dale and Manifold Valley. Hall of 17c now youth hostel, and cruciform church with 14c west tower.

Ilam (Staffs). Model village built by Jesse Watts Russell, who also rebuilt the Hall (NT), beautiful grounds of which overlook Hamps and Manifold rivers which here rise from the earth after underground journey of several miles from rugged Darfus Crags. In the church is curiously carved pre-Norman font, 13c shrine and tomb of St. Bertram and Chantrey monument to David Watts. Thors Cave (3m N), with arched 30-ft entrance, one-time home of Saxons, Romans and prehistoric man; 1m on, 200-ft high limestone mass of Beeston Tor, with St. Bertram's cave at its foot.

Kinver (Staffs). Small town with magnificent views across the Stour. Kinver Edge (NT), summit of which was formerly prehistoric stronghold.

Leek (Staffs). Ancient silk town in mountain and moorland setting above Churnet valley. Parish church of 13c with bells which ring out 14 tunes. Shaft of Saxon cross in churchyard. Gallery with works of Leek Embroidery Society. Rudyard Lake (3m NW), after which poet named, fishing and boating. The Roaches (6m NW), rugged hills rising to 1,500 ft which at certain times of year reflect double sunsets.

Leicester. County town on Soar, built on site of one of Roman Britain's richest towns, Ratae Coritanorum. Roman relics include Jewry Wall, parts of basilica and tesselated pavements. Ruined castle of 12c, of which great hall and part of keep and cellar survive. Castle Hall, with

18c additions, now assizes. Magnificently timbered 14c Guildhall, Guild of Corpus Christi, 1400 Newarke Gate and adjacent Newarke House, now museum. St. Martin's church, Norman with restorations, now cathedral. Museum and art galery, containing English paintings, hand-embroidered pictures and painted glass. On N side of town, Abbey Park with ruins of abbey and memorial to Wolsey, who died here a broken man. Beaumont Hall, with 10 acres of botanical gardens, Mons–Thurs, 10–5, Fris, 10–9. Belgrave Hall, early 18c mansion now museum of furniture, coaches and agricultural implements, weekdays 10–5, Apr–Sept, 10–6, May–Aug, 10–9, Suns 2–5.

Lichfield (Staffs). Pleasant old town with numerous historic buildings. Dr Johnson's birthplace in Market Street now museum. Daily except Mon afternoons and Suns. Three-spired cathedral dating from 1200–1370 and dedicated to St. Chad, with famous W front and 13c choir and octagonal chapter house, is one of finest in England; delicately arched interior incorporates Herkenrode stained glass windows, some beautiful Flemish glass, relics of St. Chad and many carved monuments, including the *Sleeping Children* by Chantrey. Museum of local history. Wall Roman Remains (2m SW), excavated finds (NT and AM) from Roman station of Letocetum. Staffordshire Regimental Museum (3m SE), history of two regiments, including weapons and trophies; Mons–Fris, 10–4.30.

Castle Gate, Leicester

Matlock Bath

Little Dalby (Leics). Village in wooded valley where Stilton cheese was first made by a Mrs Orton in 1730.

Loughborough (Leics). Bright, well-ordered town where the world-famous foundry was established in 1840 by John Taylor, which made the 9-ft high 17-ton bell for St. Pauls. First town to set up a carillon as a memorial of the Great War, the chimes of which were the first bell music ever to be broadcast. Prestwold Hall (2½m NE), Georgian house with painted ceilings and Chippendale furniture set in park of larches, cedars and 2,000 rose trees; selected Suns in July and Sept, 2–7.

Market Harborough (Leics). Pleasant town on river Welland arising from 12c market at ancient ford. Timber framed grammar school of 1614, with gables and ornamented bargeboards, and 13–15c St. Dionysius church, with galleried interior.

Matlock (Derbys). Of the four Matlocks, most attractive and most popular is Matlock Bath, in narrow gorge at S end of Matlock Dale. Thermal springs, warm-water swimming pool, pleasure gardens. Riber Castle, 40-acre fauna reserve on Riber Hill; all year, 10–7 or dusk. Fine views from Heights of Abraham, below which is Rutland Cavern (Easter–Sept), a series of underground caves and famous Jacob's wishing well. Mason Hill (1,100 ft) with Mason Cavern, and Heights of Jacob penetrated for 1,000 yards by Cumberland Cavern. Black Rocks (2m S), with to SE Shining Cliff (NT) and Alport Height (NT). Lea Rhododendron Gardens (5m SE), three acres of rhododendrons and azaleas, Easter–Whitsun, Sats, Suns and Bk Hols, 2–dusk.

Melton Mowbray (Leics). Bustling market town beside river Eye, fox-hunting metropolis and noted for its pork pies and Stilton cheese. Bede House of 1640. Cruciform church of 13–14c with 100-ft high central tower, superb Galilee porch, clerestorey windows, rare feature of aisles on both sides of transepts, superb monuments, stained glass and set of 18c chandeliers. Stapleford Park (5m E), curious mixture of architectural styles, with old wing dating from 1500 decorated with carved biblical and historical scenes and Flemish gables added 1663; contents include fine pictures, furnishings and Balston collection of Staffordshire portrait figures of Victorian age; grounds with lake, herons, geese and miniature passenger railway; Easter Suns and Mons, then May–Sept, Weds, Thurs, Suns and Bk Hols, 2.30–6.30.

Newark (Notts). Quaint old town of narrow streets centred on wide market square. Ruined castle of bishops of Lincoln where King John died, with 12c gateway; castle dismantled 1646 after withstanding three sieges in Royalist cause; Queen's Scone, impressive earthwork. In market place, perpendicular church of St Mary Magdalene, with 250-ft W spire, Norman crypt, late 15c chancel, screen of 1508, stalls with misericords c. 1500 and the Flemyng Brass (Flemish, dated 1363). Museum and art gallery in former Magnus grammar school. Imposing town hall and interesting old inns.

Newton Linford (Leics). Charming village of tree-shaded inn, thatched and timbered cottages and medieval church. Gateway to Bradgate Park, with 1,000 acres of forest and ruins of house in which luckless Lady Jane Grey was born. Nearby, Bardon Hill, Bronze Age stronghold and at 912 ft highest point in Leicestershire, with fine views over Charnwood Forest and hills of Derbyshire and Shropshire. Groby Pool (2m S), large lake with wildfowl, banks of which popular for picnics.

Nottingham. County city on navigable river Trent dominated by 17c castle on high rock now museum and art gallery, with collections of local artists Sandby and Bonnington, lace, embroidery and ceramics. Perpendicular 15c church of St. Mary with large central bell tower and early 15c alabaster tombs. Wollaton Hall, 16c house in huge park with deer and lake, now museum of natural history. Racecourse, Trent Bridge cricket ground, large park (surrounding university) with tennis, bowls, boating lake and children's playground. Goose Fair, first three days in October.

Rowsley (Derbys). Anglers' and artists' village at confluence of Derwent and Wye. Church with altar tomb of first Lady John Manners by Calder Marshall. Manor house of 1652 now Peacock Hotel.

Southwell (Notts). Attractive and quiet town notable for its minster created a cathedral in 1884, with early 12c nave, transepts and two towers, circular clerestorey windows, 13c choir and 14c rood screen; naturalistic carvings in chapter house, added c. 1390. Saracen's Head inn in market place where Charles I stayed shortly before his execution.

Eyam Plague Houses

Stafford. Industrial but pleasant county town on river Stowe, birthplace of Izaak Walton in 1593. Small Norman church of St. Chad with exquisite chancel arch and nave with massive pillars. Timbered High House of 1555 where Charles I and Prince Rupert lodged in 1642. Swan Hotel, where George Borrow worked as an ostler. William Salt library, a fine 18c house containing books and MSS on county. Shallowford (5m NW), with Izaak Walton's cottage by river Meece, now museum.

Taddington (Derbys). At 1,100 ft, one of highest villages in England. Restored 14c church with brasses and tombs. Nearby (1½m), Five Wells Tumulus; Taddington Dale (NT) and Millers Dale (NT).

Tissington (Derbys). Village gem of Peaks, with Tudor mansion and church with Norman doorway and font. The five wells of the parish gave rise to custom of well-dressing on Ascension Day, when biblical texts formed with flower petals pressed on wet clay are placed over each well when it has been blessed. On E (2½m), Thorpe Cloud (942 ft), Reynards Cave and Lovers' Leap.

Weston under Lizard (Staffs). Model village by Watling Street (A5). Chancel of ancient church containing two of the few oak monuments in existence. Weston Park, fine Restoration-style manor built 1671, home of Earls of Bradford for 300 years, with pictures, furniture, Gobelin and Aubusson tapestries and 17c silver and grounds incorporating three lakes, pets corner and falcons; May–mid Sept, Weds, Thurs, Sats, 2–6, Suns and Bk Hols, 2–7.

Woodhouse (Leics). Village of stone-built cottages on fringe of Charnwood Forest. Small church with monuments to the Herricks and churchyard with magnificent views.

Yorkshire Moors and Dales

Yorkshire

England's largest county, Yorkshire was divided by Danish invaders into *thryddings* or thirds; excluding the city of York, these divisions remain for administrative purposes as the Ridings, North, East and West. Beyond the Leeds-to-Hull line this is a spacious and sparsely populated region embracing a wide range of scenery, from wild and remote moorland to fells and green dales and a coast of high cliffs and sandy bays. A rich store of prehistoric, Roman and Saxon relics is matched by a profusion of grim castles and lovely abbeys and the climate is as bracing as the people are direct.

West Riding

Leg of mutton shaped area with every scenic variation except a sea coast. The dominant feature is the Pennine chain of interlocking hills, from which the streams flow eastward to the wide Vale of York. The northern part with its limestone hills is notable for its caverns, potholes and subterranean rivers, that in the NW for its beautiful vistas in which grey rocks contrast with sparkling rivers and bright green pastures separated by dry stone walls. In summer the moorlands of the Southern Pennines are covered with purple heather.

East Riding

Two basic elements in the East Riding scene, which includes the southern half of the coast, are the low-lying and fertile Holderness plain N of Hull and the Wolds, once a vast sheep-walk and now mainly devoted to wheat-growing. Highlight of the coast, the resorts along which are mostly of the modest kind, is Flamborough Head, a range of tall cliffs rising sheer from the sea.

North Riding

Within the boundary of North Riding is the northern half of the coast (from just N of Filey to the Tees) and the whole of the North York Moors and part of the Yorkshire Dales national parks. The moors take in the Hambleton and Cleveland Hills, the dales the three main valleys of Teesdale, Swaledale and, acknowledged the most inviting, Wensleydale. In the often wild and remote hinterland is a store of medieval buildings, including castles built by the Norman barons. Resorts along the coast are among the largest and most popular in Britain.

Of Special Interest

Ampleforth (S of Helmsley). Modern abbey church in romanesque style with pointed arches and unusual dome; in St. Benedict chapel, high altar stone from ruined Byland Abbey.

The Ark, Tadcaster (10m SW York). Old timbered house, restored and now museum. Tues, Weds, Thurs, 2–4.

Barden Tower (9½m NW Ilkley). Ruined 15c Tower house in beautiful Wharfedale setting, built for protection of deer in forest. All year, 9–dusk.

Beningbrough Hall (8m NW York). Brick and stone house (NT), of 1716, noteworthy interior decoration including carved friezes and oak staircase. Apr–Sept, Weds, Sats, 2–6.

Bolton Castle (4m NE Aysgarth). 14c stronghold of Scrope family, one-time Wardens of Western Marches. Folk museum. Daily, except Mon, 10–dusk, Suns, 9–5.30.

Bowes Castle (11m NW of Richmond). 12c Norman Keep (AM) on site of Roman fort. Standard hours.

Bramham Park (6m S Wetherby). Partly 17c mansion in park, damaged by fire 19c and restored with additions 20c. West front resembles Versaille, gardens in French style. Easter–Sept, Suns, 2–6 and Bk Hols.

Browsholme Hall (5½m N Clitheroe). 1507 mansion with 18c additions in landscaped garden. House contains period panelling, china, fine furniture and pictures. Good Fri–mid Oct, Thurs, Sats, Suns and Bk Hols, 2–6.30.

Burton Agnes Hall (6m SW Bridlington). Late Elizabethan manor house of red brick and stone dressings with picturesque old gatehouse, containing carvings, paintings, tapestries and four centuries of furniture. Mon–Fri, 1.45–5 (Suns till 6), May–mid Oct.

Burton Constable Hall (Sproatley, 8m NE Hull). Magnificent Tudor house with unique 18c interior of Constable family, containing furniture by Adam and Wyatt, carved panelling, paintings and statuary. Parklands by Capability Brown incorporate 22 lakes (boating and fishing), rare birds, children's zoo, dolls' museum. Easter–Sept, Tues–Fri, Suns and Bk Hols 12–6.

Castle Howard (6m W Malton). Vast Palladian mansion begun by Vanbrugh 1699 for third earl of Carlisle and completed 1726 by Hawksmoor, with richly decorated interior containing furniture, paintings and china. Costume gallery.

Castle Howard

England's greatest private mausoleum in formal gardens. Easter Sun–Oct, Tues–Thurs, Sats and Suns, 1.45–5.15. Grounds, 12.30–6.30.

Conisbrough Castle (5m SW Doncaster). Six-buttressed Keep of 12c (AM).

Cusworth Hall (1½m W Doncaster). 18c house with fine chimney pieces and Chapel. Museum, with children's section. Daily 12–5. Fishing in ponds.

East Riddleston Hall (2m NE Keighley). Stone-built 17c manor house (NT) with wheel windows and tithe barn. All year, daily, 2–6 or dusk. Closed Dec.

Harewood House (7m S Harrogate). Home of Earls of Harewood, exterior by John Carr 1759, Adam interior. Fine state rooms, pictures and Chippendale furniture. Park landscaped by Capability Brown. Easter Sat–end Sept, Suns in Oct, 11–6.

Haworth (4m SW Keighley). Bleak and windswept mecca for Bronte fans. Old Parsonage houses museum of Bronte relics. Summer, 11–5.45, Winter, 11–4.45. Sunday, 2–4.45 or 5.45.

Kirkham Priory (5m SW Malton). (AM). Beautifully situated by river Derwent. Splendid 13c sculptured gatehouse. Standard hours.

Kirkstall Abbey (3m NW Leeds). Abbey House museum, former gatehouse of ruined cistercian abbey, local archaeology and folk exhibits, including three streets; Mons–Sats, 10–5, Suns, 2–6, Oct–Mar, 10–6, Apr–Sept.

Mount Grace Priory (6m NE Northallerton). Ruined 14c priory (NT), founded Carthusian order which enjoined isolation, austerity and silence; cells of hermit monks intact. Daily, except Mons (open Bk Hols), 9.30–7, Suns from 2.

Newby Hall (4m SE Ripon). Robert Adam mansion with fine gardens reaching down to river Ure; decorated ceilings, Gobelin tapestries and classical statuary. Weds–Thurs, Sats–Suns, 2–7 and Bk Hols April–mid Oct.

Nostell Priory (Wragby, 6m SE Wakefield). Site of 12c Augustinian priory now occupied by 18c mansion (NT) designed by James Paine, with 1772 Adam wing. Chippendale furniture, paintings.

Nunnington Hall (6m SE Helmsley). 16–17c manor (NT) with panelled hall and staircase, 1580 West wing. May–end Sept, Weds and Suns, 2–6.

Harewood House

Oakwell Hall, Birstall (3m NW Dewsbury). Elizabethan house containing furniture, pottery and paintings, now a museum. Nov–end Mar, daily (exc. Fris) 12–5, Apr–end Oct, 2–7.

Ormesby Hall (3m SE Middlesbrough). 18c mansion (NT) with fine plasterwork and stables, furniture and pictures. May–end Sept, Weds and Sats, 2.30–6.30.

Pontefract Castle (Pontefract). Ruined Norman stronghold with Keep, Chapel and dungeons. Small museum of Roman and medieval relics. Mons–Fris, 8–dusk, Sats and Suns, 10–dusk.

Rievaulx Abbey and Terrace (2½m NW Helmsley). Beautifully preserved ruined white stone Cistercian abbey (AM) founded 1131 by Walter l'Espec, Lord of Helmsley (pronounced Reevo or Rivers). The terrace provides views over Hambleton and Rydale hills, gardens with two 18c temples and frescoe paintings. Terrace open daily, 9–7 or dusk.

Selby Abbey (10m N Snaith). Splendid monastic church founded for Benedictines in 1069 by William the Conqueror. Restored after fire in 1906. Perpendicular font cover and 14c stained-glass window by Jesse. Fine Norman doorway and beautiful stone screens.

Shibden Hall (Halifax). 15c half-timbered manor house, furnished in style of period with extensive grounds high above Shibden Dale, housing West Yorks Folk museum. Apr–Sept, Mons–Sats, 11–7, Suns, 2–5, Oct. 11–5, Suns, 2–5, Mar and Dec, Weds, Thurs, Sats, 2–5, and Nov, Weds, Thurs, Sat, Suns, 2–5. Closed Jan and Feb.

Sledmere House (8m NW Gt Driffield). 1751 mansion with 100-ft long library in Adam style. Chippendale, Sheraton and French furnishings, porcelain and antique statuary. One room uniquely decorated with Turkish tiles. Grounds landscaped by Capability Brown. Easter Sun and Mon, then Suns only to mid-May, 1.30–6, Mid-May–end Sept, Tues–Suns (except Fris).

Resorts and Centres of Interest

Aysgarth (8m W Leyburn). Convenient centre for Wensleydale but mainly of interest for the falls and cascades of impressive Aysgarth Force.

Bedale. Ancient market town in hunting country. Broad main street with 14c market cross. St. Gregory church with defensive tower, arcades and wall paintings. Nearby, Bedale Hall, Georgian house with museum, Tues, 10–12 and 2–4.30. Snape Castle (3m S), once home of Catherine Parr, Henry VIII's sixth wife; chapel only accessible, during daylight hours.

Beverley. Market town noted for its beautiful twin-towered 13c minster, with double transepts, Percy Shrine with Gothic canopy and frid stool on which in medieval times sat those claiming rights of sanctuary. Brick-built and castellated North Bar, rebuilt 1409, only survivor of town's five medieval gates. 17c Guildhall with ornate plasterwork. Market cross in Saturday Market. High-towered St. Mary church, with panelled ceiling in chancel depicting early kings. Art gallery and museum of local antiquities and Victorian china, paintings by the Elwells and local artists, Mons–Sats, 10–6.

Boroughbridge. Devil's Arrows (2m N), three huge standing stones erected in straight line during Bronze Age. Aldborough (1m W), site of Britain's northernmost Roman town, with fragments of boundary wall and tessellated pavements and small museum of Roman utensils; stone panel depicting Mercury built into N aisle of local church.

Bramham Moor (4m W Tadcaster). Site of battle in which army under Henry IV defeated Earl of Northumberland's forces in 1408.

Bridlington. Coast resort on sandy beach developed round ancient quay and harbour; one mile inland old market town with ruined Augustinian priory, nave of which continues as parish church. Bayle Gate Museum, 14c priory gatehouse now museum of local antiquities, June–Sept, 10–11.30 and 2.30–4.30, 6d. Boating lake. Sewerby Hall, Georgian house with gardens containing small zoo, Easter–Sept, daily 9.30–dusk, 1s, gardens and zoo all year, 6d. To N chalk cliffs, pebbly bays and caves of Flamborough Head, most prominent feature of coast.

Brimham Rocks (3m E Pateley Bridge). On moorland plateau huge stones weathered into grotesque shapes. The 200-ton Idol Rock balances on a 12-in stalk. Accessible daily.

Buckden. Dale-head village in wild, mountain-hemmed setting to SW of 2,302-ft terraced Buckden Pike. Handsome arched bridge over Wharfe. Linked with Aysgarth to N by 1392-ft Kidstone Pass. Nearby, Kelmsey Crag, rocky outcrop 200 ft high. Hubberholme Church (1m NW) has several quaint features.

149

Filey

Burnsall. Lovely views from this charming village and popular centre for exploring Wharfdale. Old Norse font in church and heathen symbols on Norse gravestones. Good angling and boating facilities.

Castleton. Trim and attractive with good shooting, fishing and excellent rides and walks over moors. 1671 Robin Hood Inn.

Cayton Bay. Wide sandy beach with good bathing and favourite spot for campers.

Clapham. Romantically placed at foot of Ingleborough and good centre for walking, climbing and potholing.

Coxwold. Exceptionally attractive village of great charm. Wide main street leading to 15c octagonal-towered church of St. Michael, with unusual 18c communion rail and pulpit; elaborate monuments to Bellasis family. 1m NE Byland Abbey, 1177, famed for its coloured glazed tiles and great wheel window, museum on site.

Filey. Peaceful resort with broad expanse of sand beneath eroding cliffs. Local fishermen use *cobles* or flat-bottomed boats. Filey Borough or Brigg, long spur of rock jutting out into the bay.

Goathland (SW Whitby). Scattered village on plateau, popular as centre for walks on magnificent heather-clad moors. Nearby waterfalls of Mallyan Spout, Thomassin Force and Nelly Ayre falls. Excavated section of Roman road known as Wade's causeway.

Glaisdale (7m E Castleton). Village at edge of 1,400-ft high moor of the same name. Centre for excursions to Eskdale, with its verdant scenery, rocky falls and rough stone bridges.

Grosmont (3m SW Sleights). At confluence of Esk and its principal tributary. Good centre for angling.

Guisborough. Ancient town situated among beautiful scenery. Ruins of great 12c priory in grounds of 19c Guisborough Hall, also horse-chestnut tree with a 150-yd span. Roseberry Topping (3m SW) most notable of Cleveland Hills, with panoramic view including that of Captain Cook's monument on Easby Moor.

Harrogate. Fashionable moorland spa and conference centre. Over 80 mineral springs (sulphur and iron) with Royal Baths and, now museum, Royal Pump Room. Notable flower gardens. Halle music festival July. Rudding Park (3m SE), ornately furnished Regency mansion housing rich collection of paintings and tapestries, park designed by Repton, Easter–Oct, daily except Fris, 2–6.

Hawes (15m E Sedbergh). At 850 ft highest town in Wensleydale. Noted touring centre for the dale and visits to Hardraw Force, the highest unbroken fall in G. Britain (100 ft in a single leap).

Helmsley. Chief town of southern Yorkshire moors, ringed by woods. Castle (AM) with fine gardens on ridge above town built in 12c by Walter l'Espec. Good trout fishing in Rye.

Hornsea. Seaside resort at centre of wide bay at edge of Holderness plain. Hornsea Mere, large freshwater lake, boating, angling, bird sanctuary.

Hovingham Spa (9m NW Malton). Lovely village for a quiet holiday. 1760 Hovingham Hall where festivals held.

Hutton-le-Hole (10m NW Pickering). Outstandingly attractive village with picturesque green and multi-bridged stream. Ryedale Folk Museum with medieval cruck house in grounds, Summer 2–8, Winter 2–5.

Ilkley. Spa and tourist centre at edge of Rombald's Moore and gateway to Upper Wharfdale with its stone circles, ancient bridges and rocks. Fine view of valley from top of steep Chevin Hill. Swimming pool, golf course. 16c Manor House Museum (local history) and art gallery, May–Sept daily except Mons. 10–12.30 and 2–5, Oct–Apr 2–5 (6d). 6m along dale, Bolton Priory, built 1154 on site of manor of Saxon Earl by Augustinian Canons. Melancholy ruins in lovely setting.

Ingleton. Popular angling, walking centre at foot of 2,373 ft Ingleborough. White Scar caverns, limestone caves beneath Ingleborough, with waterfalls and lake (guide). Ingleborough Cave with stalactite and stalagmite formations, Apr–Sept daily. Nearby, Thornton Force and Beezley waterfalls. Notorious potholes of Alum Pot, 300 ft deep, and Gaping Gill, with vertical drop of 378 ft. Ingleborough Hall, with famous rock gardens.

Kettlewell (15m N Skipton). At the foot of Great Whernside, 2,310 ft. Splendid centre for walkers, while for less energetic beautiful scenery within yards.

Kirbymoorside (8m W Pickering). Market town of red pantile-roofed houses, with moors above. Remnants of castle. Nearby, ancient Saxon church of St. Gregory's Minster (Kirkdale church) with sundial and other relics dating from 1055.

Knaresborough. Beautifully sited riverside resort on Nidd. Many 18c houses. Ruined 14c John of Gaunt's castle, keep and two baileys, guided tour. Zoological gardens. Manor house presented by James I to son Charles for fishing lodge. Riverside walks, boating. Dropping Well waterfall and Mother Shipton's wishing well.

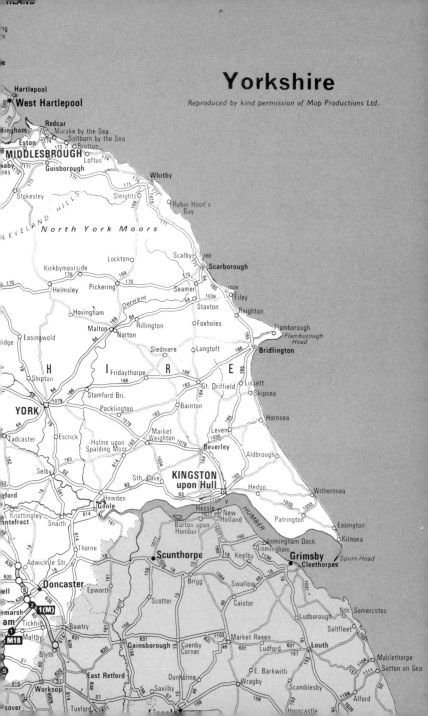

Yorkshire

Reproduced by kind permission of Map Productions Ltd.

Lastingham (7m N Pickering). Beautiful moorland village bisected by Hole Beck stream. Beneath local church is 11c crypt forming church in itself built over grave of St. Cedd, founder of monastery on the site.

Leyburn. Market town centred on broad square. SE Ure flows by ruined Jervaulx Abbey. Nearby, Masham, with 14c church with 1,000-year-old Saxon cross in churchyard.

Malham (E of Settle). Set amid some of most remarkable rock scenery in Yorkshire, at head of Airedale. Dominated by 300-ft high cliff at Malham Cove where river Aire burst into daylight after journeying underground. To E are hidden valleys and limestone gorges, typical of which is Gordale Scar, where the river has cut a cleft in 400-ft high rocks. On moors to N, Malham Tarn, large lake (NT), access to S shore only.

Malton. Old market town on W bank of Derwent. Two Norman arcaded churches. Flamingo Park, 18c house with 350-acre park, flower gardens, lakes, shrubs and trees. The zoo, set amid picnic fields, also has performing dolphins.

Middleham (13m S Richmond). Racehorse breeding centre dominated by ponderous castle (AM), the 'Windsor of the North', former home of Earl of Warwick and Duke of Gloucester, later Richard III; remains consist of rectangular stone keep surrounded by high curtain wall. Roman earthworks, unusual medieval church.

Middlesmoor (NW Pateley Bridge). Picturesquely situated on high promontory with wonderful views of Nidderdale, particularly from churchyard. Church contains interesting antiquities, including Cross of St. Chad (664).

Muker (N of Hawes). Pretty village, 'capital' of Upper Swaledale. Higher reaches of river around Muker and Keld are enclosed by heights of 2,000 ft. On hills to N 2,303 ft Rogan's Seat, vantage point for view of whole length of Swale. Nearby, Buttertubs Pass ('tubs' being deep holes in the limestone) across Pennines, 1,750 ft.

North York Moors National Park. 553 square miles of open moor covering the E half of North Riding and extending from Vale of Pickering to Tees. Moors landscape is remote and often bleak.

Pateley Bridge. Popular centre for walking and cycling and for exploring beautiful upper regions of Nidderdale. Of appeal to those interested in geology or botany. Within walking distance of immense Ravensgill Gorge and towering Guy's Cliff, topped by a mock ruin. 4½m W the extensive Stump Cross stalactite caverns, discovered in 1860 (admission charge).

Pickering. Pleasant old town to N of scenic Vale of Pickering. Ruined 12c Norman castle (AM) consisting of large shell keep on mound flanked by baileys, where Richard II imprisoned. Long low parish church with 15c frescoes on clerestory walls.

Ravenscar. On a high plateau commanding magnificent view of moors, cliffs and sea. Fishing and riding, swimming pool.

Redcar. Lively and most northerly resort on Yorkshire coast, with three sandy beaches and sand-dunes. Covered seawater swimming pool, boating lake and open air skating rink.

Richmond. Picturesque market town with cobbled streets, narrow alleys and old houses. 11c castle (AM) on rocky crag above Swale with perfectly preserved massive Norman keep. In huge market place (formerly the outside bailey of the castle) Holy Trinity church with shops built into its walls. Grey Friar tower the only remnant of a once-powerful Franciscan friary.

Ripley (4m N Harrogate). Pretty village, one-time market town, mentioned in Domesday Book, with peaceful square and market cross. 15c All Saints church has interesting tombs and monuments, and the pedestal of an ancient (2c) Weeping Cross in graveyard. Ripley Castle (1350) has 15c gatehouse and 16c tower and boasts a 600-year-old unbroken family line of descent. Fine gardens and grounds, May–Sep, Sun and Easter Mon. (2/6). Gardens only Jun–Sep, Sats, 2–6 (1/-).

Ripon. Centre for exploring soft upper reaches of Wensleydale. Small St. Wilfrid's cathedral embodies diverse architectural styles. Wakeman's House, home of 13c medieval official with the task of sounding the Wakeman's Horn at 9 each eve, a custom still followed. 3½m SW Markenfield Hall, 14c moated and castellated mansion, now farmhouse, banqueting hall, chapel, Tudor gatehouse and curious stables. May–Sep, Mons 10–3.

Robin Hood's Bay. Crazy collection of cottages tucked into fold in cliffs above sandy beach, one-time notorious smugglers haunt. Descent too steep for vehicles.

Runswick (N of Whitby). Perched on a steep cliffside overlooking beautiful bay, tightly packed cottages, narrow path-like streets and a profusion of flowers. Good bathing, boating and fishing, and offering an unconventional type of holiday.

Saltburn. Modern cliff-top resort with 8m of sands below; attractive pleasure gardens. Angling, boating, golf and tennis. On W, Skelton Castle, castellated 18c mansion.

Scarborough. Large and attractive seaside resort and conference centre on two great sandy bays separated by rocky headland on which stands ruined castle (AM) rebuilt 1155. Old houses ring fishing harbour in corner of S. Bay. Peasholme Park, with lake, Northstead Manor Gardens, also with lake and miniature railway; Italian Gardens, Holbeck Gardens, Bellevue rose gardens. Two swimming pools, open air theatre. Dutch festival each spring, cricket festival in summer. Paths along cliffs. Wood End, former home of Sitwell family, now natural history museum. Art gallery. Museum housing archaeological relics from N. Riding.

Sedberg. Remote market town ringed by fells and rolling moorland. 17c Friends meeting house. Nearby Dunkergill Cave, with subterranean stream. Baugh Fell, 2,216 ft, best climbed via Hebblethwaite Gill.

North Bay, Scarborough, from castle

Settle. Old-world town at vantage point in Upper Ribblesdale, backed by limestone headland of Castleberg. Market charter dating from 1248. Gabled houses with oriel windows and ancient market place. Two-tier Shambles, shops with houses above. NW Victoria Cave, 450 ft, finds from which are housed in local museum.

Skipton. 'Sheep town' in the centre of Craven, a limestone district of fells and dales. On rock overlooking Eller Beck fortified manor house of 13–14c (partly rebuilt in 17c) owned since 1269 by Clifford family, whose motto 'Desormais' is over keep. Sloping down from church and castle, high street with museum of relics from Craven district, Mons, Weds, Fris 2–5, Sats 10–12 and 1.30–4.30, free. Skipton is the home of famous Craven Pothole Club.

Sleights (4m SW Whitby). Charming village on river Eske and popular centre owing to its proximity to both moor and sea. Boating on river, charming riverside walk to Falling Foss, where the 50-ft fall of water has hollowed out a great rocky basin in a woodland glen.

Staithes. Cornish-style fishing village huddled in ravine-like valley below chalk cliffs.

Studley Royal and Fountains Abbey (3m SW Ripon). An avenue of limes leads through Studley Deer Park to the Abbey grounds, where the little River Skell has been utilised to form a fantastic water garden of canals and geometrically shaped pools. Temples and superb statuary. Over the lake rise the impressive ruins of 12c Fountains Abbey (AM) with its noteworthy eleven bays, lovely Chapel of Nine Altars, Chapter House and double-arched cellarium. (2/6). Nearby Fountains Hall, restored 17c mansion with interesting chapel room, minstrels' Gallery and museum. 10–6.

Thirsk. Rugged market town centred on market square, with several old coaching inns. 18c Hall, ruined Mowbray castle, 15c church with fine woodwork and stained glass. Centre for exploring 1,000-ft high Hambleton Hills.

Thornton Dale (3m E Pickering). Perhaps the prettiest village in the county and increasingly popular as walking and cycling centre. Stream flows along tree-shaded main street. c. 1300 Market Cross on green.

Wensley (4m W Leyburn). Once an important market town, pre-Norman, lying at foot of Dale which takes its name. Outstandingly picturesque village. Church has Restoration font-cover, 15c screen, medieval wall paintings and fragments of a Saxon cross.

Wetherby. Market town and summer resort on Wharfe. High street dropping to river. Unspoilt old inns hung with sporting prints recall town's place in racing calendar. Colonnaded market hall. Boating and riverside walks, angling, golf and racecourse.

Whitby. Holiday resort combined with market town and ancient fishing port enclosing natural harbour formed by Esk estuary. Old quarter on S, spa and gardens on N. On headland of E cliff gaunt ruins of Benedictine abbey, founded soon after Norman conquest, forming a tracery against the sky. Monument to Captain James Cook (1728–79) who was apprenticed to a Whitby shipowner before joining the R. Navy and sailing in the Whitby-built *Endeavour* to discover New Zealand. Art gallery and museum. Local speciality is jewellery made from black jet (hard fossilised wood). Inland, beautiful Valley of Esk, with quaint villages of Egton and Westerdale. Within walking distance, fine beach of Sandsend.

Withernsea (17m E Hull). Modest resort on Holderness coast fast being eroded by the sea. Lighthouse in main street. To S, promontory of Spurn Head, haunt of bird watchers.

York. Well-preserved medieval walled city at confluence of Fosse and Ouse. Seat of the White Rose faction. Historic crucifix-shaped Minster built 1220 stands on site of chapel built by Edwin, King of Northumbria in 627 and incorporates world-famous stained glass (notable are Five Sisters and huge E windows) and central Lantern Tower. Treasurer's House in NE corner of Minster (NT), with fine paintings and furniture, 13c Cliffords Tower built by Henry III on a high mound. Town walls punctuated by four entrance gates or 'bars', Stonegate and Micklegate being the best preserved. The walk along the top of the walls is 2½m long. Many narrow winding streets flanked by ancient timbered houses, as in Stonegate and Shambles. Ancient inns, such as the Black Swan. Castle museums (folklore) Apr–Sept., Mons–Sats, 9.30–8, Suns 2–8, Oct–Mar, 9.30–5, Suns 2–5. Castle Keep (AM). Hospitium, with Roman relics. Yorkshire Museum in grounds of ruined St. Mary's Abbey. Restored 15c Guildhall has underground passage leading to river.

Yorkshire Dales National Park. Divided equally between E and W Ridings. Covers 680 sq. miles of unspoilt dales and central Pennines. Highest point in dales is Mickle Fell, 2,991 ft.

Blackpool's famous tower

North West and Lake District

Cumberland—Lancashire and Isle of Man— Westmorland

Cumberland

The mountainous scenery of this north-western county which includes a great part of the famed Lake District, attracts many visitors and it is today one of the most famous tourist regions in Britain. Wasdale Head, near Wastwater, is a popular rock-climbing centre. Derwentwater, Buttermere, Crummock Water, Ennerdale, Wastwater and a part of Ullswater all lie within the county. Scafell, England's loftiest point, rises to 3,210 ft. Other points are Great Gable and Pillar. Cross Fell, highest peak of the Pennines, lies to the E. There is a long coastline to Solway Firth and the Irish Sea, but it is in the main given over to industry.

Lancashire

A county of great cities and sprawling industrial towns, of large tracts of wild moorland, of lakes and wooded valleys, and with a coastline of renowned holiday resorts. Chief rivers are the Mersey, the Ribble and the Lune, the latter two providing good fishing. Major resorts include Blackpool, Southport, Lytham St. Annes, Fleetwood and Morecambe. There are several nature reserves and Coniston Water and the greater part of Lake Windermere are within the county.

Westmorland

One of the smallest and least populated counties of England, but with some of the finest mountain scenery in Britain. Parts of the Lake District

National Park fall within the county and include Grasmere, Rydal Water, Haweswater and portions of Ullswater and Windermere. Along the border with Cumberland stand the high peaks of Bowfell (2,960 ft), Crinkle Crags (2,816 ft) and Helvellyn (3,118 ft). The river Lune rises on Wild Boar Fell to enter Lancashire near Kirkby Lonsdale, and the river Eden separates lakeland fells from the Pennine range to the east. Arnside and Sandside are holiday villages on Morecambe Bay, whilst Bowness and Ambleside are important tourist centres on Lake Windermere.

Of Special Interest

Borwick Hall (2m N of Carnforth). Late Elizabethan house built around defensive pele tower. Gardens, 17c gatehouse and barns. May–Sept, Weds, Suns, Bk Hols, 2.30–6.

Brougham Castle (1½m SE of Penrith). Outer walls, gatehouse and massive 12c keep. Occupies site of Roman fort of Brocavum on S bank of river Eamont. (AM Standard hours).

Brough Castle (8m SE of Appleby). Considerable remains of Norman keep with later buildings around paved courtyard. 17c restoration. (AM Standard hours).

Carlisle Castle. (See page 171).

Cartmel Priory (2m NW Grange-over-Sands). Fine specimen of Transition-Norman architecture built 1188 with remarkable upper tower. The gatehouse (NT) open always.

Castlerigg Stone Circle (1½m E of Keswick). Oval formation of 38 standing stones enclosing an oblong space of 10 other stones. (AM and NT any time).

Corby Castle (Wetheral). 17c house incorporates ancient pele tower. Extensive wooded grounds by river Eden. Grounds only, Thurs.

Cranford (Aughton). Modern garden, roses, rare trees and shrubs. Apr–mid Oct, 10–dusk.

Furness Abbey (1½m of Barrow). Cistercian abbey of 1112. Extensive remains of church and monastic buildings (AM Standard hours).

Hardnott Castle Roman Fort (9m NE of Ravenglass). Roman fort at head of Eskdale, established c. A.D. 105. Between fort and road is ruin of bathhouse (AM any time).

Heaton Hall (4m N of Manchester). (NT). Former home of Earls of Wilton by James Wyatt. Assheton Bennett collection of paintings and English silver. May–Aug, weekdays, 10–8, Suns, 2–8. Other months, 10–4 or 6 and from 2 p.m.

Hill Top Farm (Sawrey, Hawkshead). Former home of Beatrix Potter, the authoress, with personal relics. NT. Easter–Oct, weekdays, 10·30–12.30. Spring Bk. Hol–Sept, daily, 10.30–12.30 and 2–5.45.

Holker Hall (Cark-in-Cartmel). 16–19c country house set in beautiful gardens and deer park. Easter–Sept, daily (except Fris), 10.30–6.

Lancaster Castle (Lancaster). 11–15c stronghold with 14c gateway. Easter–Sept, 11–3.30.

Lanercost Priory (on river Irthing, 2m from Brampton). Church and claustral buildings of Augustinian priory of 12c. (AM Standard).

Rufford Old Hall

Leighton Hall (Carnforth). Neo–Gothic house with fine interior. Pictures and furniture. Large grounds. May–Sept, Weds, Suns, and Bk Hols, 2.30–6.

Levens Hall (5m S of Kendal). Picturesque mainly Elizabethan mansion, rich in oak carving and works of old masters. Fine topiary garden. May–Sept. Hall, Tues, Weds, Thurs, Suns, 2–5. Gardens daily (except Sat afternoons).

Muncaster Castle Gardens (Ravenglass). Large shrub garden attached to mansion wherein Henry VI took refuge. Extensive views over Lake District. Gardens only Apr–mid Sept, Weds, Sats and Suns, from 1 p.m.

Platt Hall (Rusholme, Manchester). Georgian mansion with Gallery of English Costume. Weekdays, 10–4, 6 or 8. Suns from 2.

Rufford Old Hall (Rufford). Late medieval hall of half timbered and plaster panels. Hammer beam roof. Museum. NT, weekdays (except Mons), 10–8, Suns, 1–8. Closed Weds, Oct–Mar.

Shap Abbey (1m W of Shap). Premonstratensian abbey founded c. 1080 at Preston Patrick and moved to Shap c 1199. 13c buildings with 16c W tower. (AM Standard hours).

Sizergh Castle (3½m S of Kendal). Home of Strickland family for seven centuries. Ancient pele tower (NT). Apr–Sept, Weds, 2–5.45.

Speke Hall (8m SE of Liverpool). Richly half-timbered house around square courtyard. Great hall, 16c plasterwork. Mortlake tapestries. NT. Apr–Sept, weekdays, 10–7, Mons, 2–7. Closes 5 p.m in winter.

Tullie House Museum (Carlisle). (See page 171).

Wordsworth House (Cockermouth). Birthplace of the poet in 1770. Preserves original staircase and fireplaces. (NT. Easter–Sept, Mons, Weds and Sats, 10–12, 2–5).

Wythenshawe Hall (6m S of Manchester). Restored 11–19c house, half-timbered. Furniture and pictures of 17c. Parkland. Weekdays, 10–4, 6 or 8, Suns from 2 p.m.

161

Resorts and Centres of Interest

Allonby (Cumb). Small resort on coast 5m N of Maryport with shingle beach and some sand.

Ambleside (Westm). Attractive small town with old stone houses and tumbling stream at head of Lake Windermere. There is boating and water-skiing on the lake at Waterhead and a motor vessel service to Bowness and Lake Side. Bridge House (NT) is a quaint building over the Stock Beck. Above the town is Stock Ghyll Force, a 76-ft cascade.

Appleby (Westm). County town and Royal and Ancient borough on the river Eden between high Lakeland fells and the Pennines. Trout fishing and golf. 12c–17c castle and Moot Hall.

Arnside (Westm). The only 'port' on the short Westmorland coast occupying pleasant site on the E shore of the Kent estuary. A long viaduct connects with Grange. Boating.

Askham (Westm). Picturesque village 3½m from Pooley Bridge and over-looking river Lowther. There is a part 16c hall.

Beetham (Westm). Village with ancient church of Norman to 15c work. 15–17c Beetham Hall is now farmhouse. 2m N is Milnthorpe.

Blackpool (Lancs). Unique resort with extensive sands and every con-ceivable enteprise in sport and entertainment. 7m promenade one of longest and finest in the world and its main feature, the celebrated Tower, rises 520 ft above ground. Three piers, swimming pool, Pleasure Beach. Behind the town, Stanley Park is beauty spot, with conservatories, floral displays, gardens, boating lake and sports. 5m N is Thornton Cleveleys with fine promenade, beach and entertainment.

Bolton-le-Sands (Lancs). S of Carnforth, small resort with sands and bathing.

Bowness and Windermere (Westm). Twin villages together forming small town on eastern side of Lake Windermere 4m from its head. Bowness is 'port' of the lake and good centre for fishing, yachting and boating.

Brampton (Cumb). Small town on river Irthing (fishing) near stretches of the Roman Wall. Nearby is Lanercost Priory (AM).

Brough (Westm). Village with church (12–17c) with interesting brass inscriptions. Brough castle (AM) is Norman. In Lune Forest 8m N is Mickle Fell at 2,591 ft Yorkshire's highest peak.

Buttermere (Cumb). Small lakeland village in beautiful setting between Crummock Water and Buttermere Lake. A noble setting of mountains includes Brandreth, Green Gable, Haystack, High Crag, High Stile and Red Pike. Popular excursion is to Scale Force, the loftiest fall (100 ft) in the district.

Caldbeck (Cumb). Village of interest on account of its association with John Peel, the renowned huntsman, whose gravestone is in churchyard.

Calder Bridge (Cumb). Village on river Calder 2m from the sea at Sellafield. Calder Hall was Britain's first nuclear power station. The 12c ruins of Calder Abbey (summer, weekdays 10–4) show a Norman doorway, central tower, transept and cloisters.

Cark-in-Cartmel (Lancs). Quaint village visited for Holker Hall, 16c country house in beautiful gardens.

Carlisle (Cumb). County town and busy industrial city on river Eden with prime interest in its castle and cathedral. The Castle dates from time of William Rufus; Regimental museum in keep, prison cells. (AM Standard hours). Cathedral of 12c onwards has notable 14c E window and beautifully carved capitals to choir pillars. The Tullie House Museum with Art Gallery, and the medieval Guildhall are of interest. Well-known Racecourse.

Cartmel (Lancs). Quiet old place 2m NW of Grange-over-Sands with fine old Priory church (gatehouse NT). Remarkable upper tower, beautiful E window.

Castletown (Isle of Man). Former capital in Castletown Bay towards the southern tip of the Island. On river Silverburn. The much-isolated Castle Rushen dates from 1350 (open daily). Its one-fingered Queen Elizabeth's Clock has remained in working order since 1597. The unusual Witches' Mill is museum of witchcraft. To E is Ronaldsway Airport.

Cockermouth (Cumb). Small town at northern edge of Lake District at junction of rivers Cocker and Derwent. Of interest is Wordsworth House, in main street, and birthplace of the poet in 1770. (NT Easter-Sept. Mons, Weds, Sats, 10–12, 2–5. Parts of the Norman castle are open 9.30–6, Sats, 9.30–12.

Coniston (Lancs). Village near western shore of Coniston Water at northern end. Ruskin museum with relics and pictures, his grave in churchyard. Coniston Water beautifully wooded, with Peel Island and Fir Island, both NT. Favourite excursions to Tarn Hows, Tilberthwaite, Duddon Valley. To W is Coniston Old Man (2,633 feet).

Dungeon Ghyll (Westm). Rising on Harrison Stickle (2,401 ft) and waterfall plunging to the Great Langdale Beck, 3m SW of Grasmere.

Douglas (Isle of Man). Capital and seaport through which most visitors pass, and principal resort of the Island. A 2m long sea front curves round the sheltered Douglas Bay. Firm and extensive sands, boating, fishing. Golf and many sports. The Manx museum, National Library and Art Gallery are noteworthy. There are several ballrooms, theatres, and a casino. Tower of Refuge offshore is picturesque castellated building marking position of dangerous Conister Rock. The Marine Drive is splendid roadway round Douglas Head with fine seascapes.

Fleetwood (Lancs). Busy fishing port and resort on Fylde coast 9m N of Blackpool. Boat services to Douglas, Isle of Man. Sandy beach, bowls, putting, pool, model yacht lake, golf.

Grange-over-Sands (Lancs). Pleasant coastal resort on sheltered northern shore of Morecambe Bay. Promenade nearly $1\frac{1}{2}$m long with bathing pool, tennis, bowls and putting. At 2m W is Cartmel with fine old Priory church, and 4m SW Holker Hall in its deer park.

Grasmere (Westm). Picturesque village at edge of Grasmere Lake well-known for its annual sports meeting in mid-August featuring local-style wrestling, a Guides' race and hound trail. Boating and tennis. Dove Cottage (museum) was residence of William Wordsworth from 1799. His grave is in churchyard. 3m SW is Langdale Valley beneath the towering Langdale Pikes, a popular rock-climbing region.

Hale (Lancs). Attractive village. 17c church with grave of local giant, John Middleton, 9 ft 3 in. 2m W is Liverpool Airport and Speke Hall (NT).

Haweswater (Westm). Large lake in northern Lake District now converted to artificial reservoir for Mancester's water supply. The dam, the only hollow structure of its kind in the country, is 1,550 ft long and 120 ft high. The site of the former Mardale church lies submerged beneath the water.

Hawkeshead (Lancs). Picturesque village near head of Esthwaite Water and 2m W of the larger Lake Windermere. Grammar school, founded 1585, attended by Wordsworth. 15c church.

Isle of Man. Popular holiday island in the Irish Sea, the nearest point on the mainland being Burrow Point, Wigtownshire, 16m. The length is about 32m, its breadth about 12m. The central portion is hilly and diversified; streams flow through leafy glens. The hilly region ends with the valley of the Sulby to the N of which is a flat plain, unbroken except by low sand-hills and the Curragh Mhor, once a bog. Highest point is Snaefell (2,034 ft). from which there are extensive views. On the S coast are fine sheer cliffs. Smooth sandy shores provide good bathing. Principal towns are Douglas, capital of the Island, Ramsey, Peel, Castletown and Port Erin (q.v.).

Kendal (Westm). Old stone built market town with cobbled courtyards and quaint archways. 13c castle now in ruins was birthplace of Katherine Parr, the last of Henry VIII's wives. Restored church, part 13c with high tower and good peal of bells. Sizergh Castle (NT) is $3\frac{1}{2}$m S. and at 5m is Levens Hall.

Keswick (Cumb). Prosperous market town on river Greta near northern shore of Derwentwater. Museum and Art Gallery with model of Lake District. Moot Hall built 1813. Parish church at Crosthwaite, 1m where is tomb of Robert Southey. He, S. T. Coleridge and Shelley lived in the town. To S are Falls of Lodore, to E is Castlerigg stone circle.

Kirkby Lonsdale (Westm). Grey stone houses and narrow streets of this town overlook the river Lune crossed here by ancient Devil's Bridge. Church with Norman work.

Lake District. Picturesque, mountainous region comprised in the counties of Westmorland and Cumberland and a portion of Lancashire,

Lake Windermere

within which are grouped 17 lakes and innumerable tarns and streams, and a series of mountains rising in parts to over three thousand feet. The district measures about 30 miles N to S and about 25 miles E to W and much of it is now designated a National Park. The principal lakes in order of size are Windermere, Ullswater, Coniston, Bassenthwaite, Thirlmere, Derwentwater, Wastwater, Crummock Water, Ennerdale, Haweswater, Esthwaite Water, Loweswater, Buttermere, Grasmere, Rydal Water, Brothers Water and Elterwater. Well-known heights include Scafell Pike (highest point in England), Skiddaw, Great Gable, High Stile, Helvellyn, High Street and Coniston Old Man.

Lancaster (Lancs). Historic city on river Lune with famous Norman castle and fine old parish church. R.C. Cathedral. The Shire Hall is 18c. University at Bailrigg, 2½m S.

Liverpool (Lancs). Great seaport on Mersey estuary. Busy city and University town. Anglican and R.C. cathedrals. The high Royal Liver Building dominates the 7m water front. Walker Art Gallery has fine collection. Queensway is road tunnel beneath Mersey and linking with Birkenhead.

Lytham St. Annes (Lancs). Famous golfing resort 8m S of Blackpool. Holiday town with good beaches, fine promenade, tennis, bowls, entertainment, pier.

Manchester (Lancs). Principal centre of cotton industry and important University city. The modern docks have connection with the sea via the Manchester Ship Canal and the river Mersey. The Cathedral with fine tower and good woodwork, was built 1422–1520. Chetham's Hospital is now school. Its famous library was first public library in England. John Ryland's Library and the Central Library both have rare and valuable manuscripts, the Art Gallery and Museum are of interest, and Platt Hall, Heaton Hall, Wythenshawe Hall and the Old Parsonage at Didsbury each have collections of note.

Maryport (Cumb). Sandy beach at mouth of river Ellen on Solway Firth.
Morecambe (Lancs). Much-frequented seaside resort on spacious Morecambe Bay, and gateway to Lake District. Rivals Blackpool in provision of sport and entertainment. Bathing, boating and fishing. Golf.
Newby Bridge (Lancs). Situated on river Leven 1m from foot of Lake Windermere. Quaint old-world bridge. Angling centre.
Ormskirk (Lancs). Old market town with a number of Georgian houses. The Perpendicular church is unusual in possessing two towers, one topped with a spire. The 13c Burscough Priory is 2m NE.
Patterdale (Westm). Good centre for Ullswater in Lake District nestling among wooded slopes of spurs of Helvellyn and St. Sunday Crag. Convenient for Aira Force and Gowbarrow, Grisedale Tarn, High Street, Mardale and Grasmere.
Peel (Isle of Man). Holiday resort and small fishing port on W coast of Island. Sand and pebble beach. Golf and tennis. On St. Patrick's Isle are castle ruins and, within the walls, St. German's Cathedral.
Penrith (Cumb). Town with golf and various sports activities, and a recognised centre for Northern Lakeland with excursions to Ullswater and Haweswater in particular. In churchyard is strange monument, the Giants' Grave. 1½m SE is Brougham Castle. (AM).
Port Erin (Isle of Man). Small resort on SW coast of Island with unrivalled facilities for bathing, boating and fishing. To N is Bradda Head topped by Milner's Tower. There is an aquarium.
Port St. Mary (Isle of Man). Small coastal village with picturesque harbour. Bathing at Chapel Strand. Golf. Cregneish, 1m W, is village part owned by NT and maintained as open-air folk museum. Calf of Man is islet off south-western tip of Island, where on the cliffs great colonies of sea-birds nest.
Ramsey (Isle of Man). Second largest town in the Island, with bathing sands, excellent sporting and entertainment facilities, good shops. There is good seafishing and the Sulby is excellent trout and salmon stream. Ramsey Bay sweeps for 10m between Point of Ayre and Maughold Head. Convenient for North Barrule (1,860 ft) with fine views.
Ravenglass (Cumb). Small village, 8m N of Bootle, at confluence of rivers Esk, Mite and Irt. Across estuary is a Tern and Gull sanctuary. The Eskdale narrow gauge railway connects with Dalegarth near Boot. On Muncaster fell is Muncaster Castle where the gardens are open to public. Walls is ruin of Roman bath-house. Centre for Scafell and Hardknott.
Rydal Water (Westm). One of smallest but most attractive English lakes overlooked by Nab Scar and Loughrigg. In Rydal hamlet De Quincey and Hartley Coleridge lived at the Nab. Rydal Hall stands in extensive park and at Rydal Mount Wordsworth lived and died.
St. Bees (Cumb). Small resort with sandy beach, golf and sea-fishing from rocks below St. Bees Head to the NW. Abbey church. The Head

rise 300 ft sheer from the water. Beyond the Head is Whitehaven, a busy industrial town.

Sandside (Westm). On estuary of rivers Kent and Bela. Beyond Haverbrack Common are the Fairy Steps formed by the action of water on the front of a lengthy perpendicular range of limestone. Good spot for picnics.

Seascale (Cumb). Attractive and popular seaside resort. Grassy foreshore with sands. The golf course extends along the shore. Convenient centre for Eskdale, Ennerdale and Wastwater. At Gosforth village is notable ancient cross in churchyard.

Seatoller (Cumb). Hamlet on road to Honister Hause in beautiful Borrowdale valley.

Shap (Westm). Lofty moorland village of note for its ancient abbey (AM) 1m W.

Silloth (Cumb). Holiday resort and small port on the NW coast. Bathing. Extensive views across Solway Firth to the Scottish coast.

Silverdale (Lancs). Scattered village resort on charming site on eastern side of Morecambe Bay. Fine seascapes. Wealth of wild flowers and extensive woodlands (NT).

Snaefell (Isle of Man). Highest point (2,034 ft) in the Isle of Man from which there are views of England, Scotland and Northern Ireland. An electric railway climbs to the summit from Laxey a small resort on the Island's E coast.

Southport (Lancs). Popular seaside resort with sands and extensive sand dunes, sports and entertainment. Atkinson Art Gallery with good collection. Golf.

Troutbeck (Westm). A straggling line of cottages and several good hotels including the now modern Mortal Man with famous inn sign. 4m uphill is the Kirkstone Pass with its inn, one of the highest in the kingdom. Beyond the Pass is Brothers Water.

Ulpha (Cumb). Village in Duddon valley. Westward a road leads to Birker Moor and Eskdale.

Ulverston (Lancs). Market town on Furness peninsula in close reach of Winderemere, Coniston Water and Morecambe Bay resorts. Near sea and beautiful countryside. Bathing, boating, fishing and rock climbing. Golf and other sports.

Wasdale (Cumb). Deep depression formed by the loftiest and steepest mountains in England—Wasdale Head is wild terrain amidst Great Gable and Scafell Pike, essentially for hill-walkers and climbers. Boating and fishing on Wastwater, an impressive stretch of water.

Wetheral (Cumb). Picturesque village above river Eden. Old prior gatehouse, St. Constantine's cell, three caves, by river.

Windermere, Lake (Westm). With a length of 10m N to S and a maximum width of 1m Windermere is the largest lake in England. Motor vessels ply between Lake Side in the S to Bowness on the E bank and Waterhead, Ambleside, at the northern end.

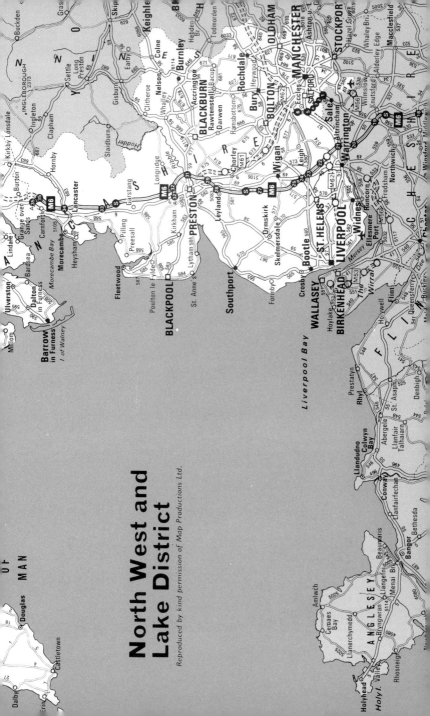

North West and Lake District

Reproduced by kind permission of Map Productions Ltd.

The North East

Northumberland—Co. Durham

Northumberland

The most northerly county in England and one of the most sparsely inhabited, with the great majority of its population concentrated in the busy industrial districts of Tyneside. The major part of the county remains unspoilt with large tracts of natural scenery. Towards the coast the land is flat or gently undulating and along the firm sandy shore there are many pleasant little villages which remain uncommercialised. Offshore are the notable Holy Island and Farne Islands group. Down the centre of the county runs the prominent sandstone outcrop known as the Great Whin Sill, whilst the western sector of the county is a tract of wild mountainous moorland. From the moors rise the rivers Till, Breamish, Aln, Coquet and the Wansbeck, all of charm and beauty. The county is immensely rich in prehistoric remains and antiquities of great interest.

Co. Durham

A palatine county in the North of England bounded on the N by the river Derwent and the Tyne, E by the North Sea, W by Cumberland and Westmorland and S by the Tees. The central area is concerned with coalmining and the eastern part heavily industrialised with the great centres of Sunderland, Middlesbrough and Stockton. But to the W is good scenery among hill ranges and fertile valleys. On the coast too, are a number of wooded valleys and sandy beaches attracting holiday-makers. Prime feature of interest, however, must be the city of Durham, with its great Norman Cathedral standing high above the winding River Wear.

Of Special Interest

Alnwick Castle. (See page 179).
Bamburgh Castle. (See page 179).
Barnard Castle (Bardnard Castle). 11c–13c ruins with circular keep of three storeys, 14c great hall, on bank of river Tees. (AM Standard hours).

Bowes Museum (Bardnard Castle). Chateau-style house built by John Bowes, son of 10th Earl of Strathmore and his wife in 1869 for display of their great art collection. Daily, 10–5.50 (earlier in winter), Suns, 2–4 or 5.

Callaly Castle (Whittingham). 15c mansion with later alterations and additions. Fine plasterwork, paintings, furnishings and grounds. Jun–Sept, Sats, Suns and Bk Hols, 2.15–6.

Cragside Grounds (Rothbury). Magnificent estate of Lord Armstrong. Rich woodlands and lakes. Grounds only Easter–Sept, daily 10–8.

Dunstanburgh Castle (8m NE of Alnwick). Early 14c ruin of Earl of Lancaster's castle strengthened by John of Gaunt. (AM and NT Standard hours).

Durham Castle (Durham). Norman structure used by University of Durham. Open throughout the year, weekdays, 10–12.30 and 2–5. Restricted in winter.

Durham Castle (Durham). (See page 180).

Finchale Priory (5½m N of Durham). Remains of 13c church and claustral buildings of Benedictine priory. (AM Standard hours).

Gibside Chapel (Gibside). Georgian building designed by Paine as mausoleum for Bowes family, now used as church. Easter–Sept, daily, except Tues. In winter, Weds, Sats and Suns only, 2–6.

Howick Gardens (near Howick, 6m NE Alnwick). Fine shrub garden, the property of Lord Howick of Glendale. Apr–Sept, daily, 2–7.

Langley Castle (1½m SW of Haydon Bridge). Restored 14c pele tower used in part as school. May–Sept, Weds, 2–7.

Lindisfarne Castle (Holy Island) (NT). Built by Prior Castell of Durham c. 1500 and restored as private dwelling. Apr–Jul and end Sept, daily (except Mons), Aug–mid Sept, Weds only, 2–6.

Norham Castle (Norham, 8m W of Berwick-on-Tweed). Built c. 1160 and since much altered. One of strongest of Border castles belonging to Bishops of Durham. (AM Standard hours).

Raby Castle (Staindrop). Mainly 14c battlemented castle home of the Nevilles. Fine pictures and grounds. Easter, then May–Sept, Weds, Sats and Bk Hols, 2–5.

Seaton Delaval Hall (Seaton Sluice). Built for the Delaval family in 1720–29 by Sir John Vanbrugh, poet-architect and one of his finest works. Furniture, pictures, porcelain. Norman church and charming gardens. May–Sept, Weds, Suns and Bk Hols, 2–6.

Wallington Hall (Cambo). (NT). Former seat of Sir Charles Trevelyan dating from 1688 with 18c alterations, noted for its rococo plaster work. Porcelain, pictures, furniture. Gardens and woods. House and gardens. Apr–Sept, daily (except Tues and Fris), 2–6. Woods at all times.

Warkworth Castle (on river Coquet, 7½m SE of Alnwick). 12c and 13c remains, 15c keep of Duke of Northumberland, rivals Alnwick and Bamburgh in internal beauty and interest. (AM Standard and Sun mornings in summer).

Washington Old Hall (Washington). Jacobean mansion incorporating parts of an earlier medieval building. The seat of the Washington family from 1183 to 1613. (NT. Daily, except Fris, 10–1, 2–6).

Resorts and Centres of Interest

Alnmouth (Nthumb). Quiet, unspoiled resort with extensive sands. There is golf, boating and good sea-fishing.

Alnwick (Nthumb). Charming old grey town in pleasant situation. Its castle is principal home of Earls and Dukes of Northumberland. The massive keep and curtain walls date from early 12c. Open May–Sept, Mons–Thurs, 1–5. Parish church with 14c tombs and effigies. In Hulne Park (Duke of Northumberland) is gatehouse of former abbey and remains of Carmelite priory in good state of preservation. Near Howick, 6m NE, are Howick Gardens.

Bamburgh (Nthumb). Colourful and unspoiled village with bracing air and firm white sands. Golf and tennis. The present parish church dates from time of Henry II and opposite W end is tomb of Grace Darling to whom a museum is dedicated. Imposing Norman Castle (Easter-Sept, daily 2–8).

Barnard Castle (Durham). Small centre on river Tees. Castle remains (AM) date from 12c and later. Bowes Museum contains fabulous art collections. To SE 1½m is Egglestone Abbey (AM).

Beadnell (Nthumb). Small fishing village 2m S of Seahouses. Tiny harbour and firm sands across Beadnell Bay. Bathing also at Newton Seahouses.

Berwick-on-Tweed (Nthumb). One of most striking of Northumberland towns with quaint hilly streets and retaining its two sets of ancient town walls, the one Edwardian, the other Elizabethan. Three bridges cross the Tweed to Tweedmouth, for Spittal, the seaside portion of that borough. From Halidon Hill are rewarding views.

Bishop Aukland (Durham). Mining town in W of the county at junction of rivers Gaunless and Wear. 16c castle, long residence of Bishops of Durham. 2m NW is Escomb with its Saxon church.

Brinkburn (Nthumb). 4m S of Rothbury with Brinkburn Priory a perfect specimen of Norman Transitional architecture.

Carter Bar (Nthumb). Notable Cheviot viewpoint on Newcastle–Jedburgh road at border with England and Scotland at altitude of 1,370 ft.

Cheviot Hills (Nthumb). Grassy range of hills forming much of the NW border of the county with Scotland and reaching highest point (The Cheviot) at 2,676 ft and the second highest hill in England outside the Lake District.

Chollerford (Nthumb). Hamlet on river N Tyne and near a section of the Roman Wall. The high-arched bridge dates from 1775. Museum. The 13c Haughton Castle with fine park is 3m N.

Corbridge (Nthumb). On river Tyne 4m E of Hexham and close to the Roman Wall. The church retains 8c masonry with a Saxon tower, and a 14c pele tower adjacent. 1½m W is Corstopitum (AM standard) a Roman site at the crossing of the Tyne on the Roman road from York to Scotland.

Craster (Nthumb). Fishing village in gap in basaltic cliff scenery. Craster Tower incorporates old pele tower. In 1½m N along cliffs is Dunstanburgh Castle.

Darlington (Durham). Industrial town in S of county with large locomotive and bridge-building works. At Bank Top station is preserved Stevenson's 'Locomotion'. The church is Early English with 15c stalls and interesting font cover. To NW 5m is Warkworth Castle.

Durham. County town and university city famed for its magnificent Norman cathedral standing high above the wooded banks of the river Wear. Of great interest are the massive Norman nave and the Galilee Porch containing tomb of the Venerable Bede. See also Chapel of Nine Altars and Nevill screen of 1380. Some monastic buildings remain, and the cloisters have been rebuilt. The former monks' dormitory is now museum with Saxon and Roman relics. Palace Green shows a number of 17c buildings. Parts of the Castle (Norman—14c) are now used by the University (weekdays 10–12.30 and 2–5. In winter, Mons, Weds and Sats only, 2–4). Gulbenkian museum with Oriental art treasures.

Egglescliffe (Durham). Pleasant village with ancient bridge across River Tees.

Embleton (Nthumb). Coast village with interesting church and fortified vicarage. 2m S is Dunstanburgh Castle.

Gateshead (Durham). Industrial town on river Tyne opposite Newcastle-upon-Tyne with which it is connected by numerous bridges. Art gallery with 18c and 19c work. 6m SE is Washington Old Hall.

Haltwhistle (Nthumb). On S Tyne river, a mining town, but finely situated. Nearby are ruins of Bellister Castle. 3½m SW is the rebuilt Featherstone Castle in a wooded park. To N is Hadrian's Wall and 4m NE Housesteads (museum) (NT) where Borcovicium is best preserved of the Roman forts.

Hexham (Nthumb). Town on river Tyne, 20m W of Newcastle-upon-Tyne, notable for its Priory church. Of particular interest are the Saxon crypt, font-bowl and frid stool, and a rare night stair to the monks' dormitory. The Moot Hall is late 12c. Eastward are the Roman remains and museum of Corstopitum (AM Standard).

Howick (Nthumb). Hamlet on fine stretch of coast 4m N of Alnmouth. Howick Haven has fine rocks and caverns. Inland is Howick Hall with gardens (open). To N is Cullernose Point and then Craster with Dunstanburgh Castle (AM).

Ingram (Nthumb). Quiet village in sequestered valley of Breamish river 14m from Alnwick. Mainly 12c church. Above the valley is Greaves Ash, an ancient British encampment. Linhope Spout is an impressive fall after rain. Views from Hedgehope Hill (2,348 ft).

Lindisfarne (Nthumb). Strange mystic island with ancient priory ruins and fairytale castle reached by causeway. One of earliest centres of Christianity in Britain.

Middleton-in-Teesdale (Durham). Attractive village on river Tees convenient for excursions to High Force, fine 70-ft waterfall 5m upstream, Lunedale and Yorkshire moors. 9m W is Cauldron Snout one of England's highest falls.

Mitford (Nthumb). Village in delightful situation at confluence of rivers Font and Wansbeck immediately W of Morpeth. In part the church shows Norman work. Only slight remains of Norman castle.

Morpeth (Nthumb). Country market town in wooded valley of river Wansbeck (boating, fishing). The church is one of the largest in the county and has some interesting medieval glass. The bridge across the river is by Telford. The attractive Carlisle Park has sports facilities. S of the river are the ruins of Newminster Abbey (Cistercian). 10m W is Wallington Hall (NT).

Newbiggin-by-the-Sea (Nthumb). Combination of fishing community, colliery village and seaside resort, 18m N of Newcastle and 9m E of Morpeth. There is bathing from sand and rocky bay and golf course on Newbiggin Moor.

Newcastle-upon-Tyne (Nthumb). County town and important manufacturing city, the industrial centre of north-east England, and great coal port occupying a strategic position on N bank of the river Tyne. Spanning the river are three bridges linking with Gateshead. The Cathedral Church of St. Nicholas, formerly the parish church, and mainly a 14c structure is noted for its spire of a type known as 'Scottish crown'. The castle was founded in 1080, but principal remains today are in the late-Norman keep and 13c outer gatehouse—the Black Gate (museum). The Guildhall in classic style was erected in 1658. The hill-top All Saints Church was rebuilt in 1789 and preserves a magnificent 15c brass of Roger Thornton, many times mayor. St. John's Church is 14c with some Norman work, but St. Andrew's is much older retaining its original late 12c nave. Jesmond

Bamburgh Castle

Dene is an attractive park in the northern suburbs. Concerts are held in the City Hall, there are cinemas and theatres and many facilities for sport including golf and racing.

Otterburn (Nthumb). Small village in picturesque situation in open, green valley of the River Rede, and site of the battle of Chevy Chase in 1388. The spot where the Scottish leader Douglas was killed is marked by the inappropriately named Percy's Cross.

Roman Wall (or Hadrian's Wall). Built during time of Emperor Hadrian c. AD 121–126 as a defence of the northernmost limit of the Roman Empire. Seventy-three and a half miles in length and some 6 to 8 ft wide and accompanied by a ditch, it stretched from Wallsend to Bowness on the Solway Firth. At every mile was a 'milecastle' and between each of these two turrets. At intervals were extensive forts capable of accomodating large garrisons. The eastern portion was of stone, and the western end originally of turf or clay but later rebuilt in stone. Long stretches are now well preserved and there is a museum at Housesteads (Borcovicium).

Rothbury (Nthumb). Picturesque market village on N bank of river Coquet to N of heathery slopes of Simonside hills. Church notable for its Saxon font pedestal. To the east is Lord Armstrong's Cragside estate (grounds open). To the SE 4m is Brinkburn Priory.

Seahouses (Nthumb). A one-time herring fishing community turned popular holiday resort with good bathing on sandy shore sheltered by St. Aidan's Dunes. Convenient for Farne Islands and Holy Island. 3m along coast is Bamburgh with its castle.

Seaton Carew (Durham). Small resort S of West Hartlepool with good bathing from firm sands.

Tynemouth (Nthumb). Sea coast resort at mouth of river Tyne with wide sandy beach and pleasant coves of Cullercoats Bay. Of its castle only a 14c fortified gatehouse remains but much of the Benedictine priory, refounded in 1090, exists (AM standard hours). Immediately N are Cullercoats and Whitley Bay.

Warkworth (Nthumb). Interesting village 2m from mouth of river Coquet, with sandy shore, boating, golf. The 12c castle (Duke of Northumberland) with later additions and fine 15c keep overlooks the village. Up river is Hermitage (AM) a small chapel and living rooms cut out from solid rock.

Whitley Bay (Nthumb). Leading seaside resort of the NE coast. Clean and bracing air. Extensive sands, boating, sea-fishing, sports and entertainment.

Whittingham (Nthumb). Pretty old-world village on river Aln. The church retains some Saxon work in spite of unfortunate restoration in 1840. There are fine mansions and Callaly Castle (17/18c) with good plasterwork, pictures and furnishings.

Wooler (Nthumb). Market town and good fishing centre. Starting point for eastern slopes of Cheviot hills. To SE is Chillingham Park with its famous white cattle.

Conway Castle

Wales

The Principality of Wales (Pop. 2,245,000) and Monmouthshire (Pop. 464,000) together cover an area of 8,006 sq. m. Its boundaries are formed by the Irish Sea, St. George's Channel, the Bristol Channel, and the English counties of Cheshire, Shropshire, and Hereford. By the Act of Union in 1536, when Wales was politically incorporated into England, the county of Monmouth became part of England, but for laws and local administration it is included in Wales.

Wales is rich in archaeological remains—cromlechs, bronze and iron relics, and evidences of Roman and Norman occupation. Offa's Dyke, an ancient rampart and fosse, was probably constructed by King Offa in the 8c as a barrier between England and Wales.

Originally an agricultural country, the discovery of extensive coal and iron fields changed the face of many areas. These have become highly industrialised with mines, smelting works, and vast docks. Much of the country, however, remains unspoilt, with splendid mountains and lovely valleys and lakes.

The people are descended from the Celts, and remained fiercely independent in spite of successive occupations by Roman, Saxon and Norman invaders. The Saxons called the natives 'Wealhas' i.e. foreigners, which became corrupted to Wales and applied to the whole country. The Welsh retained their own language, cultural independence, and way of life—still expressed in song, poetry and oratory. They are noted for their tenacity, love of fighting, music, religious fervour, and zeal for reform.

North Wales

The counties of Anglesey, Caernarvon, Denbigh, Flint, Merioneth

Isle of Anglesey

A large island connected with the mainland by suspension bridge and railway bridge across the Menai Strait, it has lush meadows, rich cornfields, delightful bays and coves, and attractive villages. From Holyhead, a steamship service runs daily to Eire.

Caernarvonshire

A county dominated by Snowdon and the large area occupied by the National Park—a region of 'mountains, lakes, cataracts, and groves, in which Nature shows herself in her most grand and beautiful forms' (Borrow). The Lleyn peninsula juts out to the SW, a pastoral area of lovely villages. Bardsey Island lies 2m beyond.

Denbighshire

The county has mainly a rugged mountainous surface. The fertile valleys watered by the rivers Dee and Conway yield excellent dairy produce. The coastal resorts are very popular, and there are National Trust areas including the beautiful Bodnant Gardens.

Flintshire

A small county on the Dee estuary, with a flat coastline, a backbone of hills, and rich agricultural areas where farming prospers. Flourishing industries of coal, iron, chemicals and textiles attract a comparatively high proportion of English workers. Flint is rich in prehistoric remains.

Merioneth

Some mines and slate quarries, but mainly a pastoral county, with lovely river valleys and unspoilt coast resorts. It has also the long mountain range of Cader Idris, and the large natural lake of Bala. On the shores of Trawsfynydd Lake a nuclear power station has been constructed.

Of Special Interest

Betws-y-Coed (Caern). Beautifully situated village in Vale of Conway, and popular centre for scenic attractions.

Beddgelert (Caern). Picturesque village near junction of Colwyn and Glaslyn rivers. Shows tomb of Llewelyn's faithful hound Gelert.

Bodnant (4m S of Conway). Famous gardens (NT) of 50 acres. Apr–Oct, Tues, Weds, Thurs, Sats and Bk Hols, 1.30–4.45.

Bardsey Island (2m off Lleyn peninsula). Ruined abbey. Bird observatory.

Capel Garmon (3m E of Betws-y-Coed). Burial chambers of long barrow type, in use before the Bronze Age. (AM any time).

Chirk Castle (7m SE of Llangollen). Has been lived in continuously since 1310. Portraits, tapestries and furniture. Gardens. Easter and May–Sept, Tues, Thurs, Sats, Suns, 2–5. Bk Hols, 11–5.

Din Lligwy (in E Anglesey). Excellent example of ancient British village, with walls and outline of stone houses. (AM any time).

Dolwyddelan Castle (7m WSW from Betws-y-Coed). Late 12c castle, birthplace of Llywelin the Great. (AM Standard hours).

Ffestiniog (Mer). The 13m narrow-gauge railway to Portmadoc is a great attraction to those interested in railway history.

Garthewin (5m SW of Abergele). Georgian mansion with period furniture. Barn converted to a theatre for Drama Festivals. Easter and Whitsun–mid Sept, Thurs, Fris and Bk Hols, 2.30–5.30.

Gop Cairn (near Prestatyn). Largest prehistoric cairn in Wales. 60 ft high and dates from 6000 B.C.

Gwydir Castle (Llanrwst). Restored 12c residence. Furniture, etc. Gardens, peacocks. Daily from 9.30.

Harlech Castle (Mer). Well preserved and finely situated castle, built by Edward I 1283–1290. (AM Standard hours).

Nant Ffrancon Pass (Caern). The main road S of Bangor follows this spectacular Pass, and its glacial lake Llyn Ogwyn.

Offa's Dyke. Constructed in 8c by Offa, king of Mercia. Extends from estuary of Dee to that of the Severn.

Penmon Priory (4m NNE of Beaumaris). Founded in 6c. Fine Norman church. The Wishing Well was originally baptismal shrine. (AM any time).

Puffin Island (off E point of Anglesey). Also called Priestholm. Once occupied by the hermit Seiriol; now a haunt of sea-birds.

Pistyll Rhaiadr (10m SE of Bala). One of the finest waterfalls in Wales, 300 ft high.

Ruthin Castle (Ruthin). 13c castle now an hotel but open to view and featuring nightly medieval style banquets.

Snowdonia (Caerns). A National Park since 1951. Covers 845 sq.m and extends from Penmaenmawr to Dovey estuary.

South Stack Lighthouse (off westernmost point of Holyhead Island). Has impressive cliff scenery.

Tre'r Ceiri (Caerns). On E peak of the 'Rivals' (Yr Eifl). A 5-acre Iron Age hill fort, with dozens of stone huts within walled compound.

Tomen-y-Mur (3¼m from Ffestiniog). Extensive remains of important Roman station and fort of 1c. Motte of medieval castle.

Colwyn Bay

Resorts and Centres of Interest

Abergele (Denb). A small market town 1m inland and midway between Colwyn Bay and Rhyl. Its suburb Pensarn lies close to the sea, and has a sand and pebble beach. The 16c church was restored in 1879. W of Abergele is the picturesque Gwrych Castle, a modern residence open to the public.

Bala (Mer). A small market town ¼m from Lake Bala—the largest sheet of natural water in Wales. The lake is used for fishing, sailing and boating, excursions, and the annual championships for long distance swimming. SW of Bala village is the old Parish Church, where Thomas Charles, founder of the Bible Society, is buried. Of the other lakes in Merionethshire, Lake Vyrnwy is important as the principal reservoir for Liverpool.

Bangor (Caern). Is an ancient settlement. A monastery was established here A.D. 525 by Deiniol, who became first bishop. A wattle fence of 'bangor' protected the monastery and became the name of the place. This busy little town is on the S coast of the Menai Strait, 2m from the Suspension Bridge that connects the mainland with Anglesey. The Pier (1,550 ft) extends two-thirds of the way across the Strait. The Cathedral was founded in 548; the later Norman structure dates from the 13c and 14c, but has been much restored. There is a University College, a Library and a Museum. Bangor mountain is attractively laid out as a recreation ground, the town and area have good transport facilities, and Bangor is an excellent centre for exploring NW Wales. Penrhyn Castle and Park (NT) lie to the E of Bangor. The castle is a Norman-style structure, developed from a medieval house built on the site of the palace of a Welsh prince of A.D. 720.

180

Barmouth (Mer). Lies on the estuary of the river Mawddach in Cardigan Bay. Barmouth has extensive sands and a long promenade. The town has quaint byways and alleys, and is a good centre for mountain walks. Barmouth Bridge, ½m long, spans the estuary. Friar's Island at the mouth is said to have been the dwelling place of a hermit. A few m to the N are interesting cromlechs at Dyffryn and Tal-y-Bont.

Beaumaris (Anglesey). A small coastal resort in the SW of Anglesey and the capital of the island. Attractively sited overlooking the Menai Strait, with superb views of the Caernarvonshire mountains. Beach is rock and shingle, with sand at low tide. The chief feature is the Castle, built in 1295 in open level country, and still almost complete—with walls, towers and moat. The church dates from the 14c and has fine carved stalls and alabaster effigies. The Grammar School was founded in 1603. The County Hall was built in 1614 and retains the original roof and many of the fittings. The 16c Bull's Head was rebuilt on the site of inn built in 1472. Baron Hill House was built by Sir Richard Bulkeley in the early 17c. The Baron Hill estate is connected with Arthurian legend; on the hill Bwrdd Arthur (Arthur's Round Table) are the remains of early British fortifications.

Caernarvon (Caern). A walled town and resort on the Menai Strait, created a Royal Borough in 1963, and noted for its fine position and historical associations. The original Roman settlement was at Segontium, ½m from the present town; excavation of this site yielded many interesting finds, now in the museum. Caernarvon is an attractive town with narrow streets, fine walls and gateways, a wide quay and a superb castle. The castle was begun in 1283. The following year, Edward II was born here, and was presented to the people as the first Prince of Wales. The Duke of Windsor when Prince of Wales was invested here in 1911, as also Prince Charles in 1969. Caernarvon Castle is one of the finest in Great Britain; it is in good repair and has many unusual and interesting features. (AM Standard hours).

Colwyn Bay (Denb). An attractive resort on a beautiful bay with fine sloping sands. There is a Pier with a Pavilion used for concerts. At the E end of the Promenade is the Dingle and the 50-acre Eirias Park. The W portion of Colwyn Bay joins up with its suburb, Rhos-on-Sea. Adjoining the swimming pool here is a hotel, formerly Rhos Fynach monastery, said to date from 1185. The monks probably tended the 13c Fishing Weir, of which traces remain on the foreshore. S of Rhos is the grassy hill Bryn Euryn (400 ft) which has traces of ancient fortifications and commands a wide view.

Conway (Caern). At the mouth of the river Conway, with two bridges spanning the estuary. Telford's suspension bridge, designed in 1821 to harmonise with the castle, has now been superseded by a modern bridge (1958). The town walls, 1¼m long, are well preserved, with fortified battlements and towers. They are probably of the same date as the Castle, i.e. between 1283 and 1287. The castle is a magnificent example of medieval architecture, and much of the interior shell remains. (Standard hours).

Close to the lower gate of the castle is Aberconway (NT), a medieval house, and outside the gate is the smallest house in Britain. Plas Mawr, in the High Street, is an Elizabethan house dated 1585. It has a fine banqueting hall, and is now the headquarters of the Royal Cambrian Academy of Art. Two nearby resorts are Penmaenmawr and Llanfair-fechan (q.v.).

Corwen (Mer). A market town on river Dee at the base of Berwyn mountain. Excellent fishing, and a market centre for Welsh mountain sheep. The fine Eisteddfod Pavilion seats over 3,000. The church, founded in 6c has a Norman font and many features of antiquarian interest.

Criccieth (Caern). A quiet resort on the NE of Cardigan Bay, with panoramic views and a sand and shingle beach. On a rocky promontory are the remains of a castle rebuilt by Edward I. In Llanystumdwy, 1½m W, Lloyd George spent his boyhood; near the bridge is his grave, and the local museum has many mementoes of him.

Denbigh (Denb). A market town and good centre for angling pleasantly sited in the vale of Clwyd, and dominated by a historic ruined castle in beautiful surroundings. This 13c castle was an important stronghold in the wars between Edward I and the Welsh. During the Civil War it was the last of the Welsh castles to hold out for Charles I, until finally starved into surrender. Other items of interest are the market cross, and the old cockpit in the yard of the 'Hawk and Buckle' inn. Eight m from Denbigh is the hillside town of Ruthin, worth visiting for its ancient buildings grouped round the market place, the 14c church, and the remains of a 13c castle.

Dolgellau (Mer). Centrally situated in Merionethshire, it is the administrative centre and principal market town of the county. A fine 17c arched bridge spans the river Wnion, and Cader Idris overlooks the town. There is a wide choice of walks and excursions—the Torrent and Precipice walks; the ascent of Cader Idris; the walk to Nannau (Georgian mansion open to public) and on to the Ganllwyd valley. To the N is Llanelltyd with its ancient church and bridge, and the ruins of the 12c Cymmer Abbey.

Hawarden (Flint) (pronounced 'Harden'). A rapidly expanding town 10 m S of Holywell. Gladstone lived here for 60 years, and the W window of the church is a memorial to him by Burne-Jones. The only parts remaining of the 13c castle are the huge keep, a well preserved chapel, and a portion of the banqueting hall.

Holyhead (Anglesey). The terminus of the short steamer route to Dublin. It is a port of Holyhead Island, now popular as a holiday resort. The causeway connecting with the mainland carries the main road and railway. One m S is a second causeway and a ferry. Holyhead town has a fine harbour; its breakwater—1½m long and 40 ft above low tide—provides a good promenade with extensive views. Salt 'Island' (not really an island) is the former site of salt works. Holyhead Mountain, 710 ft, is a rocky mass to the W. On the summit, from which there are wonderful panoramic views, are the remains of a small chapel, one of a number that once existed and justified the title 'Holy'. On the SE slopes are some circular remains of pre-Christian stone huts. S. of Holyhead town is the attractive modern resort of Trearddur Bay.

Holywell (Flint). An ancient market town 14m from Rhyl. The famous 'Well of St. Winefride' is one of the traditional seven wonders of Wales, and in the Middle Ages was one of the most famous wells in Europe. For 1,300 years it has attracted pilgrims, and miraculous cures have been claimed. The legend relates that a pious girl Winefride was decapitated by an enraged suitor. Where the head fell a spring of water gushed out, and the head was replaced on the body by St. Bueno. The well is housed in the crypt of the 15c Chapel of St. Winefride.

Llandudno (Caern). The best known resort on the N coast of Wales, in a bay bounded on the W by the bold headland (680 ft) known as the Great Orme. From here a fine promenade extends 1½m E to the Little Orme. Below Great Orme is the pier, ½m long and busy with steamer traffic. Llandudno has a pavilion, theatre, winter garden and many other amusement facilities. The sand and shingle beach provides good bathing.

There is a wide choice of walks and excursions. The Marine Drive extends 6m around Great Orme and affords magnificent views. The great castellated Lighthouse is a half-way point of the Drive. Shortly after rounding the point is Gogarth Abbey Hotel, once the home of Dean Liddell; here 'Lewis Carroll' often met the Dean's small daughter—the original 'Alice in Wonderland'. Little Orme (463 ft) has a pleasant headland walk of two hours. From the pier a path leads to Happy Valley, with extensive gardens, rockeries and lawns. Nearby at Pen-y-Dinas are walls and other indications of a British fortress, and an old rocking stone known as St. Tudno's cradle. The 15c church of St. Tudno, formerly the parish church, is plainly visible on the cliffs of Great Orme. It has a Norman font and 13c tombstones.

Llangollen (Denb). On the Dee in a secluded 7m long valley surrounded by beautiful hill scenery. Famed for another of the seven 'wonders'—the lovely bridge built in the 12c and enlarged in 1346. The parish church is mainly a 12–13c structure with a fine carved roof. Plas Newydd House (open to the public) SE from the bridge was the home of the eccentric 'Ladies of Llangollen', and contains carvings and curios. Two m N and reached by the beautiful Horseshoe Pass is the ruin of Valle Crucis Abbey founded in 1201. On the right of the road, ¼m further on, is Eliseg's Pillar, an 8c memorial stone originally 12 ft high. Llangollen is the centre for the International Music Festival held annually in July.

Llanrwst (Denb). Attractive market town 12m S of Conway in rich agricultural district amidst lofty hills and lovely woods. The bridge dates from 1636 and rises to a sharp point in the centre. Tu Hwnt I'r Bont (NT)

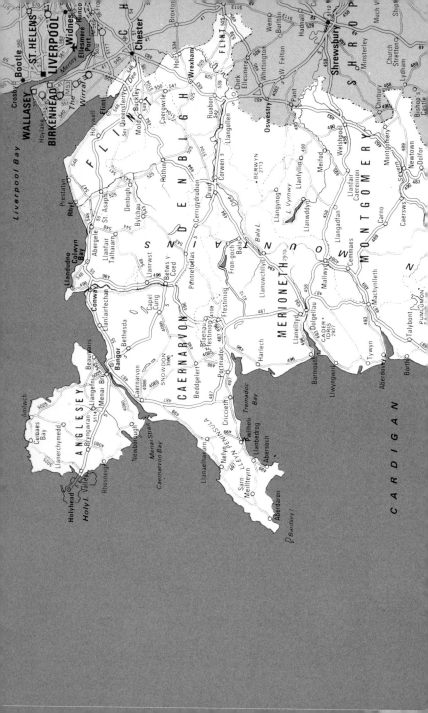

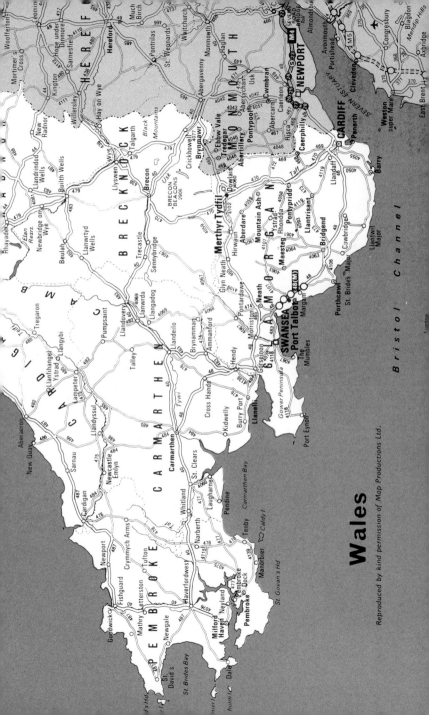

Wales

Reproduced by kind permission of Map Productions Ltd.

is 15c stone cottage, once courthouse. Adjoining the church is 17c mausoleum containing what is said to be stone coffin of Llewelyn the Great.
Nearby is Gwdyr Castle.

Llanfairfechan (Caern). A delightful small resort with ideal beach for
children, a village stream, and numerous amusement facilities. There are
two churches—St. Mary's with services in Welsh, and Christ Church
with English services. Local excursions are many, and include the Terrace
Walk, Happy Valley, Aber Lake and Falls, and the Druids' Circle.

Penmaenmawr (Caern). Five m from Conway, and a good upland walk.
It lies in a beautiful valley between two headlands, and has a bracing and
genial climate. The combination of sea, woodland, and mountain, with
a firm sandy beach and safe bathing, attracts many summer visitors.

Prestatyn (Flint). A resort 4m E of Rhyl that has long been popular
with holidaymakers. It makes ample provision for entertainment; there is
a Lido, a repertory Theatre, and a large holiday camp near the shore.
The 20-ft high Promenade has a stepped wall down to the sandy beaches,
where there is safe bathing.

One m SE is Gwaenysgor church, a fine example of Norman work.
The registers start at 1538, and an Elizabethan chalice is inscribed 'The
Cuppe of Gwaynisker'.

Pwllheli (Caern). A market town, yachting centre and resort on Tremadoc Bay. At full tide the Harbour becomes a salt-water lake of 100 acres (Pwllheli means 'Pool of Salt Water'). The fine sandy beach extends for 5m. The hill Pen-y-Garn above the town commands extensive views of the Snowdon range, the Rivals, and the Merioneth coast.

Rhyl (Flint). A popular N coast holiday resort, with fine firm sands and good bathing. The Marine Drive and Promenade extend along the front for 3m. Ample facilities for sport and recreation, and a well laid out Botanical Garden. The pier is a good viewpoint for sands, coastline, and distant mountains. To the W of the town the Foryd Bridge spans the estuary of the river Clwyd, and S of the bridge is the Marine Lake.

Less than 3m up river and easily reached by road is the interesting small town of Rhuddlan, which has a 16c bridge. In the High Street is Old Parliament House, incorporating part of the building in which Edward I held a Parliament in 1283 which secured the judicial rights and independence of Wales. Rhuddlan Castle, founded in 10c was burnt by Harold in 1063. The existing castle was built in 1277, and has towers, twin gatehouses and a moat. In 1645 it was laid in ruin by the Roundheads. On Rhuddlan marsh, between Rhuddlan and Rhyl, Offa, King of Mercia, defeated the Welsh in 795.

Ruabon (Denb). The centre of an ironworking and colliery district that has now lost its rural character. The Church, founded in the 6c has interesting memorials. The mining suburb of Ruabon is Rhosllannerchrugog, which has a population of over 10,000, and a vigorous cultural life.

St. Asaph (Flint). Lies 5m S of Rhyl in the Clwyd valley. Its Cathedral is the smallest in England and Wales, and occupies the site of a monastery and church of 560. It was largely repaired in the 15c and again restored in 1870. It has many interesting features, including 15c stalls and a collection of curious Bibles. A monument in front of the Cathedral commemorates the translation of the Bible into Welsh.

Towyn (Mer). The town stands ¾m back from the sea on an extensive plain backed by hills. The holiday area is nearer to the sea, and there is a long sand and shingle beach. Walks include the river Dysynni to the N, and Aberdovey to the S. A railway runs 7m inland to Abergynolwyn. The extensive ruins of Bere Castle lie 2m NW; this was once one of the largest and most richly ornamented Welsh castles.

Wrexham (Denb). A market and industrial town, and a good centre for N. Wales and bordering areas. It is noted for its glorious church tower, 135 ft. high, and another of the 'Seven Wonders of Wales'. The church dates from 1525, replacing earlier structures. Elihu Yale, the founder of Yale University, gave the altar piece, and his tomb is in the churchyard. Erddig Hall, 1½m E was his early home. One m N is Acton Hall, where Judge Jeffreys was born.

Central Wales

The counties of Brecon, Cardigan, Montgomery, Radnor

Breconshire

A mountainous area with magnificent scenery but few towns—Welshpool, the largest, has a population of only 6,500. The upper valleys of the Towy and Usk are wild and beautiful, and the river Wye flows along the northern border. In the E are the Black Mountains, and S of these the Brecon Beacons rise to 3,000 ft.

Cardiganshire

The long coast line on Cardigan Bay offers attractions to holidaymakers, Aberystwyth being the chief resort. Inland is more mountainous, and hill streams flow through fertile valleys to the sea. In the Plynlimon area lead was mined by the Romans.

Montgomeryshire

The county extends from the borders of Shropshire almost to the W coast. It formed much of the ancient kingdom of Powys. The land is mountainous and not very fertile, so that sheep rearing and manufacture of woollens were for long the main occupations; the latter dwindled in competition with Yorkshire.

Radnorshire

A thinly populated county, like Montgomeryshire, and devoted mainly to hill farming and sheep rearing. The beautiful Elan Valley has been flooded to provide a water supply for Birmingham. In Victorian times a number of spas developed in this area, Llandrindod Wells being the most frequented.

Powis Castle

Of Special Interest

Abbey Cwmhir (9m N of Llandrindod Wells). Remains of very large Cistercian Abbey in delightful surroundings. Burnt by Owen Glendower in 1401.

Brecon Beacons (SW of Brecon). Highest is Pen-y-Fan. Good viewpoint, included in National Park.

Breiddin Hill. Viewpoint overlooking Shropshire plains. Multiple ramparts of Iron Age fort.

Cefnllys (2m E of Llandrindod Wells). 13c church and remains of castle. 1m N is the Alpine Bridge in beautiful surroundings.

Devil's Bridge (Card). Reached by narrow-gauge railway from Aberystwyth. Here three bridges (the lowest 800 years old) span the river Mynach over a deep gorge with series of waterfalls.

Llandegley. (6½m E of Llandrindod Wells). Has mineral springs and Well House. The thatched 'Pales' is the oldest Quaker meeting-house in Wales.

Llananno (6m N of Llandrindod Wells). Has 15c church with very fine rood loft and screen.

Lake Vyrnwy (Mont). A beauty spot and favourite with anglers, as well as a reservoir for the Liverpool water supply.

Nanteos (4m SE of Aberystwyth). Georgian mansion with fine furniture and paintings, and 'Cup of Nant Eos', chalice with a legendary history. Weds and Sats, 2.30–5.30. Weds only in winter.

Powis Castle (Welshpool). Restored 16c castle and terraced gardens. Plasterwork, tapestries. Jun–Sept, daily, 1–6, except Mons and Tues, Bk Hols, 10.30–5.30. Also gardens in May.

Plynlimon (Cards). Source of Severn, Wye and Rheidol rivers. Tracks lead to the summit (2,649 ft) from which there is a view of most of Wales.

Strata Florida Abbey (8m S of Devil's Bridge). Remains of once magnificent Cistercian Abbey, a former place of pilgrimage. (AM Standard hours).

Tregaron (Cards). Small Cardiganshire town. An adjacent bog area 4m long and 1m wide is now a Nature Reserve.

Tretower Court (9m NW of Abergavenny). Fortified medieval manor house, once home of Vaughan family. Beside it is the tall keep of former fortress, destroyed by Owen Glendower in 1403. (AM Standard hours).

189

Resorts and Centres of Interest

Aberystwyth (Cards). A popular Cardigan Bay holiday resort and University town. It is a rather sprawling town, in a beautiful setting with far-reaching views, and sheltered at the back by mountains. The foreshore is of sand and pebbles, rocks and coves. At the S end are the ruins of Aberystwyth Castle in pleasant gardens. The castle, on a rocky promontory, was built in the time of Edward I and was often the scene of fierce fighting. During the Civil War it was blown up by the Parliamentarians in 1646. On Penglais Hill are the fine new buildings of the University, and of the National Library of Wales with its extensive collection of books, manuscripts, records and maps. The modern building near by is the Welsh Plant Breeding Station, which continues the work inaugurated by Sir George Stapledon. There are many rewarding walks—to Constitution Hill (also served by funicular railway); to Clarach Bay and Valley; to Cym Woods via Panorama Walk and Constitution Hill; and to Pen Dinas (413 ft). S of the town and easily distinguished by its tall commemorative column to the victory of Waterloo.

Brecon (Brecs). The alternative name of Brecknock is a nearer approach to the Welsh form. A touring centre and one of the principal inland towns of central Wales. Situated on the river Usk where this is joined by the river Honddu. Brecon has a cathedral that is second only to that of St. Davids; it was begun in the early 13c. S of the cathedral are Christ College, founded by Henry VIII, and the ruins of Brecon Castle. 2½m W was the Roman fort of Y Gaer.

Builth Wells (Brecs). A busy little town picturesquely situated on the Breconshire bank of the Wye. Beside the Wye and overlooked from the stone bridge of six arches is the Groe, a grassy recreation ground and favourite promenade. The Parish Church has a 14c squat massive tower. Only a mound remains to mark the site of Builth Castle. It was whilst reconnoitring to secure the surrender of this castle that in 1282 Llywelyn (the Last, grandson of Llywelyn the Great) was surprised and killed by the English. The mineral springs that made Builth a spa are about a mile from the town. Two other spas, both lying SW of Builth, are Llanwrtyd Wells (whose waters are sulphurous) and the smaller Llangammarch Wells, whose waters are peculiar in that they contain barium chloride.

Cardigan (Cards). A rural Welsh market town with narrow streets, situated near the mouth of the river Teifi. It is a convenient centre for touring by road or river, and the ancient bridge provides a good viewpoint. On a woody knoll repose the ruins of the ancient Norman castle 'Aberteifi'. Cilgerran Castle, 3m up river, is picturesquely poised on the brink of a gorge. It has often been the subject of painters, including Turner and R. Wilson. The present structure was built in 1223, and has most of the curtain walls and towers intact.

Hay-on-Wye (Brecs). A pleasant country town on the Wye at the junction of the counties of Brecon, Radnor, and Hereford. The name is derived from Norman-French 'haie' meaning hedge or enclosure. English and Welsh have met here for a weekly market for many centuries. Of the Norman castle only the fine gateway remains. 4m to the NW is Pains-castle, where the motte and bailey, with moat and earthworks, are all that remain of a famous castle. The 13c church has a Norman font.

Knighton (Rad). An attractive small town by the river Teme, where Radnor borders on Shropshire. Its Welsh name means 'Town-on-the-Dyke' and there are well preserved traces of the rampart of Offa's Dyke extending for several m both N and S of the town. The church is partly 12c and traces of the castle can be seen on Castle Bank. There are many of the black-timbered houses so characteristic of Border towns. At Stowe, a short distance from Knighton, are traces of a Roman villa.

Lampeter (Cards). An assize town, situated on a gentle hill beside the Teifi. Its full name is Lampeter-Pont-Stephen—a bridge was built here by King Stephen. Lampeter is a good centre for salmon and trout fishing. St. David's College, founded 1822 for theological students and now an open University, has links with the Universities of Oxford, Cambridge and Cardiff.

Llanidloes (Mont). An ancient and picturesque small hill town with old half-timbered Market Hall (now a museum); a 13c church; and a delightful waterfall. Well situated at a main road junction and on the Severn. It is the market centre of a large sheep-rearing area.

Llandrindod Wells (Rad). Attractively situated 700 ft above sea-level. It was developed by the exploitation of its natural waters when spas were more popular, and became a fashionable resort like Bath. Now 'taking the waters' is less obligatory, but the town remains a popular holiday resort, and a centre for exploring the Upper Wye and mid-Wales. Hotels and guest-houses abound, and attract many conferences etc. Llandrindod Wells is a spacious town, with plenty of playing fields, a 50-acre Common with putting greens; a 14-acre boating lake with island; and beyond the Lake is the Golf Club's 18-hole course. To the W of the town the picturesque Rock Park, with Pump Room and Winter Gardens, extends to the river Ithon. At Castell Collen, 2m N, is a recently excavated Roman camp.

Llanwrtyd Wells (Brecs). An attractive and very small town on both banks of the Irfon, surrounded by mountains. A short distance up the valley were the springs whose unpalatable sulphurous waters were at one time credited with sufficient healing powers to justify a spa. Llanwrtyd is a good centre for walking and for pony-trekking.

Machynlleth (Mont). A flourishing market town in the Dovey Valley, occupied with agriculture and slate-quarrying. There is good fishing in the neighbourhood. The town is pleasantly situated at the base of a group of rounded hills that gradually rise to Plynlimon; being at the junction of

several road routes it is a good centre for excursions. Owen Glyndwr held a parliament here in 1402–4, and a building in Maengwyn Street is said to have been the meeting place. E of the town is a modern stone circle erected for the National Eisteddfod of 1937. The beautiful Llyfnant Valley lies a few miles to the S.

Montgomery (Mont). Once of important strategic value during the long Border struggles between English and Welsh. The Norman castle was destroyed and rebuilt many times, and finally dismantled by the Parliamentary forces during the Civil War. Montgomery has now a population of less than 1,000, and although it is nominally the county town, the county assizes are now held at Welshpool. Montgomery is an attractive place, with some fine old houses and a 14c church.

Newtown (Mont). On river Severn, in the centre of an agricultural and sheep rearing district. Up to the beginning of the present century it was a notable wool trading centre. Still an important market town, where markets have been held continuously for nearly 700 years. Robert Owen, the social reformer, was born here in 1771 and returned here to die in his old age. His tomb is in the old churchyard of St. Mary's Church (now in ruins), and on the site of his birthplace is the Robert Owen Memorial

192

Museum. In and around the town are some fine timbered houses, of which Maesmaur Hall, 5m W, is a good example.

New Quay (Cards). An attractive resort with bathing, fishing and sailing facilities. Cardigan Bay Regatta is an annual event. There are fine sandy beaches, a sheltered bay with a pier, a tidal harbour, and cliffs inhabited by many sea birds. Neighbouring coastal resorts are Aberayron to the N —an unspoilt village with a shingle beach; and Llangranog to the S—a secluded village with an ancient church and fine coast scenery.

Presteigne (Rad). County town of Radnor. On the river Lugg, a tributary of the Wye. There are facilities for fishing, shooting, golf, bowls and tennis, and a Floral and Agricultural Show is held every August. The Norman church has much of interest; from its belfry the curfew has been rung for 400 years. The timbered 'Radnorshire Arms', once an Elizabethan residence, became a coaching inn in 1792. The site of the Norman castle is now a wooded eminence called the Warden and forms a fine viewpoint. The ruins of Stapledon Castle are 1m away. At Wapley Hill ($2\frac{1}{2}$m) there is an early British earthwork fortification.

Radnor (Rad). SE of Radnor Forest (which is not tree-clad but a bare uncultivated mountain 2,160 ft high) is New Radnor, once an important place commanded by an 11c castle of which traces still exist. It is now a small village, and superseded as county town by Presteigne. Nearby is an 80-ft fall called 'Water-break-its-neck'. $2\frac{1}{2}$m SE of New Radnor on a hill is the equally small village of Old Radnor, with its fine old church with a unique Celtic font.

Rhayader (and Elan Valley). Originally Rhaiadr-Gwy, the 'Waterfall on the Wye', is a small market town that is said to have existed since the 6c. It lies at an altitude of 700 ft on the upper Wye, among deep ravines and high hills—one of which bears the ruins of a 12c castle. The river is spanned by an 18c bridge. A few m to the W are the valleys of the Elan and Claerwen rivers, where artificial lakes have been constructed to supply the city of Birmingham with water. The reservoirs of the Elan valley were completed in 1904. More recently the Claerwen reservoir has been constructed. A road 12 ft wide with footpaths across the long curving dam provides fine viewpoints of the lakes and lovely wooded surroundings.

Welshpool (Mont). Lies near the W bank of the river Severn. It was the capital of the old kingdom of Powys, and is now the assize town of Montgomeryshire. Was once an important agricultural centre and market for wool trade; its weekly market has been held since 1406. Welshpool has many attractive old houses and inns. St. Mary's church dates from the 13c. Powys Castle (NT) of red sandstone, dates from the early 12c and has been continuously inhabited. It is open to the public.

South Wales

The counties of Carmarthen, Glamorgan, Monmouth, Pembroke

Carmarthenshire

The largest of the Welsh counties. Carmarthen Van, at the eastern border, rises to 2,632 ft, but most of the area is fertile lowland, traversed by the rivers Towy, Taf and Teifi. Industrialisation is confined to the SE, where there is some exploitation of minerals and slate.

Glamorganshire

The most populous area of Wales. The north of the county is mountainous, and from here the Taff, Neath and other rivers descend to the Bristol Channel. Exploitation of mineral wealth has destroyed the beauty of many of the valleys, bringing alternate prosperity and destitution. But the beauty of the Gower Peninsula and the Vale of Glamorgan remain unimpaired.

Monmouthshire

Where Wales merges into England. The county is mostly lowland country except in the NW. Though heavily industrialised in parts, it has the beautiful valleys of the lower Usk and Wye. From near Chepstow the fine new bridge now crosses the Severn.

Pembrokeshire

Ever since the extensive settlement by English and Flemings after the Norman conquest, Pembroke has remained the most English part of Wales. The Welsh language is seldom heard except in the N. Its fine harbours were known to the Vikings, as the name Milford Haven suggests. Most of the county is beautiful and fertile, undulating but only really hilly in the Prescelly range.

Of Special Interest

Caerleon. (See under Newport).
Caerphilly Castle (6m N of Cardiff). 13/14c castle with great leaning tower. (AM Standard hours).
Caldey Island (2½m off Tenby). Covers over 500 acres. Has housed religious communities since the 6c.
Carew Castle (Pembs. 6m W of Tenby). By an inlet of Milford Haven. Imposing roofless ruins. Destroyed during Civil War. Daily, 10–7, Sun afternoons in Aug.
Castell Coch (5m NW of Cardiff). Restored medieval castle on wooded height. (AM Standard hours).
Cefntilla Court (3m E of Usk). Seat of Raglan family, built 1616. Contains souvenirs of Peninsula campaign and Crimean War. Bk Hols, Suns, Mons and Tues, 2.30–6.30.
Clwydach Gorge (6m W of Abergavenny). Sometimes known as the Fairy Glen. Well wooded with streams and waterfall.
Crickhowell (6m from Abergavenny) on river Usk. Has an arched bridge, 14c gatehouse and remains of 13c castle.
Grosmont (11m NE of Abergavenny). Its castle, with Skenfrith and the imposing White Castle, formed the 'Trilateral' defence of the English frontier. (AM).
Kidwelly Castle (Kidwelly). Impressive remains of Norman castle, with many features still intact. (AM Standard hours).
Llanthony Priory (11m N of Abergavenny). Ruins of 12c priory, in beautiful setting. Much of the church remains.
Manorbier Castle (5½m SW of Tenby). An inhabited Norman castle (12c) on the coast W of Tenby. Apr–Sept, daily, 10.30–7.
Margam Abbey (2½m SE of Port Talbot). 12c Cistercian abbey, whose W end is still used as parish church.
Pentre Ifan (1½m SE of Nevern). Fine example of cromlech-type burial chamber. The cap-stone, 16 ft long, is supported on three uprights. (AM any time).
Raglan Castle (7m SW of Monmouth). The picturesque ruins are mainly of the 15c castle that replaced the 12c structure. (AM Standard hours).
St. Fagan's (4m W of Cardiff). Picturesque village with a Tudor mansion, and a very interesting Welsh Folk Museum and exhibition. Daily (except Mons).
St. Govan's Head (Pembs). At most southerly point of county. Magnificent cliff scenery. Note 13c Chapel; the chasm called Huntsman's Leap; and Stack Rocks.
Severn Bridge. Opened 1966, 3,240 ft in length and carries M4 over river, super-seding old Beechley-Aust ferry. Unique suspension design of wires hanging in V-form to provide rigidity.
Skenfrith (Mon). On river Monnow. Has 13c church and castle, the latter being one of the 'Trilateral' with Grosmont and White Castle. (AM Standard hours).
Skomer and Skokholm Islands off SW coast of Pembroke. Both are Nature Reserves for the study of sea-birds.
Sugarloaf (Mon). A conical mountain 3½m N of Abergavenny. There are extensive views from the summit, 1955 ft. (NT).
Tintern Abbey (5m N of Chepstow). Founded in 1131 for Cistercian monks. These elegant graceful ruins are admirably sited in the lovely Wye valley. (AM. Standard hours).
Usk (Mon). Small town, an angling centre of river Usk, with shell of a Norman castle and a priory church of interest.

Resorts and Centres of Interest

Abergavenny (Mon). A flourishing market town on the river Usk. Being close to the Monmouth-Welsh border, it is often described as the 'Gateway of Wales'. It lies in a hollow, sheltered by three mountains, and is a good centre for walks and climbing. The town is interesting for its ruin of an ancient castle, and for a church founded in the 11c and much enlarged in the 14c. This has old choir stalls and some magnificent monuments. About 5½m ENE, just beyond Llanvetherine, is White Castle. This, with Grosmont and Skenfrith Castles, formed a trio built to keep the Welsh in check.

Barry (Glam). Nine m SW of Cardiff, Barry is a modern town with three large docks. Less than a century ago the population was 85. The construction of the docks, and the growing custom of taking summer holidays, combined to make it both a thriving city and a popular resort. It is a convenient centre for exploring the vale of Glamorgan with its picturesque villages. The town is on a slope 300 ft above sea-level. The gateway and portcullis chamber are all that remain of a Norman castle. Separated from the mainland by the width of a dock is 'Barry Island'. Here are gently sloping sands that provide safe bathing; a long pebble beach; a good promenade; a large unspoilt park, and many holiday amenities. Prehistoric burial mounds, a Roman well, and remains of an ancient abbey, attract the antiquarian.

Bridgend (Glam). A market town and industrial centre well situated on the river Ogmore, between hills and sea. There are good transport services to Swansea and Cardiff, and within easy distance are many coastal resorts and the Vale of Glamorgan. Two m to the NE are the substantial remains of a 12–14c Coity Castle, and the attractive 14c church of Coity. Ewenny Priory, a fine fortified monastery, lies 2m S. It is well preserved, with an embattled wall and an interesting church. Other places to visit are the 12c ruins of Ogmore Castle, near Ewenny; and St. Donat's Castle, on the coast 9m S of Bridgend.

Caerphilly (Glam). An industrial town 7m N of Cardiff. Once a market town, noted for the cheese that bears its name. Caerphilly is rich in musical tradition; noted for its Nantgarw porcelain; and above all famous for its 13c castle. This is a magnificent fortress, the largest in Wales, with a 50-ft high leaning tower—the result of an attempt to demolish the castle during the Civil War.

Cardiff (Glam). Cardiff, the capital of Wales, is on the Bristol Channel. It is a University and industrial city, and a port, with extensive docks, for the S Wales coalfields. Cardiff airport lies 10m SW of the city. The Romans established a military centre here in the 1c, and a thousand years later the Normans made it their stronghold, incorporating the Roman walls into their castle. The great octagonal tower is 15c and the

The Coast at Tenby

spire quite modern. The castle was the residence of the Marquess of Bute, who in 1947 presented it to the City. The Banqueting Hall, the Chaucer Room, and the Private Chapel are richly decorated. The rapid development of Cardiff in the 19c was due to its geographical position combined with the mineral wealth of the neighbourhood. Modern Cardiff has a great variety of industries, and is a well planned city with fine buildings. The beautiful civic centre is overlooked by the great castle. The City Hall, its huge dome surmounted by the Welsh Dragon, contains good paintings and statuary. Other buildings worthy of mention are the National Museum, the University College, the College of Advanced Technology, the Law Courts, the County Hall, and the Hall of Nations. The city has well planned open spaces. Roath Park covers 102 acres and includes a botanic garden. See also Llandaff.

Chepstow (Mon). Beautifully situated on the steep slope of a hill overlooking the Wye. Once it was a bustling port, with shipbuilding yards. Today it is a quiet town, largely occupied with salmon fishing and tourists who are attracted by its beauty and historic associations, or its convenience as a centre for road or river trips. The extensive remains of the 12c castle are on a rocky eminence beside the Wye. Much of the city walls still remains; the Town Gate was rebuilt in the 16c—once used as a prison it now houses a local museum. The old Beachley-Aust ferry has been replaced by the fine new bridge over the Severn. Five m SW is Caerwent, the Roman city of Venta Silurum. This was the only Romano-British walled civilian town in Wales. The walls and N and S gates are still in good preservation. The Parish Church is an interesting medieval structure incorporating Roman work; in the porch are two inscribed altar stones.

Fishguard (Pemb). A small port on the N coast of Pembroke, with a bay, a shingle beach with excellent bathing, and fishing facilities. The steamers for Eire leave from Goodwick, $1\frac{1}{2}$m W. The sheltered bay can float the largest liner, and a massive breakwater runs out $\frac{1}{2}$m from Goodwick.

The Gower Peninsula. W. of Swansea is Gower—an unspoilt peninsula 15m long and averaging 5m in breadth, scheduled as an area of outstanding beauty. It has a magnificent coastline of 50m, all of which is accessible by road or footpath. On the S coast are smooth sandy bays; lovely inlets such as Mewslade backed by richly wooded cliffs; coves, caves, and blowholes. Mumbles, with a pier and promenade, good beaches, and the fine castle of Oystermouth, is becoming a very popular resort. The N foreshore is flatter, with sand-dunes. Cockles have for centuries been gathered at Penclawdd. The sandy marsh of Whiteford Burrows, sheltered by Whiteford headland, is rich in wild life and the area is now a nature reserve. Inland are picturesque glens and narrow country lanes leading to small villages of thatched and whitewashed cottages. The peninsula has many prehistoric and later remains. There are cromlechs and traces of old encampments, castle ruins such as those of Weobley Castle, and ancient churches such as Llangennith that was once a priory founded by Henry I.

Gower is ideal for walkers, anglers, bathers, speleologists, nature lovers, and antiquarians.

Haverfordwest (Pemb). A busy inland market town and the seat of county government. On the slope of a steep hill beside the river West Claddon. There are the ruins of a 12c castle, and four ancient churches, notably St. Mary's. Both church and castle were used as a temporary gaol for the French prisoners taken in the last and bloodless invasion of Britain at Strumble Head in 1797.

Llandaff (Glam). Two m to the NW of Cardiff is the suburb of Llandaff, dominated by its Cathedral. This was originally founded in the 6c, and after various restorations was badly damaged during the last War, but has again been restored. The Norman tower and doorways have survived, and there are interesting monuments.

Llandeilo (Carms). A market town built on high ground in the Towy valley. In a walled park W of the town is the modern Dynevor Castle, with the ruins of the former castle in its grounds. Two other spectacular castles not to be missed, and within easy distance, are at Carreg Cennan, about 5m SE; and at Dryslwyn, 5m W and perched above the Towy.

Llandovery (Carms). This town, whose name means 'Church among the Waters', is situated between the Towy and Bran rivers amid beautiful scenery. It is mainly concerned with sheep-rearing, although this is now being replaced by afforestation in certain parts of the area. Llandovery is on the site of the Roman station Lovertium. Only a fragment remains of the Norman castle that once dominated the neighbourhood.

Llanelly (Carms). A large industrial town on the Burry inlet, once a flourishing port exporting coal, iron and tinplate. Now the port is closed, and Llanelly is mainly concerned with the steel industry and allied products, and the producing of anthracite coal. The large number of churches and chapels, and most of the houses, are early Victorian. There is a fine municipal park and a museum.

Merthyr Tydfil (Glam). Once a most important industrial centre. Exploitation of the coalfields, limestone quarries, and iron ore led to industrialisation, prosperity and increase in population. After the closing of the ironworks in 1930, Merthyr dwindled in importance in favour of the unlovely Rhondda Valley that stretches from Pontypridd to Porth. Merthyr now hopes to become popular as a mountain resort noted for its bracing air.

Milford Haven (Pemb). The town takes its name from the magnificent natural harbour, which covers 20 sq. m. Milford in 1800–1814 preceded Pembroke as a royal dockyard, and the church has interesting mementoes of Nelson. It is now a trawler port and oil port, but is also a holiday resort with a mild sheltered climate, and is increasing in favour as a yachting centre. E. of Milford is Neyland, where the ferry crosses to Pembroke.

Monmouth (Mon). An ancient county town in picturesque surroundings, bounded by the Monnow and Wye rivers. The unique 13c bridge has a fortified gatehouse and is rich in historical associations. Henry V was born in 1387 at the Castle, part of which is still standing. Castle House, dating from 1673, has interesting architectural features. St. Thomas Church originally belonged to a priory; it has Norman and Saxon work and interesting galleries. St. Mary's Church, of Norman origin, is notable for its fine spire and the bells that Henry V brought from Calais. N of the church are the remains of a Priory. The R.C. Church has many relics, including a 13c cross. The museum houses a large collection of Nelson relics. The Grammar School was founded in 1614. Monmouth is a splendid centre for exploring the Wye Valley.

Neath (Glam). Neath, at the mouth of the river of that name, originated from the Roman station at Nidum. Recent excavations have revealed the site of two gateways of the fort. One m W is the ruin of a 12c abbey founded by Richard de Granville. The Castle, at the W side of the town, is also a ruin; its main gateway is flanked by towers. Neath is an industrialised town of collieries, and steel and tinplate works. In contrast, the Vale of Neath, stretching out to the NE, is a valley of beauty with winding rivers, high waterfalls, lush dales, caves and steep gorges. S of Neath the borough includes the industrial towns of Briton Ferry and Port Talbot, and the resort of Aberavon.

Newport (Mon). An assize town and thriving industrial town at the mouth of the Usk. It is a coal and steel area, with modern docks, a transporter bridge, and a civic centre. The Cathedral church of St.

Pembroke Castle

Woolos has some fine Norman and Gothic work. The shell of the Norman castle is interesting for its towers, one of which has a water-gate with a chapel above. Three m to the W is the Roman fort of **Caerleon**, also known as Isca, founded in A.D. 75 and a fortress and seaport town for three centuries. Extensive remains exist. Excavations have revealed that outside the fortress wall there developed a busy walled town with shops, houses, temples, baths, and a remarkable amphitheatre to seat 6,000. A modern town with a population of 5,000 is now on the site, and has a Legionary Museum, a Norman motte, and a 15c church of Norman origin. Caerleon has associations with Arthurian legends and Tennyson.

Pembroke (Pemb) lies on a creek of Milford Haven. Its castle, on a rocky promontory overhanging the river Pembroke, was one of the largest and strongest fortresses in Wales, and is still very impressive. Henry VII was born here. The keep, built about 1200, is 75 ft in height, with walls 15–20 ft in thickness. Near the castle, beyond Monkton Bridge, are the remains of Monkton Priory, founded in 1098. Two m from Pembroke is Pembroke Dockyard, which was a naval dockyard from 1814 to 1925. During the second World War it was used by the R.A.F. as a flying-boat base, from which Sunderlands and other aircraft made their sea patrols.

Penarth (Glam). Four m S of Cardiff. Developed from a small village during the shipping and coal trade boom period, and was made one of the customs ports of Cardiff. Is becoming increasingly popular as a holiday resort with pebble beaches, a wide esplanade, pier, harbour and dock. Penarth is built on a headland which provides a splendid viewpoint. There are pleasant cliff and field walks, and steamer trips to numerous places of interest.

Pontypridd (Glam). At the junction of the Rhondda with the Taff, it has a graceful single-arched bridge built in 1756. The town lies at the S end of the Rhondda Valley, and after many years of depression, now shows increasing prosperity from its new industries and the power station. It has the largest industrial estate in Wales, also cinemas, shops and a fine park.

Porthcawl (Glam). A popular seaside resort on the Bristol Channel, well positioned for serving the mining valleys. It is a well kept town, with good sands and a fine esplanade; sand dunes, rocks and woodland; and ample provisions for sport and entertainment. The interesting village of Newton is now part of Porthcawl, and its 13c church is well worth visiting. Stone, bronze and iron age relics have been unearthed in the neighbourhood. Also incorporated in Porthcawl is Nottage, a former walled village. Nottage Court is an Elizabethan manor of special architectural and historic interest.

Port Talbot (Glam). A coal and iron port on Swansea Bay. To the N it joins up with Aberavon, where there are excellent sands, good bathing, and traces of a castle.

St. Davids (Pemb). Though the population is very small (about 1700) St. Davids ranks as a city by virtue of its magnificent Cathedral. The see was founded by St. David in the 6c. The city lies a mile or so inland from St. Davids Head, a rugged promontory with several cromlechs and stone circles. From here there is a good view of Whitesand Bay to the S, and of Ramsey Island beyond this. The Cathedral is approached by the Pebbles, a thoroughfare lined with ancient houses and leading through a 13c gateway to the Close. The stone staircase descending from here to the Cathedral is known as the Thirty-nine Articles since it has this number of steps.

St. Davids Cathedral has a severe exterior, but a rich and ornate interior. The oldest part is the nave, dating from the 12c when the Cathedral was rebuilt after having been burnt down by the Danes in 1087. W of the Cathedral are the ruins of the 14c Bishop's Palace, still beautiful although a later bishop stripped off its leaden roof to provide dowries for his five daughters.

Swansea (Glam). Is the second largest town in Wales and has two distinct aspects. To the E it is wholly industrialised, is an important oil port, and has practically a monopoly in exporting anthracite. To the W are fine sands and panoramic views. The remains of the 14c castle have been incorporated into a modern office building. After heavy War damage much rebuilding was necessary. St. Mary's church has been restored and a fine Civic Centre built.

Railway and road skirt the coast to **Mumbles,** a popular resort with good sands, a pier, many amusements, and fine coastal views. Near the shore are the ruins of Oystermouth Castle, and the Parish Church is of Norman origin.

Tenby (Pemb). Splendidly sited on the W side of Carmarthen Bay. To the E of the town is a rocky peninsula culminating on Castle Hill, a fine viewpoint. To the S is an excellent sandy beach extending 2m to Giltar Point. St. Catherine's Island is accessible at low water. The Harbour is protected by a stone pier, and the North Sands extend 2m to Monkstone Point. In past centuries Tenby was successively colonised by Romans, Danes, English and Flemish. After the Tudors, Tenby's prosperity dwindled, and only recovered when it became a popular holiday resort. On Castle Hill, now a recreation ground, are the remains of the 13c castle; the keep houses a museum. Tenby was a walled town in the 14c, the walls being later enlarged and rebuilt. Sections remain along the E side of the Parade; the interesting SW gateway is known locally as the Five Arches. St. Mary's is the largest parish church in the county, and dates from 13–14c. It has a medieval tower and spire 152 ft high, a fine wagon-roof, and beautiful windows. The pleasant stone-built town has many old houses—the Tudor Merchants' House, the adjoining Plantagenet House, and several good examples of Georgian architecture.

The Lowlands of Scotland

The Lowlands of Scotland are generally regarded as being that part of the country lying between the lines linking Helensburgh with Stonehaven and Girvan with Dunbar.

Across the Border some 9m N of Carlisle is a flattish belt of land which embraces Annan, Dumfries and, generally speaking, the area falling within the course of the rivers Sark and Nith. Dumfries, a county town with 27,988 inhabitants, is worth visiting on account of its many associations with Robert Burns, and also as a touring centre from which to explore the counties of Kirkcudbright and Wigtown. Lying off the main traffic routes this rather neglected part of Scotland (often referred to as Galloway) offers much fine scenery ranging from the inland beauty of Glen Trool National Forest Park in the N to the great sand wastes of Luce Bay in the S. Whithorn, Castle Douglas, Kirkudbright, Wigtown and Portpatrick are just some of the places worthy of attention.

N of Galloway is Ayrshire and with it the Burns Country which radiates from Ayr—Kilmarnock, Mauchline, Tarbolton Kirkoswald and, not least, Alloway, the poet's birthplace. The county's main coastal resorts are Largs, Troon, Prestwick, Ayr and Girvan.

N Dumfriesshire and S Lanarkshire have many delightful villages set in pleasant rolling countryside. Moffat, Wanlockhead, Elvanfoot, Crawford and Abington are to be recommended.

The county of Bute which includes the islands of Bute, Arran and the Great and Little Cumbrae is well served by frequent steamer/car ferry services from the mainland. Bute itself has a lively county town in Rothesay. Close at hand are the famous Kyles of Bute, possibly the greatest attraction for the discerning visitor. Arran, with the possible exception of Brodick its chief town, has many uncommercialised parts and is popular with those seeking a quiet holiday. Great Cumbrae (Millport is the only resort) offers a generally rugged coastline, though there are one or two pleasant sand beaches.

In the SE is Berwickshire, an agricultural county with few large towns. Coldstream, Duns and Chirnside are noted angling resorts; Eyemouth and Coldingham are for the sea-lover.

The Lothians (E, W and Midlothian) are vastly different in many respects. North Berwick, Dunbar and Gullane offer an abundance of sea, sand and golf; Midlothian is, to all intents and purposes, an 'inland' county where all roads lead to Edinburgh (or so it would seem) while

W Lothian is a composition of good farming land merging with a landscape of derelict coal bings and the like. The introduction of giant undertakings such as the B.M.C. factory at Bathgate have, however, done much to improve the county's contribution to Scotland.

One of the main approach roads to Scotland from the N of England crosses the Border at Carter Bar and thereafter enters Roxburghshire, a county which, like its neighbours Selkirkshire and Peeblesshire, is entirely landlocked. At Jedburgh, the first town of any size in from Carter Bar, there are a dozen or so routes all of which will lead to the romantic names of the Scottish Borders—the Abbeys (Jedburgh, Dryburgh, Kelso, Melrose); the towns and villages (Hawick, Selkirk, Galashiels, Peebles, Denholm, Cardona, Cappercleuch) and the rivers and hills (Tweed, Ettrick, Yarrow, Dollar Law, Ettrick Pen). Hawick, Selkirk and Galashiels are the chief woollen manufacturing centres—each has its annual Common Riding (or Riding of the Marches) ceremony—and, while this is of great importance to the country's economy, tourists generally speaking ignore the present and turn their attention on the Scott country and the great Abbotsford House. Dryburgh Abbey, Scott's place of burial, is visited by upwards of 40,000 persons each year.

Scenically, the best countryside is generally considered to lie along the valleys of the Ettrick and Yarrow Waters (Selkirkshire), the upper reaches of the Tweed at Cadrona and Stobo (Peeblesshire) and in Teviotdale (Roxburghshire).

Of Special Interest

Dumfriesshire

Burn's House (Dumfries). Home of Scotland's national poet from 1793 until his death in 1796. Museum of books and relics. May–Sept, 2–8.
Carlyle's Birthplace (Ecclefechan). (NT). Thomas Carlyle born here in 1795. Letters and some of the writer's belongings can be viewed. Apr–Oct, 10–6, Nov.–Mar, 10–4.
Caerlaverock Castle (Dumfries 7m). Besieged by Edward I in 1300. Outstanding medieval secular architecture. Apr–Sept, 10–7, Oct–Mar, 10–4.
Ruthwell Cross (Dumfries 8m). Richly carved 18-ft high stone cross dating from 7c. Can be seen at any time.

Kirkcudbrightshire

Dundrennan Abbey (Kirkcudbright 6½m). Founded by David I in 1142, this Cistercian house was where Mary Queen of Scots last stayed in Scotland. Apr–Sept, 10–7, Oct–Mar, 10–4.

Wigtownshire

Whithorn Priory (Whithorn). 12c priory this later became the cathedral church of Galloway. Doorway of nave (Norman) is chief feature. Apr–Sept, 10–7; Oct–Mar, 10–4.

Ayrshire

Burns' Cottage (Alloway). Birthplace in 1759 of Scotland's national poet. Cottage includes a museum with Burns relics. Apr–Sept, 9–7, Oct, 9–6, Nov–Mar, 9–4.
Souter Johnnie's House (Kirkoswald). (NT). Home of John Davidson (died 1806) the original Souter Johnnie in Burns' 'Tam o' Shanter'. Life-size stone figures of the Souter, Tam and other characters stand in the garden. Burns relics. Apr–Sept, 2.30–dusk.
Culzean Castle (Maybole 4m). (NT). Built between 1772 and 1792 this is generally regarded as being one of the finest of Robert Adam's works. Mar–Oct, 10–dusk.

Berwickshire

Mellerstain (Kelso 7½m). Georgian mansion built by William and Robert Adam. 18c. Fine plaster ceilings; period furniture and paintings. May–Sept, 2–5.30 (except Sats).
Dryburgh Abbey (Melrose 5m). Founded by David I the remains date from 12 and 13c. Sir Walter Scott and Earl Haig buried here. Apr–Sept, 10–7, Oct–Mar, 10–4.

Roxburghshire

Melrose Abbey (Melrose). One of the most visited of the Border Abbeys. Fine sculpture and window tracery are among the notable features. Founded 1136. Apr–Sept, 10–7, Oct–Mar, 10–4.
Abbotsford House (Galashiels 2m). Sir Walter Scott's 19c home. Many of Scott's books and relics are on view. Apr–end Oct, 10–5.

Peeblesshire

Traquair House (Peebles 6m). A 10c Scottish mansion said to be the oldest inhabited house in Scotland. Fine embroideries, silver, glass. Jun–Sept, 2–5.30.

East Lothian

Dirleton Castle (Dirleton). Ancient stronghold of the de Vaux now one of the most beautiful ruins in Scotland. Imposing group of towers dating from 13c. Apr–Sept, 10–7, Oct–Mar, 10–4.

205

West Lothian

House of the Binns (Linlithgow 3½m). (NT). 15c home of the Dalyells; famous on account of its moulded plaster ceilings and interesting pictures. Mid-June–mid-Sept, 2–5.
Linlithgow Palace (Linlithgow). Birthplace of Mary Queen of Scots. Some of the existing pile dates from around 1400. Fine architecture. Apr–Sept, 10–7, Oct–Mar, 10–4.

Lanarkshire

David Livingstone Memorial (Blantyre). In Shuttle Row is the restored tenement in which Livingstone was born (1813). Relics associated with the great missionary-explorer are on view. Weekdays (summer), 10–9, weekdays (winter), 10–dusk.

Bute (Isle of Arran)

Brodick Castle (Brodick 1m). (NT). Ancient seat of the Dukes of Hamilton. Outstanding collection of paintings, porcelain, furniture and silver. May–Sept, 1–5.

Resorts and Centres of Interest

Annan (Dumf). Pleasant market town on river Annan 16m SE of Dumfries. Nearby is the Atomic Energy Establishment at Chapelcross and the 8c Ruthwell Cross.
Ardrossan (Ayr). On Firth of Clyde 28m SW of Glasgow it is one of the main Scottish ports for steamer services to Ireland. Car ferries operate to Isle of Arran, 15m offshore.
Ayr (Ayr). County town 33m SW of Glasgow. It is one of Scotland's leading holiday resorts. The famous Burns country is close at hand as is the international airport at Prestwick. A racing course and skating rink are among the many amenities offered.
Brodick (Bute). The largest resort on I. of Arran it is also the steamer port for services to and from the Ayrshire coast. Coach tours include the popular 'Round the Island' trip. Brodick Castle attracts some 25,000 visitors each year.
Castle Douglas (Kirk). Market town 18m SW of Dumfries. The park at Carlingwark Loch is a local attraction whilst at no great distance is the 14c Threave Castle, stronghold of the Douglases.

Traquair House

Coldstream (Bwerw). On the Scottish–English border 13½m SW of Berwick-upon-Tweed. Good hill-walking centre. See house where Coldstream Guards were raised.

Dalbeattie (Kirk). Small town 5m ESE of Castle Douglas. Good freshwater fishing in pleasant surroundings. The SE corner of Kirkcudbrightshire is easy of access—see Sweetheart Abbey, 1273 (near New Abbey village) and Kirkbean, home of John Paul Jones founder of the American navy.

Dumfries (Dumf). County town on River Nith 33m WNW of Carlisle. It has many associations with Robert Burns—see Burns' House, Mausoleum, Globe and Hole in the Wa' taverns. Excellent touring centre with many amenities, not least of which is the fine freshwater fishing.

Dunbar (E Loth). Coastal resort 28m E of Edinburgh much favoured by holidaymakers on account of its good sunshine record.

Duns (Berw). County and market town 15½m W of Berwick-upon-Tweed. Noted as an angling centre it lies amidst lovely countryside.

Ecclefechan (Dumf). Small village just off the A74 Carlisle–Glasgow road, 13½m E of Dumfries. Thomas Carlyle's birthplace (1795) has been the property of the National Trust for Scotland since 1935.

Eyemouth (Berw). Popular coastal resort on Berwickshire seaboard 49m SE of Edinburgh. Coldingham and St. Abb's Head (see Fast Castle 3½m NW) are among the interesting places nearby.

Galashiels (Selk). Tweed manufacturing town 33m SE of Edinburgh it is a good touring and angling centre (Tweed and Gala Water meet here). It has a famous 'Braw Lads' gathering each year.

Gatehouse of Fleet (Kirk). This old world town lies in the valley of the Water of Fleet 8m NW of Kirkcudbright. See 15c Cardoness Castle, ancient home of the McCullochs. Burns composed 'Scots wha ha'e' in town's Murray Arms Hotel.

Gourock (Renf). Holiday resort on Firth of Clyde 26m NW of Glasgow. Headquarters of Clyde pleasure steamers it is also a yachting centre. Magnificent views of Cowal hills from nearby Fort Matilda and Cloch Point. See Cross of Lorraine.

Gretna (Dumf). Village on the Scottish–English border 9m NW of Carlisle. The old smiddy (Blacksmith's Shop) was where runaway marriages were once performed in thousands.

Hawick (Rox). Tweed manufacturing town on river Teviot 51m S of Edinburgh and roughly that same distance NNE of Carlisle. Given the tag of 'Queen o' a' the Borders', Hawick has a well-known annual Common Riding ceremony. Noted angling centre.

Jedburgh (Rox). County town on Jed Water 48m SSW of Edinburgh. Jedburgh Abbey, founded by David I in 1118, Queen Mary's House 16c (now a museum) and Blackfriars Church (1746) are among the most interesting sights.

Kelso (Rox). Situated at the confluence of the rivers Tweed and Teviot, this market town is 43m SW of Edinburgh and 11m NE of Jedburgh. It has a famous 12c Abbey; the John Rennie bridge across the Tweed (erected 1803) and, to the NW off A6089, the magnificent Floors Castle (gardens and grounds open during summer). Kelso is also a noted angling centre.

Kirkcudbright (Kirk). County and market town at mouth of river Dee 27m SW of Dumfries. The 16c Maclellan's Castle (ruin) and the Tolbooth (16–17c) are among the historical interests of the town. See also 18c houses. Noted artist's community.

Langholm (Dumf). On the banks of the Border Esk this pleasant little town lies 23m SW of Hawick and about that same distance N of Carlisle. It is much favoured by anglers and has an annual Common Riding ceremony.

Largs (Ayr). Sometimes referred to as the 'Gem of the Clye', Largs (30m SW of Glasgow) is probably the finest coastal resort in N Ayrshire. The town offers splendid views of the Cumbraes, Bute and Arran and has many attractions such as steamer cruises, sea fishing trips and illuminations. The 'Pencil' monument commemorates the Battle of Largs (1263), fought between Alexander III and Haco, King of Norway.

Melrose (Rox). Famous on account of its associations with Sir Walter Scott, this little town lies 4m E of Galashiels and 38m SE of Edinburgh. See Melrose Abbey (the best preserved of the four great Border Abbeys,

Abbotsford House (3m W), Dryburgh Abbey (3½m SE) and Scott's View (7m E).

Millport (Bute). Holiday resort on Great Cumbrae island. There are many amenities, good seascapes and an interesting Marine Biological Research station near Keppel pier.

Moffat (Dumf). Inland resort on river Annan 19m N of Dumfries. Good hill walking and angling centre. See Devil's Beeftub (A701) and Grey Mare's Tail (A708) to the N and NE of the town respectively.

New Galloway (Kirk). Small village at head of Loch Ken 19m N of Kirkcudbright. Fishing, golf and climbing (Rhinns of Kells) are the chief attractions. See unusual carvings and inscriptions in Kells churchyard, ½m N of village.

Newton Stewart (Wig). Market town on river Cree 25m E of Stranraer and 44m SW of Dumfries. Noted touring and angling centre. See lovely Glen Trool National Forest Park, 10m away to the N.

North Berwick (E Loth). One of the country's leading seaside resorts, North Berwick is also a noted golfing centre. Tantallon Castle (3m E) a stronghold of the Douglases, is boldly situated on a rocky headland facing the conspicuous Bass Rock.

Peebles (Peeb). Built upon a peninsula where the rivers Tweed and Eddleston mingle, this county town is a good centre for both touring and angling. 23m S of Edinburgh it is well known as an inland holiday resort of some distinction. Nearby (1m W) is the picturesque Neidpath Castle (15c) while, more distant (at 7m ESE of the town) is Traquair House, reputed to be the oldest inhabited house in Scotland.

Portpatrick (Wig). Attractive little resort 8m SW of Stranraer it is said to be the show place of the Mull of Galloway's coast. Good cliff scenery. The ruined Dunskey Castle (early 16c) faces the sea a little way S of the resort.

Rothesay (Bute). County town on I. of Bute, Rothesay is also an extremely popular holiday resort. Pleasure steamers to Kyles of Bute, Dunoon and other Clyde coast resorts. See 13c Rothesay Castle, Bute Museum and the Church of St. Mary. Etterick (or Ettrick) Bay has the island's best beach.

Selkirk (Selk). County town on Ettrick Water 38m SE of Edinburgh. Good touring and angling centre. See lovely St Mary's Loch and (nearby) the monument of James Hogg, the Ettrick Shepherd. Ceremony of Common Riding is held each year.

Troon (Ayr). Seaside resort 8m N of Ayr, it is largely a residential town. Good beaches and excellent golf courses are among the main attractions.

Turnberry (Ayr). Small resort 6m N of Girvan it is best known for its excellent hotel and golf courses. The famous Culzean Castle is but a short distance to the north. Ten miles offshore is the prominent Ailsa Craig.

Edinburgh

Edinburgh (Pop. 467,986), county town of Midlothian and capital of Scotland, is sometimes referred to as the 'Athens of the North'. One's first impressions on arriving at the city's Waverley station are certainly highly favourable for here are the wide open spaces of Princes Street Gardens; fine buildings and monuments such as the Royal Scottish Academy, Register House and the prominent Scott Monument and, not least, the centuries-old Edinburgh Castle vying as it were in competition with the modern shops and stores of Princes Street, the most highly rated thoroughfare in Scotland. But these are merely the first impressions . . . cross the 'Bridges' and walk the 'Royal Mile' (Edinburgh's oldest and most interesting area) from the Castle to the Palace of Holyroodhouse; see Parliament House, Gladstone's Land, St. Giles Cathedral and John Knox's House; visit the city at Festival time and hear the great symphony orchestras of the world; go to Edinburgh in the dead of winter when Scotland's international Rugby XV are playing at Murrayfield—or when Hearts and Hibernian are fighting for a place in the soccer league. All this is Edinburgh, a city of many contrasts.

Of Special Interest

Edinburgh Castle. Taken in 1296 by Edward I the castle was later (1341) captured by the Scots. See St. Margaret's Chapel, Mons Meg, Scottish National War Memorial, King's Bastion and Half Moon Bastion. Weekdays (winter), 9.30–4.30, from Whitsun, 9.30–6.

Gladstone's Land (Lawnmarket). A 17c tenement house, it has been beautifully restored. See tempera painting on walls and ceilings. (NT). Mon–Fris, 2–5.

Palace of Holyroodhouse. Dating back to James IV (building about 1500) this is the official residence of the Royal Family in Scotland. State rooms and Picture Gallery of great beauty and interest. Jun–Sept, 9.30–6, Oct, 10–5, Nov–Jan, 10–4.

John Knox's House (High Street). Built in 1490 it is thought to have been lived in by John Knox from 1561 to 1562. Regarded as being among the most picturesque of Edinburgh's historic buildings. Mons–Sats, 10–5.

St. Giles (Royal Mile). Built in 14 and 15c this is by far the most famous of Edinburgh's churches. See Thistle Chapel designed by Sir Robert Lorimer. Weekdays, 10–5.

Register House (Princes Street). Repository of Scottish archives dating back to 1292. Although originally designed by Robert Adam (1772) it was later modified by Robert Reid (1814). Among the interesting collection of papers is the Articles of Union of 1706. Mons–Fris, 10–4.

Parliament House. Dates from 1640. This was where the Scottish Parliament sat until the Union of 1707. Mons–Fris, 10–5, Sats, 10–1.

Mercat Cross (Royal Mile). It is from here that Royal Proclamations are read and have been read since Cross was restored in 1885 by Gladstone.
Greyfriar's Church. Originally built in 1612 this was where the Solemn League and Covenant was signed in 1638. Martyrs' Memorial commemorates Covenantor prisoners. Mons–Fris, 10–12.30, 2–4.45, Sats, 10–2.

Near Edinburgh—

Rosslyn Chapel (Roslin). Founded in 1446 the chapel has fine stone carving. The exquisitely decorated 'Prentice' (or Apprentice) Pillar is world famous. Weekdays 10–1, 2–5.
Craigmillar Castle (2½m). Once the home of Mary Queen of Scots. See massive 14c keep. Here was signed in 1567 the plot to murder Darnley. Apr–Sept, 10–7, Oct–Mar, 10–4.
Laurieston Castle (4m). Built in late 16c this was for a time the home of John Law, the financier who founded the first bank in France. Furniture, wood mosaics and paintings on view. Apr–Oct, 10–1 and 2–5, Nov–Mar, 2–4.

Resorts and Centres of Interest in the Edinburgh District

Dalkeith (Midloth). Market town 6½m SE of Edinburgh. St. Nicholas Church has in its roofless eastern apse the grave of Monmouth's widow. See (2m SW) Newbattle Abbey formerly a Cistercian Abbey (1140) and now a residential college.
Dalmeny (W Loth). Village at approaches of Forth Bridge 9½m NW of Edinburgh. It has a 12c parish Church with exceptionally rich carvings.
Dirleton (E. Loth). Claims to be one of the prettiest villages in Scotland, it lies 20m NE of Edinburgh. Nearby is the famous golfing resort of Gullane. See impressive remains of 13c Dirleton Castle and the 17c Church.
East Linton (E Loth). A picturesque old-world village 22m E of Edinburgh. Nearby is Preston Mill 17c (NT) believed to be the oldest water-mill still working in Scotland. Hailes Castle (see fine 16c chapel) is 2m SW of the village.
Edinburgh (Midloth). Capital of Scotland, historic Edinburgh is often called the 'Athens of the North' on account of its very fine setting. The world famous Princes Street with its impressive Scott Monument and Royal Scottish Academy; its 'Royal Mile' with Edinburgh Castle at one end and the Palace of Holyroodhouse at the other; St. Giles, John Knox's House, Gladstone's Land, Parliament House, Edinburgh University and many other well known buildings—it is these which have made the Edinburgh of yesterday the even finer Edinburgh of today. The city offers all modern recreational facilities including a three weeks long International Festival of Music and Drama.

Gifford (E Loth). Attractive little village on Gifford Water 19½m E of Edinburgh. It has an early 18c Church. To the S is Lammer Law (1,773 ft), a fine viewpoint.

Haddington (E Loth). County town on river Tyne 17m E of Edinburgh, it has several fine buildings. See town library with valuable 17c collection, St. Mary's Church (14c) and 1m S Lennoxlove, ancient home of the Maitlands now residence of the Duke of Hamilton. John Knox is believed to have been born in Haddington (1505).

Linlithgow (W Loth). County town of W Lothian 16m W of Edinburgh. It has a fine 16c Palace, birthplace (1542) of Mary Queen of Scots. See St. Michael's pre-Reformation parish Church and 3m NE The Binns (NT) 15c seat of the Dalyells.

Prestonpans (E Loth). Small town on Firth of Forth 8m E of Edinburgh. Battle of Prestonpans (1745). Hamilton House, dating from 1628, has been restored by the National Trust for Scotland. See town's fine 17c Mercat Cross.

Roslin (Midloth). Small village on river N Esk 7m S of Edinburgh. Rosslyn Chapel dates from 1446 and contains the world famous Apprentice Pillar. The 14c Castle was formerly a seat of the St Clairs, Earls of Orkney.

South Queensferry. Small port at approaches of Forth rail bridge 9m NW of Edinburgh. Near here is the 2,000 yards long Forth road bridge opened in 1964. Hopetoun House, a fine mansion containing magnificent paintings and furnishings, is 3m W of the town.

Edinburgh

Glasgow

Glasgow, it is said 'made the Clyde and the Clyde made Glasgow'. Here, on both sides of this world famous river sprawls a city whose associations with shipbuilding, heavy engineering industries and the like go back almost 200 years. The really old Glasgow lies around the High Street wherein was built (1471) Provand's Lordship, the city's oldest house; twenty years earlier saw the founding of Glasgow University while much further back in the 12c (1197 to be precise) the present Cathedral was built. Other interesting buildings are the Kelvingrove Art Gallery and Museum, the Mitchell Library, City Chambers (Municipal Offices), and, on the outskirts, Crookston Castle and Provan Hall. Glasgow, well provided for in the sense of its recreational facilities, is additionally, an excellent touring centre. Sauchiehall Street at lunch time for a half-day trip to Loch Lomond or the Trossachs and home again for tea—this is how fortunate Glaswegians really are. It is the other aspect of the 'biggest, the oldest, the most maligned and best liked town in Scotland'.

Of Special Interest

Glasgow Cathedral. This fine building dates 1197. It is unique in the sense that it is the only complete medieval cathedral still surviving on the Scottish mainland. Notable features are the elaborate vaulting in the crypt and the 14c timber roof. Apr–May, 10–6, June–Sept, 10–7, Oct–Mar, 10–5.
Provand's Lordship. Built in 1471 this is the city's oldest house. Among the famous people who have stayed here are James II, James IV and Mary Queen of Scots. There is some interesting period furniture on view. Apr–Sept, 10–5, Oct–Mar, 11–4. Closed Thurs and Suns.
Crookston Castle (Glasgow 4m). Dates from 13c. Lord Darnley and Mary Queen of Scots are said to have stayed here. See remains of unusual 15c tower. (NT). Apr–Sept, 10–7, Oct–Mar, 10–5.
Provan Hall (Stepps). 15c mansion house once closely associated with Provand's Lordship. The house is regarded as being one of the most perfect pre-Reformation mansions in Scotland. (NT). Daily (except Tues) throughout the year.
Pollok House (Built in 1752 by William Adam, this privately-owned house (seat of the Maxwells) contains fine Spanish and other pictures. Apr–Sept, 10–7, Oct–Mar, 10–5.
David Livingstone Memorial See Lowlands section—Lanarkshire.

Resorts and Centres of Interest in the Glasgow District

Balloch (Dunb). Small town on river Leven 18m NW of Glasgow. From the nearby Balloch pier steamer tours operate (summer only) on lovely Loch Lomond. There is a fine park owned by Glasgow Corporation.

Blantyre (Lanark). Mining town 8½m SE of Glasgow. Birthplace of David Livingstone (1813–1873), the famous missionary and explorer.

Cumbernauld (Dunb). 13½m NE of Glasgow and roughly that same distance S of Stirling the Cumbernauld of today holds the distinction of being a prize-winning 'New Town'.

Drymen (Stir). Attractive little village near river Endrick 18m NNW of Glasgow. The picturesque hamlet of Balmaha on a sheltered bay of Loch Lomond, is 3½m distant.

Dumbarton (Dunb). Shipbuilding town at mouth of river Leven 15m NW of Glasgow. It has a famous thousand-year-old Castle, now a National monument. See Glencairn House (1623) and the Cunninghame Graham Memorial (Nat Trust for Scotland).

Fintry (Stir). Picturesque village on river Endrick 18½m N of Glasgow. Fine hill walking country with much fine scenery. The Loup of Fintry, a 100-ft waterfall, is 3m E of the village.

Glasgow (Lanark). City and seaport on river Clyde, Glasgow has by far the largest population in Scotland (1,018,582). It is extremely important by world standards as a major industrial and commercial centre. The 55 main public parks are acknowledged as being among the best kept in Britain. Dating from the 12c is the Cathedral with its fine crypt, choir and tower whilst, also of interest, is Provand's Lordship (1471), Glasgow University (1450) and Kelvingrove Art Gallery and Museum which houses the famous Burrell Collection. The city's Mitchell Library—the largest free library in Scotland—has an important Burns collection. See also Tolbooth Steeple, Old Glasgow Museum and Transport Museum. Touring centre for Loch Lomond, the Trossachs and Burns country.

Kilmacolm (Renf). Residential resort on Gryfe Water 17½m W of Glasgow. Good golf course set in pleasant surroundings. See 2m SE the ruined church of St. Fillan (1635) and 2m SW the scanty remains of Duchall Castle (formerly the Lords Lyle).

Paisley (Renf). Important town 6½m WSW of Glasgow. It is the world's biggest thread-producing centre. Paisley Abbey, destroyed by the English in 1307, was restored in the mid-15c. See also Museum and Art Gallery. 3m E of the town are the remains of 14c Crookston Castle.

Strathblane (Stir). Picturesque village in Blane Valley 10½m N of Glasgow. Good hill walking country on Campsie Fells and Fintry Hills. See the medieval stocks and dungeons of Duntreath Castle 2m NW of the village.

Loch Ailort

Highlands of Scotland

Argyll—Invernessshire

Leaving Dunbartonshire at Arrochar the A82 to Campbeltown enters Argyll and is soon climbing to Rest and Be Thankful, a point which affords magnificent views of the Croe valley and much of the surrounding countryside. Near here the visitor would do well to take the left fork for St. Catherines, Strachur, Loch Eck and Dunoon (Tighnabruaich may be reached by the B8000). Dunoon itself, an attractive holiday resort on the Firth of Clyde, offers many amenities not least of which are the highly popular steamer and bus trips to such places as Rothesay, Kyles of Bute, Glendaruel and Ardentinny.

But back at Rest and Be Thankful the route to Campbeltown follows Loch Fyneside to Inveraray, county town of Argyll. The famous Castle, home of the Duke of Argyll, has a magnificent collection of Arms and some very fine tapestries, furniture and portraits.

Continuing S we pass Lochgilphead, Ardrishaig and Tarbert before touching the Atlantic proper at Tayinloan opposite Gigha island. Campbeltown, a busy fishing port, holds no lasting memories for most visitors though close to the town there is much to delight the eye. Southend, Machrihanish, Carradale are to be recommended.

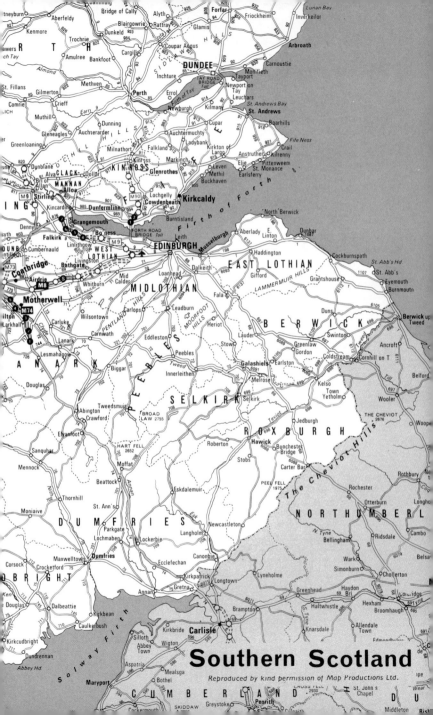

Southern Scotland

Reproduced by kind permission of Map Productions Ltd.

W Loch Tabbert, 1m W of Tarbert village, has a pier from which operates the MacBrayne steamer to Gigha, Jura, Islay and Colonsay whilst 3 miles further W (at Kennacraig) is the terminal of the recently introduced drive-on drive-off car ferry service to Port Askaig (Islay).

Islay, second largest island of the Inner Hebrides (after Mull), is noted for its whisky distilleries and splendid sand beaches; Jura is a land of hills—the well known 'Paps' dominate the island—and privately-owned estates on which roam an estimated 5,000 deer whilst Gigha and Colonsay, comparatively small islands, are perhaps most noted for their splendid 'Gardens' at Achamore and Kiloran respectively.

Continuing beyond Glen Falloch and Crianlarich we cross the Perth/Argyll county boundary just W of Tyndrum. From this point, taking the left fork to Oban, we pass Dalmally (Kilchurn Castle), Loch Awe and the Pass of Brander (see Hydro Electric power station) before reaching the delightfully situated village of Taynuilt near to which is Loch Etive and the great mass of 3,689-ft Ben Cruachan.

Oban as a town has much to commend it. Here from its wide bay (fine views of Mull and Lismore) one can marvel at the glorious sunsets of which Oban is justly famous. As a touring centre it has few rivals. Steamer services operate to Tobermory where one would do well to prolong one's visit and thereby see some of the beauties of Mull and Iona; to Lochaline, port for the Morven and Ardnamurchan districts of Argyle and to Coll, Tiree and Barra all of which have beaches and seascapes of a very high order. Yet these are just some of the things which attract visitors to this lovely town. Ashore, either N or S there are many more to discover—Ganavan sands, Benderloch, Appin, Kilninver, Kilmelfort and Ford can all be recommended.

Glencoe, reached from the S by the A82 from Tyndrum is, in addition to its being famous on account of the Massacre (1692), now well known as a popular winter sports centre. W and SW of Kingshouse hotel are the great Argyllshire mountains of Bidean nam Bian (3,766 ft) and the Buchailles or Shepherds of Etive whilst to the SE are the vast wastes of Rannoch Moor.

Ballachulish on the shores of Loch Leven is important in that it has a ferry to the Lochaber side of the loch. E of this is the road which passes Kinlochleven, a centre of no small importance as regards its aluminium industry.

Fort William (Invernessshire) a much-visited town on the shores of Loch Linnhe is picturesquely set near the foot of Scotland's highest mountain, the 4,406 ft Ben Nevis. Here is the ideal place from which tourists can explore the regions made legendary by Bonnie Prince Charlie —Moidart, Arisaig and Morar with their own historic place names, Glenfinnan, Lochailort, Kinlochmoidart. Mallaig, port for Skye and the Small Isles, is reached by the recently improved A830 which passes the famous Sands of Morar.

Fort William

Reaching still deeper into Invernessshire we continue NE from Fort William by the A82 which goes on to Invergarry, Fort Augustus, Loch Ness-side and Inverness itself, a town which rightly takes the 'tag' of 'Capital of the Highlands'. Scenically, some of the best countryside along this route is to be found near Spean Bridge, Invergarry and Drumna-drochit (Loch Ness).

SE of Inverness, where the A9 meets the river Spey, is Aviemore, a village which in recent years has become the leading winter sports centre in Britain. Hereabouts are many other delightful villages such as Kingussie, Newtonmore, Carrbridge and Boat of Garten. The Glen More National Forest Park, which includes lovely Loch Morlich, is to be recommended.

Beauly, an attractive little town 13m W of Inverness, has in the river Beauly, one of the most famous salmon waters of Scotland.

The other important road from Fort William (or, more correctly from Invergarry) is the A87 which runs NW to Kyle of Lochalsh via Cluanie Bridge, Glen Shiel and Loch Duich (see Eilean Donan Castle). It is worth noting that Kyle of Lochalsh (Ross & Cromarty), together with Mallaig, handles much of the traffic to Skye, an island perhaps best known for its spectacular hills (the Cuillins) and 13c Castle (Dunvegan).

N and S Uist, for many years now linked by causeway from Benbecula, are popular with those seeking first-rate angling or merely relaxation on the miles of sandy beaches which are offered.

Still further N are Harris and Lewis which, though joined one to the other, come under separate administrations. Harris, famous on account of its tweed industry, is a part of Invernessshire whilst Lewis, probably best known for its busy fishing port and capital Stornoway, is an insular region of Ross and Cromarty.

Of Special Interest

Argyll

Inveraray Castle (Inveraray). Residence of the Duke of Argyll, and built in the 18c. Fine tapestries, French furniture and outstanding collection of early Scottish Arms. Daily (except Fris) Apr–Jun. Daily thereafter till mid-Oct, 10–12.30 and 2–6, Suns, 2–6.

Castle Sween (50m S of Oban). Built about 12c this is said to be the earliest stone castle in Scotland. Destroyed by Sir Alexander Macdonald in 1647. Open at all times.

Carnasserie Castle (Kilmartin). Dates from 16c. Captured and partly blown-up during Argyll's rebellion in 1685. It has fine architectural details. Open at all times.

Iona Abbey (Isle of Iona). Founded by St. Columba in 563. The 17-ft high Iona Cross faces the Abbey. Steamer from Oban during summer. Ferry from Fionphort.

Duart Castle (Isle of Mull). Dates from 14c. Home of the chiefs of Clan Maclean. Well restored. Daily from May 1.

Kildalton Cross, Islay (Isle of Islay). Cross (9c) is generally regarded as being the finest Celtic cross still in existence. St. Martin's Cross in Iona is comparable for fine carving.

Invernessshire

Beauly Priory (Beauly). Founded in 1230 this ruined Priory has monuments and graves to the Chisholms, Frasers and the Mackenzies of Kintail. Apr–Sept, 10–7, Oct–Mar, 10–4.

Culloden (Inverness 5m). (NT). Site of the famous battle in 1746 when the Jacobite Rising was crushed by the Duke of Cumberland's forces. NT information office open daily, Apr–Sept.

Stones of Clava (opposite Culloden Field). These stones and cairns date from the late Neolithic or Early Bronze Age (possibly about 1600 B.C.) and are some of the most extensive in the country. (NT).

Urquhart Castle (near Drumnadrochit). The castle (now ruined) was one of the largest in Scotland. Blown up in 1692 to escape being occupied by the Jacobites. Dates from 16c. Apr–Sept, 10–7, Oct–Mar, 10–4.

Glenfinnan Monument (Fort William 18½m). (NT). Erected in 1815 to commemorate the men who followed Prince Charles Edward in the '45. NT Information Centre daily, Apr–mid-Oct, 10–dusk.

Dunvegan Castle (Isle of Skye, Portree 15m). Privately owned by John MacLeod of MacLeod this has been a residence of the Clan MacLeod since 1200. The Fairy Flag, drinking horn and an Irish communion Cup are among the most famous treasures. Apr–mid-Oct, 2–5.

Kisimul Castle (Castle Bay, Isle of Barra). 15c seat of the Macneils of Barra. Largely restored by the 45th Chief, The Macneil of Barra, it is the largest castle in the Outer Hebrides. May–Sept, Sats, 3–6. Boats may be hired from Post Office at Castlebay.

Resorts and Centres of Interest

Acharacle (Argyll). Well-known angling centre at western end of Loch Shiel, 62m (ferry 33m) WSW of Fort William. Steamer services to Glenfinnan start from here.

Ardrishaig (Argyll). Pleasantly situated village at N end of Kintyre peninsula, 26m SW of Inveraray. Here, linking Loch Fyne with the Sound of Jura, is the Crinan Canal.

Aviemore (Inver). Popular winter sports centre on river Spey, 31m SE of Inverness. Good facilities for pony-trekking, sailing (L. Morlich), and mountaineering. See famous Larig Ghru and Glenmore National Park.

Ballachulish (Argyll). Village on L. Leven from which ferry links the Appin and Lochaber districts of Argyll. Excellent mountaineering centre it is 12m S of Fort William.

Beauly (Inver). Small resort at western end of Beauly Firth, 13m W of Inverness. Beauly Priory is one of the three monastic houses of the Valliscaulian Order founded in Scotland.

Carradale (Argyll). Small village on east coast of Kintyre peninsula 13m NE of Campbeltown. It has an attractive little harbour with splendid sands nearby.

Connel Ferry (Argyll). Oban, 6m SW. From Connel a toll bridge carries traffic to the Benderloch and Appin districts of Argyll. Falls of Lora (beneath the bridge) are best seen at low tides. Ardchattan Priory (13c) NE of the village has associations with Bruce's Parliament of 1308.

Culloden (Inver). The battle of 1746 in which the Jacobite rebellion was crushed is here commemorated by a cairn. Inverness is 5m W.

Dalmally (Argyll). Noted angling centre near river Orchy and L. Awe, 25m E of Oban. Good mountaineering country nearby. See 15c Kilchurn Castle (2½m W) and 2m SW monument to Duncan Ban MacIntyre, the famous bard.

Drumnadrochit (Inver). Hamlet near mouth of river Enrick W side of Loch Ness, 15m SW of Inverness. Nearby are the ruins of 16c Urquhart Castle.

Dunoon (Argyll). One of the main coastal resorts of Argyll, Dunoon is 26m (ferry from Gourock) W of Glasgow. It offers splendid views of the Firth of Clyde and is a good centre for pleasure sailings. See (7m N) the Botanic Gardens of Benmore House.

Fort Augustus (Inver). Touring and fishing centre at S end of Loch Ness, 34m SW of Inverness and roughly that same distance NE of Fort William. Original fort is now a Benedictine Abbey through which visitors may be shown.

Fort William (Inver). One of the chief touring centres for the Lochaber district of Invernessshire it lies at the head of L. Linnhe, 65½m SW of Inverness. Nearby is the famous Ben Nevis (4,406 ft). See W Highland Museum.

Glencoe (Argyll). Scene of the famous Massacre (1692). Excellent mountaineering (notably Bidean nam Bian (3,766 ft) and the Shepherds of Etive) and winter sports centre. 35m S is the Perthshire village of Crianlarich.

Glenfinnan (Inver). Good angling centre at head of Loch Shiel, 18m W of Fort William. The prominent Prince Charles Edward monument (NT) is nearby.

Iona (Argyll). One of the most famous of the Inner Hebridean isles, it is reached by ferry from Fionphort, SW Mull. Iona Abbey dating from 1203 attracts many thousands of visitors each year. See also the famous St. Martin's Cross. There are many excellent beaches.

Inveraray (Argyll). County town of Argyll on W shore of Loch Fyne, 16m SW of Dalmally. It has a fine situation and a splendid Castle—headquarters since the early 15c of the Clan Campbell.

Inverness (Inver). Attractively set on both banks of river Ness (fine fishing) this town is often referred to as the 'Capital of the Highlands'. An excellent touring centre it offers many amenities including the annual Highland Games. See 19c St. Andrew's Cathedral, Town Steeple, Queen Mary's House and (5m E) the field of Culloden. Glasgow 167m. Edinburgh 157m.

Kingussie (Inver). On the river Spey 27m SSE of Inverness this picturesque resort offers golf, fishing and pony-trekking. There is an interesting Highland Folk Museum.

Lochaline (Argyll). Village with pier at mouth of Loch Aline 19m SW of Strontian. Good touring centre for Morven and Ardnamurchan areas of Argyll.

Lochgilphead (Argyll). Small town at head of Loch Gilp 24m SW of Inveraray. Administrative capital of Argyll it is a good touring centre for Knapdale.

Mallaig (Inver). Fishing port 42m NW of Fort William it also has a pier from which steamers operate to Skye and the Small Isles. See (2m S) Sands and Falls of Morar.

Newtonmore (Inver). Pony trekking, angling and mountaineering centre 45m S of Inverness. See Clan Museum with interesting Macpherson treasures.

Oban (Argyll). Popular coastal resort in the Lorne district of Argyll, it is also important as a steamer terminal for services to Mull, Coll, Tiree and Barra. Oban, 93m NW of Glasgow, has a famous Argyllshire Gathering each September. See Cathedral, McCaig's Folly and (3½m N) the 13c Dunstaffnage Castle.

Portree (Inver). Capital of I. of Skye it can be reached by boat from

Kyle of Lochalsh. Excellent touring centre offering good access to Cuillin Hills. See Flora Macdonald's monument and (14m W) Dunvegan Castle (13c home of the Clan MacLeod).

Spean Bridge (Inver). Probably most famous nowadays on account of its memorial to the Commandos, many of whom did their wartime training here. From this small village (10m NE of Fort William) there are impressive views of Ben Nevis and the Lochaber mountains.

Taychreggan (Argyll). Hamlet on Loch Awe opposite Portsonachan it lies 18½m SSE of Oban. Good angling centre. Ferry to Portsonachan.

Tayinloan (Argyll). Small village on W coast of Kintyre peninsula 18m SW of Tarbert. Here is passenger ferry to Gigha island, 3m W.

Tarbert (Argyll). Well-known fishing village on W shore of Loch Fyne, 36m SW of Inveraray. A well-known yachting centre, it is separated from W Loch Tarbert by a mile-wide isthmus. See ruined 14c Castle.

Taynuilt (Argyll). Picturesque village near shore of Loch Etive, 12m E of Oban. Magnificent views of nearby Ben Cruachan (3,689 ft). See Pass of Brander and Falls of Cruachan midway between Taynuilt and Loch Awe villages.

Tighnabruaich (Argyll). Delightfully situated resort on Kyles of Bute 46m WSW of Dunoon. Noted yachting centre.

Tobermory (Argyll). Chief village of Island of Mull it is also a port for steamer services to Oban/Coll, Tiree and Barra. Beautifully set on a wide bay the resort is an ideal touring centre for the island.

Tomdoun (Inver). Noted angling centre with fine situation in Glen Garry, 10½m W of Invergarry village. Outstanding mountain scenery.

223

Central Scotland

The counties of Dunbarton, Stirling, Clackmannan, Kinross, Fife, Perth and Angus

N and NW of Glasgow we have, within a 35-mile radius of the city centre, some of the most beautiful scenery in Scotland. Loch Lomond itself (its southern extremity is at Balloch and its northern limits 22m further N at Ardliu) is, of course, a great attraction with neatly-set little villages such as Luss, Tarbet and Balmaha fringing its western and eastern shores. Rowardennan, starting-point for those wishing to climb the famous 'Ben' (3,192 ft) is reached by road from Balmaha or by ferry from Inverbeg whilst Inversnaid, worth visiting on account of its rather spectacular waterfall, is best reached by the B829 to Stronachlachar (near) and thence by the Glen Arklet road—(it is from Aberfoyle that this route commences). Throughout the summer a pleasure steamer plies the entire length of Loch Lomond from its broad island-studded southern half to its narrows at, and beyond, Inveruglas. Here is the power station of the Loch Sloy hydro-electric scheme. The busy A82 road which skirts the 'Bonnie Banks' for more or less the entire length of the loch quits the waterside at Ardlui and proceeds northwards into Glen Falloch. Here runs the turbulent river Falloch flanked on either side by thickly-wooded countryside; N of this again we meet the mountainous regions around Crianlarich and Tyndrum.

E of Loch Lomond, roughly along a line running from Inversnaid to Callander (via Loch Ard) is the country made famous by Rob Roy the famous freebooter. Aberfoyle, an excellent touring centre for this district, is also a favourite place from which to visit the famed Trossachs, an area reached by the picturesque Duke's Road (A821) to Loch Achray. A popular excursion is the sail (summer only) from Trossachs pier (Loch Katrine) to Stronachlachar. The Lake of Menteith, Scotland's only 'lake', lies 3½m E of Aberfoyle village.

Stirling, county town 26m NE of Glasgow, is an extremely important historical and touring centre; nearby is the Field of Bannockburn and Cambuskenneth Abbey (scene of Bruce's Parliament of 1326).

The road running NW from the town (A84) via Doune and the picturesque town of Callander on the banks of the Teith river goes on to the Pass of Leny, Strathyre and Lochearnhead where one should deviate (Lix Toll A827) for Killin with its much-photographed Falls of Dochart. E and NE of this are the highly recommended towns and villages of St. Fillans, Crieff, Perth (ancient capital of Scotland), Aberfeldy, Pitlochry and Dunkeld. Perth, by far the largest of these, is a noted touring centre with many interesting buildings (see St. Ninian's Cathedral, St. John's Kirk, Fair Maid of Perth's House and (2m NE) Scone Palace).

Leaving Stirling by the A91 which winds past the Wallace Monument (fine views of the town and its 15–16c Castle) we pass Menstrie (see restored 16c Castle) and are soon running alongside the Ochill Hills at the easternmost end of which is Dollar, possibly the most attractive little town in Clackmannanshire. 3½m NE we enter Kinross-shire at the picturesque hamlet of Rumbling Bridge. Kinross, the county town, is famous on account of its excellent trout fishing (Loch Leven) and historically as being the scene of Mary Queen of Scots dramatic escape (1568) from that loch's Castle.

The Kingdom of Fife has, in St. Andrews, one of the most interesting seaside resorts in Scotland. Steeped in history with many finely preserved buildings to remind us of the past (e.g. Cathedral, Castle, St. Rule's Church, University), this famous town is also the recognised 'home of Golf' . . . Royal and Ancient Club founded in 1754. Ten miles down the coast from St. Andrews, in the district known as the East Neuk of Fife, is the quaint fishing village of Crail—a place much frequented by artists.

Apart from Dunfermline (the residence of early Scottish kings) and one or two pleasant little villages (Elie, Lundin Links, Kinghorn, Aberdour) the SE region of Fife holds little appeal to the visitor. Kirkcaldy, the largest town in this area, is extremely important on account of its linoleum industry. Near N Queensferry are the two great Bridges (rail and road) which link Fife with the S of Scotland.

Tayport and Wormit on Fife's northern coast (more accurately the Firth of Tay) are the stepping-off points for the Tay road and rail Bridges. Angus, a county which was formerly known as Forfarshire, lies across the 2½m wide estuary with Dundee (Scotland's third largest city after Glasgow and Edinburgh) occupying a commanding position along the waterfront. Notable buildings—there are many—include the Albert Institute, St. Andrew's Church, Museum and Art Gallery and the Old Steeple of St. Mary.

NE of the city is the famous golfing resort of Carnoustie with, beyond it, Arbroath, a fishing port renowned for its ruined 13c Abbey in which was signed (1320) the Declaration of Arbroath. Montrose, well known for its fine sandy beaches, is a lively holiday town near the Kincardineshire border.

Away from the coast there is a wealth of exquisite scenery to be found in such areas as the Carse of Gowrie (a great fruit-growing centre), Edzell, Glamis and, not least, Glens Clova, Prosen and Shee. The SW corner of the county is famous for its prize cattle.

Of Special Interest

Dunbarton

Dumbarton Castle (Dumbarton). A stronghold since the 5c. It was, until 1008, the centre of the independent British kingdom of Strathclyde. Apr–Sept, 10–7, Oct–Mar, 10–4.

Stirlingshire

Bannockburn Monument (Stirling 2m). (NT). Monument marks the spot where Robert the Bruce raised his standard before the Battle of Bannockburn (1314). Field of Bannockburn lies between here and river Forth.

Cambuskenneth Abbey (Stirling 1m). Augustinian house founded in 1147 by David I. Scene of Bruce's Parliament in 1326. James III buried here. Apr–Sept, 10–7.

Stirling Castle (Stirling). Early Renaissance Palace with many interesting features . . . see 15c hall, gatehouse, Chapel Royal and bastioned outworks. Apr–Sept, 10–6.45, Suns, 11–6, Oct–Mar, 10–4, Suns, 1–4.

Clackmannan

Menstrie Castle (Menstrie). Restored 16c castle in which was born Sir William Alexander, a 17c North American colonist, founder of Nova Scotia. Weds, Sats and Suns, 2.30–5.

Castle Campbell (Dollar 1m). (NT). Dates from late 15c. John Knox visited castle in 1556. There are some 16/17c additions. Apr–Sept, 10–7, Oct–Mar, 10–4.

Perthshire

Doune Castle (Doune). 15c. It has two fine towers. Restored in 1883. Privately owned by the Earl of Moray and Lord Doune. Daily, 10–1, 2–6. Closed December, also Thurs in Jan, Feb, Mar, Apr, Oct and Nov.

Dunblane Cathedral (Dunblane). Dates from 13c; see the lady chapel, the E and W gables and the nave arcade. Apr–Sept, 10–7, Oct–Mar, 10–4.

Killin Church (Killin). Dates from 1744 though has a 9c baptismal font. Apr–Sept.

Dunkeld Cathedral (Dunkeld). This beautifully situated 15c Cathedral contains some interesting wall paintings and a chapter-house which is now a mausoleum of the Dukes of Atholl. Apr–Sept, 10–7, Oct–Mar, 10–4.

Blair Castle (Blair Atholl). Privately owned by the Duke of Atholl this Castle contains a fine collection of furniture, porcelain, arms and, not least, jewellery, lace and miniatures in the treasure rooms. Open Easter, Suns and Mons in Apr, and daily from May–Oct, 10–6, Suns, 2–6.

Scone Palace (Scone—Perth 2m). Privately owned by the Earl of Mansfield, the present building dates from about 1803–1812. Treasures include ivory statuettes and Vernis Martin Vases. Open Apr–Oct, Mon–Sat, 11–5, Suns, 2–5. Closed Fris.

Kinrossshire

Loch Leven Castle (Loch Leven, Kinross). Dates from late 14–early 15c. In 1568 Mary Queen of Scots made her dramatic escape from here. Apr–Sept, 10–6. (Ferry service from Kinross).

Fife

Inchcolm Abbey (Inchcolm Is. near Aberdour). Founded by Alexander I in 1123 this Augustinian monastery has in its choir the best example of 13c wall painting left in Scotland. Apr–Sept, 10–7, Oct–Mar, 10–4. (Boats may be hired from Aberdour).

Dunfermline Abbey (Dunfermline). The Abbey, founded about 1070 was closely associated with Queen Margaret. Robert the Bruce is buried in the choir. Charles I born in guest-house (1600) which later became Royal palace.

Falkland Palace (Falkland). (NT). Built during 15 and 16c as a hunting lodge for Stewart kings. There is some fine early Renaissance work. Apr–Oct, 10–6. Suns, 2–6.

Culross Palace (Culross). (NT). Built between 1597 and 1611 this mansion contains fine 16c Renaissance paintings on wooden walls and ceilings. Apr–Sept, 10–7, Oct–Mar, 10–4.

Angus

Glamis Castle (Glamis). Privately owned by the Earl of Strathmore and Kinghorne; Castle dates from 14c. 17c plasterwork, furniture, china and tapestries. May–Sept, Weds and Thurs, 2–5.30, Jul–Sept, Suns, 2–5.30.

Barrie's Birthplace (Kirriemuir). (NT). Sir James M. Barrie born here in 1860; many of the writer's original manuscripts and personal possessions are on view. Apr–Oct, 10–12.30, 2–6, Suns, 2–6.

Arbroath Abbey (Arbroath). Declaration of Arbroath signed here in 1320; imposing remains (cloisters) date from founding in 1176. Apr–Sept, 10–7, Oct–Mar, 10–4.

Queen's View, Loch Tummel

Resorts and Centres of Interest

Aberdour (Fife). Seaside resort on Firth of Forth, 8m E of Dunfermline. It has an interesting 14c Castle and a restored Norman Church. 1½m offshore is the little island of Inchcolm on which are remains of Inchcolm Abbey (founded 1123).

Aberfeldy (Perth). Noted angling centre on river Tay 32m NW of Perth. Spanning the river is one of General Wade's most famous bridges (built 1733). Village offers good access to Loch Rannoch, Glen Lyon and Strathtay.

Aberfoyle (Perth). Picturesque village set in the heart of the Rob Roy country, 27m N of Glasgow. Excellent touring centre for Trossachs by famous Duke's road. Fishing and pony trekking are among the attractions offered.

Arbroath (Angus). Fishing port and holiday resort on Angus coast 17m NE of Dundee. It has a famous Abbey (founded 1176) in which the Declaration of Arbroath was signed (1320).

Arrochar (Dunb). At the head of Loch Long 17m N of Helensburgh, this village gives easy access to nearby (1m E) Loch Lomond and (13m WSW) via Rest and be Thankful, the picturesque Lochgoilhead. The unusually shaped Ben Arthur (2,891 ft)—the Cobbler—is noted for rock-climbing.

Balquhidder (Perth). Small village near the E end of Loch Voil, 13m NNW of Callander. See Rob Roy's grave marked by three stones. The wild and beautiful Braes of Balquhidder lie to the N and NW of the village.

Blair Atholl (Perth). Delightful Highland village 6½m NW of Pitlochry on the A9 road to Inverness. Fishing and pony-trekking centre. See nearby Blair Castle, seat of the Duke of Atholl.

Blairgowrie (Perth). Holiday town on river Ericht, 15m N of Perth. Centre of fruit-growing district. To the N is Glenshee, popular for winter sports. There is a fish pass on the river Ericht.

Callander (Perth). One of the most popular of Perthshire's inland resorts this town lies on the river Teith 38m N of Glasgow. Excellent touring centre for Trossachs, Strathyre, etc. The picturesque Falls of Leny are close at hand.

Carnoustie (Angus). Well-known golfing resort on Angus coast 11m E of Dundee. Excellent sands are an additional attraction.

Crianlarich (Perth). Good mountaineering centre 6m SE of Perth/ Argyll county boundary and 52m N of Glasgow. Mallaig and Oban rail routes meet here. Picturesque Glen Falloch is near at hand.

Crieff (Perth). Inland resort on river Earn 17m W of Perth. Good touring and angling centre. See (6m SE) Tullibardine Chapel one of the few unaltered Collegiate churches in Scotland.

Dollar (Clack). Holiday resort at foot of Ochil Hills, 12m NE of Stirling.

Dollar Academy, a well-known Scottish school, was built in 1818. Good hill-walking country.

Doune (Perth). Village on river Teith 8m NW of Stirling. The 14c Doune Castle is owned by the Earl of Moray and Lord Doune.

Dunblane (Perth). Famous on account of its 13c Cathedral, this pleasant little town lies on the Allan Water, 6m N of Stirling. 2½m E is the site of the Battle of Sheriffmuir (1715).

Dundee (Angus). Major Scottish city and port on Firth of Tay 22m E of Perth. Best known for its jute industry the city also has considerable interests in engineering, shipbuilding and preserve-manufacturing. Here, running S from the waterfront, are the two great Tay bridges which carry traffic to Fife and the S. There are many interesting buildings including the Albert Institute, the Old Steeple of St. Mary and St. Andrew's Church.

Dunfermline (Fife). One of the largest towns in Fife this Royal Burgh (16½m NW of Edinburgh by the Forth Bridge), was once a favourite residence of the early Scottish kings. Andrew Carnegie was born here in 1835. See 12c Abbey and the picturesque Pittencrieff Glen.

Dunkeld (Perth). Splendidly set on the banks of the river Tay, Dunkeld is 15m N of Perth on the main A9 road to Inverness. Noted angling centre. See 15c Cathedral and restored 'Little Houses' (NT).

Edzell (Angus). Holiday village near Kincardine border, 6m N of Brechin and 12m NW of Montrose. Good hill-walking centre. See 16c Edzell Castle, ancient seat of the Lindsays of Glenesk.

Elie (Fife). Holiday resort of Firth of Forth 13m S of St. Andrews. Good sand beach. See finely carved doorway of Gillespie House (1862).

Falkland (Fife). Small village (Royal Burgh) 11m N of Kirkcaldy. It has a famous Palace (16c) which is the property of the National Trust for Scotland.

Glamis (Angus). Small village 5½m SW of Forfar. Glamis (pronounced 'Glams') is best known for its notable Castle, childhood home of Queen Elizabeth the Queen Mother.

Helensburgh (Dunb). Residential town on upper reaches of Firth of Clyde, 22m NW of Glasgow. It has picturesque surroundings notably along the Gare Loch and in Glen Fruin. Birthplace (in 1888) of James Logie Baird, inventor of television. See obelisk commemorating Henry Bell, designer of the 'Comet'.

Inversnaid (Stir). Attractively set hamlet on eastern shore of Loch Lomond, 15m NW of Aberfoyle. The nearby Arklet Waterfall is well known to visitors as is the 1,762-ft Cruachan, a notable viewpoint.

Kenmore (Perth). Attractive little village at eastern end of Loch Tay, 6m SW of Aberfeldy. Good angling and boating centre. Taymouth Castle, once visited by Queen Victoria in 1842, is nearby.

Killin (Perth). Picturesque little Highland village at western end of Loch Tay, 20m NNW of Callander. The beautiful Falls of Dochart are

229

nearby. Ben Lawers (3,984 ft) to the NE of the village is noted for its rare alpine plants.

Kinross (Kinross). County town near western shore of Loch Leven, 12½m N of Dunfermline. Famous trout fishing centre. See island castle (Loch Leven) where Mary Queen of Scots was imprisoned. Also of interest is the carved Town Cross and (3½m E) the village of Kinnesswood, birth-place (in 1746) of Michael Bruce, the poet.

Kirriemuir (Angus). Holiday town 6m NW of Forfar. Birthplace (NT) of Sir James Barrie (1860–1937). Good touring centre for Glen Clova, also Isla and Prosen.

Lochearnhead (Perth). Attractive little village at western end of Loch Earn 10m NNW of Callander. It is one of Scotland's leading water ski-ing centres.

Luss (Dunb). Sometimes regarded as being Scotland's prettiest village, Luss on the western shores of Loch Lomond, lies 12m N of Dumbarton and 10m SSE of Arrochar. It has well-known Highland Games each July.

Montrose (Angus). Royal Burgh and leading seaside resort on Angus coast, 31m NE of Dundee. Good sands and bathing are among the attractions offered. See Town Hall (1,763) and 18c Medicine Well.

Perth (Perth) Ancient capital of Scotland. It lies on the river Tay 22m W of Dundee. Excellent touring and fishing centre. The many interesting buildings include St. John's Church (15c), the Fair Maid of Perth's House and the Art Gallery and Museum. See (2m N) Scone Palace.

Pitlochry (Perth). Leading inland holiday resort 28m N of Perth on the main A9 road to Inverness. It has many fine hotels and a famous 'Theatre in the Hills'. See hydro-electric scheme (also fish ladder) at nearby Loch Faskally. The spectacular Queen's View at Loch Tummel is close at hand.

St. Andrews (Fife). Popular holiday resort 12½m SSE of Dundee. It is the recognised home of golf (Royal and Ancient Golf Club founded 1754). Apart from the two splendid beaches there is an attractive park at Craigton. See St. Andrews Castle, St. Rule's Church (tower), Cathedral ruins, Holy Trinity Church and University. Good touring centre for the E Neuk of Fife.

Stirling (Stirl). County town of great historical importance, it lies 26m NE of Glasgow and 36m NW of Edinburgh. Excellent touring centre. Nearby is the river Forth with its Old Bridge where Wallace won the famous Battle of 1297. See Stirling Castle, Church of the Holy Rude, Bannockburn Monument, Cambuskenneth Abbey and Wallace Monument.

Trossachs (Perth). Renowned beauty spot lying between Lochs Achray and Katrine, 9m W of Callander. Steamer sailings (summer only) operate from Trossachs pier to Stronachlachar (Loch Katrine).

Northern Scotland

The counties of Kincardine, Aberdeen, Banff, Moray, Nairn, Ross and Cromarty, Sutherland, Caithness, Orkney and Shetland

Crossing the Angus/Aberdeenshire boundary near the Devil's Elbow (Perthshire border also meets here) we soon reach Braemar, setting each year of the Royal Highland Gathering. NW of this village are the Cairngorm mountains, the highest of which, Ben Macdhui, reaches 4,296 ft. Deeside is followed throughout much of the 52-mile journey from Braemar to Aberdeen and within this area are several delightful villages —Crathie (Balmoral Castle), Ballater, Aboyne and Banchory to mention but a few.

Aberdeen, an exceptionally clean city set between the rivers Dee and Don, is perhaps most known on account of its thriving fishing industry and its splendid granite buildings (St. Machar's Cathedral, Marischal College). Because of its first-rate amenities Aberdeen ranks as the leading seaside holiday resort of Scotland.

The less visited Donside (in terms that is, of Deeside) has many attractive villages, notably Alford, Strathdon, Monymusk and Kemnay.

Taking the coast road N from Aberdeen we reach Newburgh, a small village noted for its sea-trout fishing (River Ythan). N of this again we enter the district of Buchan and, with it, Cruden Bay, Boddam and Peterhead. From here the A952/A92 goes on to Fraserburgh, a town of no small importance as regards its fishing industry.

Crossing the river Dee at the southern approaches to Aberdeen, we enter the small county of Kincardine. Stonehaven, the county town and chief coastal resort, is a good centre from which to see something of the interior (Fettercairn, Cairn o' Mount, Bridge of Dye and the greatly contrasting Banchory).

In order to reach Inverness from Aberdeen by the recognised main road route it is necessary to traverse the counties of Banff, Moray and Nairn. Here in an area often referred to collectively as the Moray Firth and Speyside, are a score of places well known throughout Scotland. Banff, Cullen, Buckie, Lossiemouth, Nairn, on the coast; Keith, Fochabers, Elgin, Forres inland, and the famous angling centres of Craigellachie and Grantown-on-Spey.

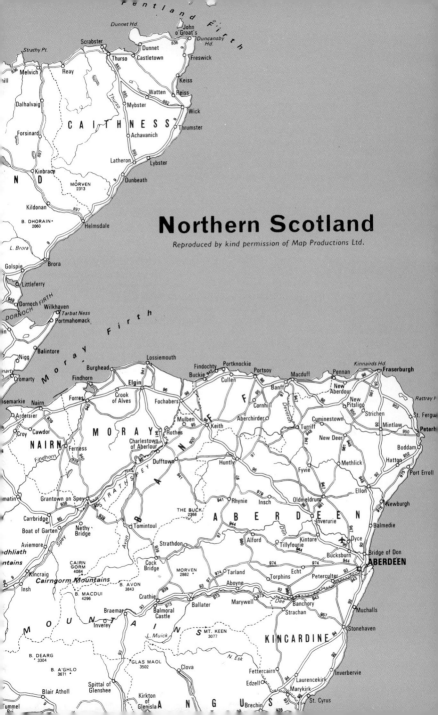

Northern Scotland

Reproduced by kind permission of Map Productions Ltd.

Leaving Inverness by the A9 road running north we cross the Inverness-shire/Ross and Cromarty boundary beyond Beauly, a village noted for its fine salmon river. From here, one can with ease see the Black Isle area of Easter Ross (chief resorts, Fortrose, Rosemarkie and Cromarty) and, immediately W of it, the attractive villages of Strathpeffer and Garve, the former being a much favoured spa within reach of the 3,429-ft Ben Wyvis.

Gairloch, often regarded as being one of the best centres for touring Wester Ross, can be reached by the A832 which runs (from Strathpeffer) via Achnasheen, Kinlochewe and Loch Maree. Hereabouts there is much outstanding scenery though it should be noted that this also applies to the areas both N and S of this road—that is, around Gruinard Bay, Loch Broom and Ullapool on the one hand and Lochs Torridon, Carron and Duich on the other. Poolewe, a village at the head of Loch Ewe, is well known for its tropical Gardens of Inverewe.

Sutherland, a county of first-rate salmon, sea-trout and trout waters is unique in that it is the only Scottish shire whose boundaries extend to the true N, W and E coasts of the county . . . (being non-mainland counties, Orkney and Shetland are, of course, excluded).

The area W of Loch Shin and the A838 Durness road has, around Lochinver, Scourie and Rhiconich literally hundreds of freshwater lochs varying in size from the 6¼m long Loch Assynt to the tiny Loch Inshore (near Cape Wrath). This, however, is only part of the scene—there are the beautiful sand beaches at Achmelvich, Stoer, Sandwood Bay and Durness and the really outstanding feature, the prominent mountains of Suilven, Canisp and Quinag.

Durness, on the N coast of Sutherland, is a good centre from which to visit the lonely Cape Wrath lighthouse (12m W) and, in the other direction, lovely Loch Eriboll, scene of the surrender of many German U-boats at the end of World War II. Tongue, Bettyhill and Melvich, further E along the coast, are good centres for those wishing to see the Loch Loyal, Strath Naver and Strath Halladale areas of the county.

Lairg, railhead for the W Sutherland villages, is pleasantly situated at the SE end of Loch Shin. Some six miles S are the picturesque Falls of Shin whilst to the E and SE are the three popular seaside resorts of Brora, Golspie and Dornoch—the last-mentioned place being well known on account of its championship golf course.

Thurso and Wick, the two largest towns in Caithness, have a common denominator in that both places link the mainland with Orkney and Shetland (steamer Thurso/Scrabster–Stromness; air Wick–Kirkwall/ Orkney, Sumburgh/Shetland).

Wick, the county town of Caithness, has an important fishing industry and a small factory which produces some extremely fine glassware, while Thurso, until recent years of no major significance, is now an integral part of the Atomic Energy Research Station at Dounreay. Touring in Caithness generally means the area E of Thurso (via Dunnet Bay and

Castle of Mey) to John o' Groats though while on this subject one should not omit mentioning the excellent trout fishing which is to be had in the interior regions of the county—e.g. Lochs Watten, Heilen and Calder.

Orkney, a group of about 70 islands the chief one of which is called Mainland, offers some very fine coastal scenery, spectacular cliffs and unusual pillar-like rocks such as the 450-ft Old Man of Hoy. Trout fishing is of a very high order. Kirkwall, the county town and Stromness 14m W are the only places of any size.

Lerwick, capital of the Shetland islands, is probably best known on account of its sea fishing industry. The town itself makes a splendid base from which to explore Mainland island and, time permitting, some of the other islands of the group. Sea-trout fishing on the voes is one of Shetland's main attractions. Another is, for some, the trip to Unst, the most northerly island in Britain.

Of Special Interest

Kincardineshire

Crathes Castle (Banchory 2m). (NT). The painted ceilings are a feature of this fine 16c Jacobean castle. May–Sept, 2–7, Oct–Apr, Weds and Suns, 2–7 (or dusk).
Dunottar Castle (Stonehaven 1½m). 14c ruined fortress, stronghold of the Earls Marischal. It is now privately owned by the Rt. Hon. Viscount Cowdray. Weekdays, 9–5, Suns, 2–5.
Muchalls Castle (Stonehaven 5m). This Castle was built in 1619. Fine plaster work ceilings and fireplaces. May–Sept, Tues and Suns, 3–5.30.

Aberdeenshire

St Machar's Cathedral (Aberdeen). Founded about 1136, the most notable features are the W front, the nave ceiling and the monuments to Bishops Scougal and Dunbar. Free entry daily.
Provost Ross's House (Aberdeen). (NT). Dating from 1593 this is the oldest house in the city. It has been carefully restored. Mons and Fris, 2.30–4.30.
Kildrummy Castle (Kildrummy). Ruins of 13c secular building (probably the best example in Scotland) with interesting barbican. Free entry at any time.
Haddo House (Ellon 6m). Georgian House built in 1732 by William Adam. Beautiful interiors, valuable paintings, also private chapel. Generally open on Suns in Jun, Jul, Aug and Sept, 2.30–5.

Banff

Cullen House (Cullen). Castellated architecture; part of this privately owned house is 700 years old. Many art treasures, paintings, tapestries and carvings. Jun–Aug, Weds, Thurs and Suns, 2–5.
Balvenie Castle (Dufftown ½m). Probably of 15c date, this castle (one of the best preserved in N Scotland) possesses a remarkable iron Yett. Apr–Sept, 10–7, Oct–Mar, 10–4.
Deskford Church (Cullen 4m). 16c ruined building possessing a rich sacrament house.

Moray

Elgin Cathedral (Elgin). Founded in 1224, the 15c chapter-house is said to be the finest of its kind in Scotland. See Celtic cross-slab with Pictish symbols in the nave. Apr–Sept, 10–7, Oct–Mar, 10–4.
Duffus Castle (Elgin 5m). Original seat of the de Moravia family. It is the finest example of a mount and bailey castle in N Scotland. Apply to custodian.

Ross and Cromarty

Hugh Miller's Cottage (Cromarty). Dates from 17c. Here was born (1802) Hugh Miller, the geologist. Geological collection on view. Cottage under the care of the NT for Scotland. Weekdays, 10–12, 2–5.
Eilean Donan Castle (Kyle of Lochalsh 7½m). This 13c castle (now privately owned) has many Jacobite relics and a War Memorial to the Clan Macrae. Apr–Oct, weekdays, 10–12.30, 2–6.
Callanish Standing Stones (Isle of Lewis). 16m W of Stornoway, these Standing Stones (numbering about 50 in all) are the most remarkable antiquity in the Western Isles. There is a well-marked avenue and circle. Free entry at any time.

Sutherland

Dornoch Cathedral (Dornoch). This ancient Cathedral (1222) was rebuilt in 1837. To this day it is in constant use. Open daily. Public worship on Suns.

Orkney

Earl Patrick's Palace (Kirkwall). Built in 1600 this magnificent Palace, though roofless, is otherwise almost intact. Excellent architectural details. Apr–Sept, 10–7, Oct–Mar, 10–dusk.
Skara Brae (Stromness 6m). Stone age village engulfed by drifting sand. Stone furniture, fireplaces and drains are still well preserved. Apr–Sept, 10–7, Oct–Mar, 10–4.

Shetland

Jarlshof (Lerwick 20½m). Remains of three stone built villages occupied from the Bronze Age to Viking times. This is generally considered to be one of the most remarkable archaeological sites in Britain. Apr–Sept, 10–7, Oct–Mar, 10–4.
Mousa Broch (Mousa Isle near Sandwick). A remarkable 45-ft high Iron Age broch tower. Can be reached by boat from Leebotten (near Sandwick).

Resorts and Centres of Interest

Aberdeen (Aber). One of the major cities of Scotland, Aberdeen is also a leading holiday resort and touring centre. Lying between the rivers Dee and Don at the southern end of the county's coastline, the 'Granite City' is 130m NE of Edinburgh, 140m NE of Glasgow and 58m ENE of Braemar (Royal Deeside). All modern recreational facilities are available. Notable among the many famous buildings are King's and Marischal Colleges (Aberdeen University); St. Machar's Cathedral; Provost Ross's House (the oldest house in the city—1593) and the 14c St. Nicholas' Church. An impressive 7-arched bridge crosses the river Dee 2m SSW of the city centre.

Aboyne (Aber). Holiday resort on river Dee, 30½m WSW of Aberdeen. This attractive village stages one of the country's most important Highland Games (Sept).

Ballater (Aber). Popular Deeside holiday centre 37m W of Aberdeen. It was formerly the railhead for Royal Deeside. Crathie Church and Balmoral Castle are 8 and 9m W of the town.

Banchory (Kinc). Pleasantly situated holiday resort on river Dee 18m W of Aberdeen. Nearby is the Bridge and Water of Feugh. See 16c Crathes Castle (NT) 3m E of the town.

Banff (Banff). County town and coastal resort at mouth of river Deveron, 46m NNW of Aberdeen. Immediately across the river is the fishing port of Macduff. See 18c Duff House, former seat of Earl of Fife.

Braemar (Aber). Attractive holiday village on river Dee, 58m W of Aberdeen and 9m W of Balmoral Castle. Here is held (Sept) the famous Royal Highland Gathering. Excellent mountaineering centre.

Brora (Suth). Coastal village of E Sutherland roughly midway between Dornoch and Helmsdale. Good sands and bathing.

Craigellachie (Banff). Picturesque village and well-known angling centre on river Spey, 12m SE of Elgin. Hereabouts are many of Scotland's most famous whisky distilleries.

Cruden Bay (Aber). Small holiday village on Buchan coast, 22m NNE of Aberdeen. It has a splendid golf course and good beach.

Cullen (Banff). Popular coastal resort with good sands, it lies 12m W of Banff. Worth seeing is Cullen House, a seat of the Countess of Seafield and (4m S) the ruined Deskford Church.

Dornoch (Suth). County town and coastal resort of SE Sutherland, it lies 6m NE of Tain. An excellent golf course and splendid beach are among the attractions offered. See 13c Dornoch Cathedral.

Durness (Suth). Pleasantly situated village in remote NW corner of county. Fine angling centre and excellent base from which to visit (12m W) the lonely Cape Wrath lighthouse. Balnakeil and Sango Bays have magnificent sands. See remarkable Smoo Caves 2m E of village.

Elgin (Moray). Historical county town and popular holiday centre of Moray, it lies 6m S of Lossiemouth and 38m NE of Inverness. Elgin Cathedral, founded in 1224, has a 15c chapter-house considered by many to be the finest of its kind in Scotland. See (5m NE) Duffus Castle and (5m SW) Pluscarden Priory, a 13c Cistercian monastery.

Fochabers (Moray). Small township on river Spey, 9m SE of Elgin. Good angling centre.

Forres (Moray). Attractive holiday resort on river Findhorn, 12½m W of Elgin. See Sueno's Stone, a remarkable carved pillar of unknown origin. NE of the town (4m) are the Culbin Sands, an area now afforested with Scots and Corsican pine.

Gairloch (Ross). Set in one of the most scenically attractive areas of Britain, Gairloch is a splendid centre for touring Wester Ross. See (3m NE) lovely Loch Maree and (6m N) the tropical Gardens of Inverewe.

Golspie (Suth). Small seaside resort 5m SW of Brora and 20m E of Lairg. Good sand beach. Dunrobin Castle, seat of the Duke of Sutherland, is 2½m NE of the village.

Grantown-on-Spey (Moray). Highland holiday resort in Spey Valley, 15m NE of Aviemore and 34m SE of Inverness. Noted angling and winter sports centre. See (3m N) Castle Grant, seat of Countess of Seafield.

Kirkwall (Ork). County town and seaport of Orkney (SE Mainland). It lies on an isthmus 14m E of Stromness. Good touring centre and an interesting place in its own right. See 12c St. Magnus Cathedral, Earl Patrick's Palace, Bishop's Palace (13c) and Tankerness House (1,574). Scapa Flow (former wartime naval base) and the Churchill Barriers are within easy reach of the town.

Kyle of Lochalsh (Ross). Coastal village in SW corner of the county, it is 55m WSW of Inverness and 79m NW of Fort William. From here steamer services operate to Skye, Applecross and Lewis I. See lovely Loch Carron (Strome ferry 13½m NE) and (near Dornie 10½m E) the famous Eilean Donan Castle.

Lairg (Suth). Village at S eastern end of Loch Shin, 9m N of Bonar Bridge. It is the railhead for the W and NW Sutherland villages. Nearby is the tree-lined river Shin, a famous salmon water.

Lerwick (Shet). County town with fine natural harbour on E coast of Mainland island. It is a busy fishing port and excellent centre from which to explore the island. Good sea-trout fishing in voes. Up Helly A' festival held each year (Jan). Lerwick Town Hall has interesting stained glass windows. See (7m W) Scalloway Castle built about 1600, and (25m S) near Sumburgh, the remains of three extensive village settlements (Jarlshof) dating from the Bronze Age.

Lochinvar (Suth). Attractive holiday village in Assynt district of Sutherland, 46m WNW of Lairg. Noted angling centre. Good beaches at nearby Achmelvich and Stoer. The peculiarly shaped mountains of Suilven

(2,399 ft), Canisp (2,779 ft) and Quinag (2,653 ft) are within each reach of the village.

Lossiemouth (Moray). Popular holiday resort and fishing port 5m N of Elgin. Good sands. Near here is the famous public school for boys, Gordonstoun. Lossiemouth was the birthplace (1866) of Ramsey Mac-Donald, first labour Prime Minister.

Nairn (Nairn). County town and seaside resort at mouth of river Nairn, 15½m NE of Inverness. It has an excellent bathing beach. Dulsie Bridge (10m SSE of town) is well-known beauty spot. Cawdor Castle (dating from 1454) and Culloden Moor lie to the SW.

Poolewe (Ross). Small village at head of Loch Ewe, Wester Ross, 5m NE of Gairloch. See well-known tropical gardens (NT) of Inverewe House.

Stonehaven (Kinc). County town and seaside resort 15m SSW of Aberdeen. It has a 15c Tolbooth now restored as a folk museum. See (1½m S) the impressive Dunnottar Castle (16c) and (5m N) Muchalls Castle, noted for its elaborate plasterwork ceilings and fireplaces.

Stornoway (Ross). A busy fishing port and terminal for steamer services from Kyle of Lochalsh, Stornoway (on E coast of Lewis Island) is by far the largest town in the Outer Isles. There are many attractive sand beaches nearby. See (13m W) Callanish Standing Stones and (62m SW in Harris) the 16c St. Clements Church at Rodel.

Strathpeffer (Ross). A favourite holiday resort on River Peffery, 5m W of Dingwall. It is a good touring centre for much of the county (especially the Black Isle and Easter Ross). Ben Wyvis (3,429 ft) is 10m N of the village.

Tain (Ross). A Royal Burgh on S shore of Dornoch Firth, 25m NE of Dingwall. A fine golf course is among its holiday attractions. See Mercat Cross, 14c Church of St. Duthas and Gothic Memorial. Tarbat Ness and the little villages of Portmahomack and Balintore are within easy reach.

Thurso (Caith). Residential town 20½m NW of Wick. Due to the setting up of the Atomic Research Station at Dounreay, Thurso (Pop. 9,190) is now largest place in Caithness. Scrabster (2m NW) is the port for the Orkneys. See Town Hall and Church of St. Peter.

Tongue (Suth). Small village on Kyle of Tongue 37m N of Lairg. Good centre from which to explore Loch Loyal and Strath Naver areas of Sutherland. The ruined Castle Varrich is nearby.

Ullapool (Ross). Popular little resort on Loch Broom, 47m NW of Dingwall. It is a good touring centre with much spectacular scenery nearby. First-rate sea angling is also one of the attractions offered.

Wick (Caith). County town and fishing port, 38m NE of Helmsdale, it is also a touring centre of some note. The much-visited John o' Groats is 17½m N. See Museum and Parish Church. 1m S is the 14c Castle of Old Wick.

Northern Ireland

Reproduced by kind permission of Map Productions Ltd.

Northern Ireland

The 'Six Counties' of Armagh, Antrim, Down, Fermanagh, Londonderry and Tyrone which together form the Province of Northern Ireland cover a total area of about 5,238 square miles—roughly a sixth of the total area of Ireland. The modern city of Belfast is both the chief industrial centre and the capital. Though certain fiscal powers are reserved to the British Parliament, Northern Ireland is administered by a separate local Parliament which meets in the very fine Parliament Building at Stormont, 4m E of the capital. Historic Londonderry on Lough Foyle has the second largest population. Main geographic features include a magnificent coastline along much of which runs the fine Antrim Coast Road, the beautiful Antrim Glens, Lough Neagh, the largest inland water in the British Isles, the unique Giant's Causeway, and the easily accessible Mourne Mountains.

Of Special Interest

Ardress House (Co. Armagh, 7m from Portadown). 17c house with plasterwork. 100-acre estate. (NT). Apr–Sept, Weds, Thurs, Sats and Bk Hols, 2–6, Suns, 2.30–5.30.

Carrickfergus Castle (Co. Antrim, 10m NE of Belfast). Notable Norman fortress with fine keep and gatehouse. (AM). Weekdays, 10–4 or 6, Suns from 2.

Castlecoole (Co. Fermanagh, 1½ SE of Enniskillen). 18c classical house built by James Wyatt. Park. (NT). Apr–Sept, daily except Mons other than Bk Hols, 2–6.

Derrymore House (Co. Armagh, 1½m NW of Newry). 18c thatched manor house where Act of Union of 1800 was drafted. Park. (NT). Apr–Oct, Weds, Thurs, Sats and Bk Hols, 2–6, Suns, 2.30–5.30.

Dunluce Castle (Co. Antrim, 4m E of Portrush). 14c stronghold on bold black headland overhanging the sea. (AM). Apr–Sept, 10–6, Suns, 2–6. Oct–Mar, Sats, 10–4, Suns, 2–4.

Florence Court (Co. Fermanagh, 7m SW of Enniskillen). 18c house built by John Cole. Fine plasterwork. Furniture, pictures. (NT). Apr-Sept, Tues, Weds, Fris, Sats and Bk Hols, 2–6.

Giant's Causeway (Co. Antrim, 9m from Portrush). Unique basalt rock formation. Of the three main projections, the Grand Causeway protrudes seaward for about 700 ft. (NT). Freely accessible.

Mount Stewart Gardens (Co. Down, 5m SE of Newtownards). Fine garden with many delicate plants and shrubs. Temple of the Winds is elegant folly. (NT). Apr–Sept, Weds, Sats, Suns and Bk Hols, 2–6.

Rowallane (Co. Down, 11m SE Belfast). Fine grounds including connoisseur's garden of trees, shrubs, plants and bulbs. Walled garden. (NT). Apr–Sept, daily, 9–6.

Springhill (Co. Derry. Close Moneymore). Example of 17c fortified manor house built by settlers in Ulster. Furniture, paintings, costume museum. (NT). Apr–Sept, Tues, Weds, Fris, Sats and Bk Hols, 2–6.

Resorts and Centres of Interest

Antrim (Antrim). Small but fast developing county town to NE of Lough Neagh, at mouth of Six Mile Water. Golf, tennis, sailing. Fishing on Lough Neagh, and in Six Mile Water and local reservoir. The Round Tower in grounds of Steeple estate is 93 ft high and one of the best examples of its type in Ireland. The castle is in ruins but the grounds, now the beautiful Massereene Park, extend for 2m along the lough shore. Lough Neagh is largest fresh-water lake in United Kingdom. 5m NW is Randalstown and along road is Shane's Castle with its beautiful park and gardens.

Ardglass (Down). Attractive small resort at head of little creek with high green hills on either side. There are several sandy nooks along its rock-bound bay. The Downs is a high common along the coast with golf course. Overlooking harbour is Jordan Castle (12c). Among several castles are also Cowd Castle and Ardglass Castle, a strange building with tower at each end.

Armagh (Armagh). Ancient city, county town and ecclesiastical capital of Ireland. St. Patrick's Cathedral (C.I.) built of red sandstone stands on a hill in the centre of the city on the site of the church first founded by St. Patrick in 445. St. Patrick's Cathedral (R.C.) is imposing modern structure on Knockadrain Hill in the north-west of the city. The Mall is tree-lined recreation ground with sports facilities. There is a County Museum with pictures, costume and folklore collections. Off College Hill, to NE, is the Observatory (open) with planetarium.

Ballintoy (Antrim). Small old-world village with quaint harbour and sea angling from rocks. Nearby is Carrick-a-rede, an isolated rock divided from the mainland by a 60-ft chasm through which the sea rushes violently. Above the chasm swings the awesome cable bridge, 90 ft above water level. To W is Whitepark Bay, a golden sandy strand with interesting caves.

Ballycastle (Antrim). Holiday town on wide sandy bay between Fair Head and Ballycastle Head. Behind the town rises Knocklayd (1,695 ft). There is golf, fishing for trout and salmon, and sea-fishing. Bowls and tennis (annual tournament). Bonamargy Abbey is ruin of Franciscan friary of 15c date. Inland is Glenshesk, one of the Antrim glens which runs for

Armagh

6m to Armoy with its round tower. To N of cliffs is Clare Park with the ruins of Duneany Castle, an early home of the MacDonnells. Kenbane Head, further N, is good picnic spot. Offshore 7m is Rathlin Island (boat service).

Ballymena (Antrim). Busy marketing and linen centre in the Braid Valley. There is golf, tennis and other sports and fishing in Rivers Main, Braid and Clogh. To W is Galgorm Castle. To NW is Cullybackey where Chester Arthur, U.S. President (1830–36) was born. 8m E is Slemish Mountain (1,437 ft).

Bangor (Down). Largest resort and fourth largest town in Northern Ireland. The seafront extends for 4m around Smelt Mill Bay to the west, Bangor Bay, and Ballyholme Bay to the east. Bathing from sand at Bally-holme Bay or swimming pool at Pickie. Golf, tennis, bowls, yachting, boating, sea-angling. Drama and variety theatres, cinemas, ballrooms.

Belfast (Antrim). With a population of over 400,000 Belfast is the second city in size in Ireland. Capital and seat of Northern Ireland Government, with cathedral, university, and many thriving industries, it is a place of leading importance. The city is well situated on the River Laggan close to Belfast Lough and there is a fine harbour. The impressive City Hall is great-domed Renaissance-style palace in Donegall Square. In nearby Bedford Street is the Ulster Hall, scene of many famous assemblies. The Royal Court of Justice is regarded as the most beautiful public building in Belfast. Its central Court Hall has walls and floor of travertine marble. St. Anne's Cathedral is commandingly noble building (1904), its nave is the widest in Ireland. Queen's University received its charter in 1908 and now has about 5,000 students. Nearby are the well-known Botanic Gardens (daily). In the park is the Ulster Museum, the State Museum of Northern Ireland. At Bellevic is modern Zoo. To the E, 4m, at Stormont, is the Northern Ireland Parliament Building, completed in 1932, in Greek Classical style (open Mons–Fris, 9.30–1.30. When House not sitting, to 4.30).

Belleek (Fermanagh). Popular angling village on River Erne (trout). The river flows westward through picturesque gorge to Ballyshannon on Donegal Bay. The place is well-known for its hand-made Parian pottery. 4m S is pretty village of Garrison at eastern end of Lough Melvin in which Gillaroo trout abound. To E is Lower Lough Erne along both north and south shores of which roads run to Enniskillen. Near the northern shore is Boa Island, 4m in length, giving good views.

Carrickfergus (Antrim). Busy resort and popular yachting centre on Belfast Lough 11m NE of Belfast. Once a port of some importance and remains of its ancient walls including the nearby perfect Spital Gate can still be seen. The Norman castle (AM, 10–6) is one of the best preserved fortresses in Ireland. It is built on a basaltic dyke with the sea on three sides. The square keep is 90 ft high with walls 9 ft thick. In 12c Parish Church is fine monument to Sir Arthur Chichester, first English Governor of Ulster. 3m NE is Kilroot in the church of which Dean Swift began his clerical career. 5m NE along the coast is the modern seaside resort of Whitehead, and still further the peninsula Island Magee.

Castlerock (Derry). Quiet seaside resort with good rock and surf bathing. Golf. On cliffs is Mussenden Temple (NT) of 1783. To W is Downhill with the sandhills and raised sand beach of Magilligan Strand beyond.

Coleraine (Derry). Prosperous Ulster business town and market centre on River Bann 4m from mouth at Ballyaghran Point. Good touring centre. Fishing for salmon and trout in river and boating is popular. Annual regatta, bowls, tennis. Golf nearby. 1½m S along river is interesting Salmon Leap. 6m N is Portstewart.

Cushendall (Antrim). Tiny village among high hills and splendid centre for some of the best scenery in the county. Bathing, boating, fishing in three rivers, golf, and some climbing. At nearby Lubietavish a half-circle of stones marks the reputed grave of Ossian, the pagan poet (c. 430). 3½m N is Cushendun, a favourite spot with artists. To N of Red Bay are slight remains of 16c castle of the Macdonnells. Inland are the vales of Glenaan and Glencorp.

Cushendun (Antrim). Tiny village, now NT property, in a hollow at mouth of River Glendun, 3½m S of Cushendall. To W are Glencorp and Glendun, the latter with the deep gorge of the Dun river. To N is Green Hill with fine views to the Scottish islands of Jura and Islay.

Downpatrick (Down). County capital and cathedral city with history dating back to a period long before the Christian era. The cathedral is fine specimen of the Pointed style with nave, choir and aisles, and lofty square tower. To E of cathedral is 10c granite cross. To NW is the mound or

"Dun" from which the city derives its name. NW is Inch Abbey on N bank of the Quoile river.

Enniskillen (Fermanagh). County town and thriving market centre of a busy stock-raising county. Cattle market on Thurs. For the most part the town is situated on an island between channels of the river connecting Upper and Lower Lough Erne (trout). In the cathedral (1840) is the Pokrich Stone, an inscribed slab (1628) to one of the founders of the town. In the chancel are the colours of the Inniskilling regiment. Remains of a 15c castle are in the barrack yard. To SE is Castlecoole (NT, open), seat of the Earls of Beemore.

Kilkeel (Down). Small and pleasant town facing open Irish sea with extensive sand and shingle beach. The town stands on River Aughrim (trout), tributary of Kilkeel river at mouth of which is small harbour. There are several dolmens in neighbourhood. To the N are the Mourne Mountains. 5m W is Greencastle on Carlingford Lough. Its ruined castle keep is a conspicuous feature of the shore.

Larne (Antrim). Busy terminal of the Stranraer steamer service and manufacturing town. There are, however, facilities for holiday visitors including golf, tennis, bathing, fishing and sailing. Offshore a sickle-shaped gravel spit called the Curran (reaping hook) curves round to the S. To W is Ballyclare on the Six Mile Water. From Larne begins the magnificent Antrim Coast Road running through grand coastal scenery for 25 miles to Cushendall. 12m along the road is picturesque Glenarm with Glenarm Castle and its beautifully wooded grounds (Earl of Antrim, open).

Londonderry

The Loom, Giant's Causeway

Limavady (Derry). Small town in beautiful valley of River Roe, a one-time important centre in the territory of the O'Cahans. It was here in 1851 that Miss Jane Ross heard a strolling fiddler play the melody later to become famous as the "Londonderry Air". N of the town rises Benevenagh Mountain (1,260 ft).

Londonderry (Derry). County town and cathedral city well situated on the River Foyle. Sports facilities include golf at Prehen and bowls and tennis in Brooke Park. The city walls, built early 17c, survive in their entirety and encircle the old city. They are flanked by bastions and provide an interesting promenade. Several old guns of the famous siege of 1689 are preserved including the famous Roaring Meg at the Double Bastion. The Diamond is a square laid out as a garden with a war memorial. From the Square streets run off to reach the walls at gates of similar name. St. Columba's Anglican Cathedral was erected in 1633 by the Irish Society. There is a fine peal of 13 bells. The County Courthouse is fine building of white sandstone modelled on the Erechtheum at Athens. The Guildhall is striking Gothic building dating from 1890. Crossing the river to Waterside is the two-level Craigavon Bridge.

Lough Neagh. Largest fresh-water lake in the United Kingdom, 17m long and 11m broad. Five of the six counties of Northern Ireland contribute to the 80 miles of its shores. Fishing for trout, pollan (fresh-water herring) and eels. Ram's Island, offshore near Glenavy, is a good picnic resort.

Mourne Mountains (Down). A fine mountain range occupying an elliptical area 14m long and 7m broad immediately SW of Newcastle. At the northern end is Slieve Donard (2,796 ft) by Newcastle and at southern tip is Rostrevor. The group is bisected by the Spelga Pass through which a road runs from Hilltown to Kilkeel.

Newcastle (Down). Among the principal seaside resorts in the north of Ireland. The town nestles at the foot of Slieve Donard at 2,796 ft the highest point in the Mourne Mountains range. The town stretches for 2m along the most westerly curve of Dundrum Bay, with broad beach of smooth sand backed by dunes. Among holiday facilities are golf, bowls, tennis, boating, bathing and mountain climbing. Swimming pool at Blackrock. Nearby trout streams. 2m W is Tollymore Forest Park (open).

Newry (Down). Thriving commercial and market town with port facilities at head of Carlingford Lough. The R.C. Cathedral is imposing building in Gothic style with some good wood-carving. St. Patrick's Church is oldest Protestant church in Ireland (1578). The Newry Canal, with many miles of navigation, connects to the north with Lough Neagh and southward with Carlingford Lough. 3m NW is Bessbrook, a picturesque Armagh village with some good angling (salmon, trout). Close by is Derrymore House (NT) in which was drafted the Act of Union of 1800.

Newtownards (Down). Prosperous industrial town and capital of the Ards Peninsula. The Town Hall dates from 1770. There are remains of a 13c abbey church showing graceful arcading and a square tower built in 17c. In High Street is old town cross (1636). To W is Scrabo, a lofty crag crowned by a monument to third Marquess of Londonderry. 5m S are the beautiful Mount Stewart gardens and beyond is Grey Abbey where the old abbey dates back to Norman times.

Newtownstewart (Tyrone). Popular angling centre on River Mourne. ½m SW is Harry Avery's Castle (AM) with two towers.

Omagh (Tyrone). County town and administrative centre at junction of River Drumnagh and River Camowen which here unite to become the Strule. Centre of extensive agricultural district. Buildings include a two-steepled R.C. church, a Church of Ireland, an attractive courthouse, and barracks of the Royal Inniskilling Fusiliers. There is golf and angling for salmon and trout. To N is Gortin Gap between the high hills of Mullaghcarn (1,778 ft) and Curraghchosaly (1,372 ft).

Portadown (Armagh). Prosperous town 10m NE of Armagh noted for linen and rose-growing. The town is also centre of the Armagh apple-growing district. Fishing for trout in Bann and Cusher streams. Golf, and other recreational activities. 5m NE is Lurgan another important linen town. 8m NW is Maghery, a good fishing spot on the shore of Lough Neagh.

Portaferry (Down). Quaint little town near southern extremity of Ards

247

Peninsula with long main street running parallel to Strangford Lough and a steep hill leading up from its quay. There is bathing and sailing and a golf course. Clams and lobsters are plentiful. Across the lough is Strangford, a charming village with its ancient castle (AM, NT, open).

Portballintrae (Antrim). Small seaside resort of some beauty on sandy bay. To NE is Runkerry Point beyond which is the famous Giant's Causeway. 1½m W is Dunluce Castle. A little inland is Bushmills, on the river Bush (fishing).

Portrush (Antrim). One of Ireland's leading holiday resorts situated on bold promontory jutting a mile into the Atlantic. Fine sandy bays either side provide good bathing. Famous Blue Pool on E side. Golf (2 courses, championships play), Recreation Gardens at Ramore Head (bowls, tennis, putting), seafishing, and local reservoirs for trout, dancing, cinema and theatre. 1m offshore are the Skerry Islands with bathing and fishing. 2m E are White Rock Caves and farther E is Dunluce Castle. 4m W is Portstewart.

Portstewart (Derry). Pleasing resort and fishing harbour 4m W of Portrush. Bathing, boating, fishing, 2 golf courses, cinema. The old castle once the home of the O'Haras is now convent school. To W is magnificent Agherton Strand.

Rostrevor (Down). Charming little resort on Carlingford Lough with background of wooded mountains sheltering it from N and E winds. On mound to NW of village is obelisk commemorating Major-General Ross (d. 1914) who distinguished himself in a number of campaigns. To N are ruins of Kilbroney church. St. Brigid's Well is reputed to possess powers of granting eternal youth and beauty. The Fairy Glen is richly wooded valley through which flows the Kilbroney stream.

Strabane (Tyrone). Border town 15m from Derry in agricultural district. Good salmon fishing in River Mourne which is here crossed by a picturesque red bridge. 1m SW is Carricklee, popular for point-to-point races. To the E are the Sperrin Mountains.

Warrenpoint (Down). Seaside resort at head of Carlingford Lough, and fine centre for the various beauty spots around the lough. Motor launches to Rostrevor, Greenore and Carlingford. Bathing, boating, golf, bowls. Pier. Constant ferry links with Omeath. 2m NW is Narrow Water Castle with fine grounds.

Whitehead (Antrim). Modern seaside resort with numerous amenities and facilities for holiday recreation, including boating, bathing, seafishing, bowls, tennis, golf and cinema. Pebble beach with some sand. The fine esplanade faces sea and gives prospect of shipping and yachts as well as Bangor, Belfast Lough, the coast of Co. Down and the Copeland Islands. On Blackhead promontory is lighthouse. To N is peninsula of Island Magee.

Index

INDEX

INDEX

252

INDEX

INDEX